Leaving Birmingham
King of the Road
Me and the Boy
The Sixkiller Chronicles
Too Old to Cry
Long Gone
The Good Old Boys
Mayor: Notes on the Sixties (with Ivan Allen, Jr.)
The Nashville Sound

THE

THE EDUCATION

HEART

OF A MINOR-LEAGUE

OF THE

BALLPLAYER

GAME

Paul Hemphill

Simon & Schuster

New York London Toronto Sydney Tokyo Singapore

SIMON & SCHUSTER
Rockefeller Center
1230 Avenue of the Americas
New York, NY 10020

Designed by Chris Welch

Manufactured in the United States of America

10   9   8   7   6   5   4   3   2   1

Library of Congress Cataloging-in-Publication Data

Hemphill, Paul
The heart of the game: the education of a minor league ballplayer/Paul
Hemphill.
p.   cm.
1. Malloy, Marty. 2. Baseball players—United States—Biography. 3. Minor
league baseball—United States. I. Title.
GV856.M323H45   1996
796.357'092—dc20   95–40225
[B]   CIP

ISBN 0-684-81172-3

For Lisa and Lloyd and the kid, Darden David Shadrach,
now in his rookie season at Little Rock.

Shoot a cuff
At Billy Goat Gruff,
   and come back home a winner.
      Joseph Bryan Cumming Jr., 1926–

THE
HEART
OF THE GAME

THE DURHAM BULLS

OPENING DAY, 1994

NAME, AGE	HT.,	WT.	B/T	EXP.*	HOMETOWN
PITCHERS					
Jamie Arnold, 20	6'2",	185	R/R	2	Kissimmee, FL
Jeff Bock, 23	6'5",	200	R/R	1	Cary, NC
Jason Butler, 23	5'11",	170	L/L	3	Harrisburg, IL
Matt Byrd, 22	6'2"	200	R/R	1	Brighton, MI
Mike D'Andrea, 24	5'10",	195	R/R	2	Old Town, ME
Ken Giard, 21	6'3",	200	R/R	3	Warwick, RI
Matt Murray, 23	6'6",	235	L/R	5	Swampscott, MA
Carl Schutz, 22	5'11",	200	L/L	1	Paulina, LA
John Simmons, 23	6'6",	220	L/L	2	Tinley Park, IL
Blase Sparma, 23	6'2",	185	R/R	3	Dublin, OH
Tony Stoecklin, 23	6'1",	175	R/L	2	Champaign, IL
CATCHERS					
Adrian Garcia, 21	5'11",	180	R/R	4	Elizabeth, N.J.
Brad Rippelmeyer, 24	6'2",	190	R/R	3	Valmeyer, IL
David Toth, 24	6'1",	195	R/R	4	West Keansburg, NJ
INFIELDERS					
Jason Keeline, 25	6'2",	170	R/R	3	San Jacinto, CA
Marty Malloy, 21	5'10",	160	L/R	2	Trenton, FL
Raymond Nunez, 21	6'0",	180	R/R	2	Manzanillo, DR
Nelson Paulino, 21	5'11",	155	S/R	3	San Pedro de Macoris, DR
Bobby Smith, 20	6'3",	190	R/R	2	Oakland, CA
Julio Trapaga, 19	6'0",	190	R/R	1	Veracruz, MX

OUTFIELDERS

Kevin Grijak, 23	6'2",	195	L/R	3	Sterling Heights, MI
Damon Hollins, 19	5'11",	180	R/L	2	Vallejo, CA
Tom Waldrop, 24	6'3",	195	L/L	2	Decatur, IL
Mike Warner, 22	5'10",	170	L/L	2	Palm Beach Gardens, FL
Juan Williams, 21	6'0",	180	L/R	4	Riverside, CA

*Years in pro ball prior to '94

FOREWORD

On a Tuesday in October of 1946, as I got home from school, I was surprised to find my father sprawled in the big chair in the living room, shrouded in a cloud of cigar smoke, peering intently at the Motorola radio at his side. He was a long-distance trucker, usually far from our house in Birmingham, Alabama, at that time of the week, and I had no idea what he was up to. I was ten years old, a scrawny kid without any particular passions for anything except shooting marbles and hoarding comic books, and I thought that only mothers and kids listened to the radio in the middle of the afternoon, when the soap operas and *Henry Aldrich* were on the air. "You might be interested in this, son," he said, inviting me to pull up a footstool beside him.

With the same intensity with which he had listened to FDR's

fireside chats during the war, he was leaning forward to catch every word. It was the seventh game of the World Series, he said, between the Boston Red Sox and the St. Louis Cardinals at Sportsman's Park in St. Louis. Knowing nothing whatsoever about baseball at that point in my life, thinking I couldn't care less, I obeyed him and took a seat. I'll never know whether it was his way of luring me to the game of baseball, but in the next half hour, between his instructions and Mel Allen's dramatic description of the events nearly six hundred miles away, I would be transported to ethereal realms.

Soon the game reached the bottom of the eighth inning, score tied at 3-3, Cardinals at bat, the world championship on the line. Suddenly there was the crack of a bat and a roar from the crowd as a Cardinals outfielder named Enos "Country" Slaughter, a farm boy from North Carolina, lined a single. We leaned forward to hear Mel Allen paint the picture: two outs, a runner on first, bedlam in the stands, the dangerous Harry "The Hat" Walker (from Leeds, Alabama, as it turned out, not ten miles from our house) at bat. In a flash, Walker shot a single to left field and Slaughter was off and flying. When the Red Sox shortstop, Johnny Pesky, took the relay throw from the outfield, he was startled to see Slaughter rounding third base; his moment of hesitation allowed Slaughter to slide across home plate in a cloud of dust to score the go-ahead run. We counted the pitches in the top of the ninth when the Cardinals' Harry "The Cat" Brecheen—ah, those nicknames—mowed down the final three Boston batters to lock up the Series.

Thus began my obsession with baseball. What I had heard over the radio wasn't so much a game as it was theater: an elaborate stage, costumes and props and sound effects, a dramatic plot, an ensemble of supporting actors—good guys and bad guys—a rapt audience, many twists and turns in the story line until, finally, a thrilling denouement. From that instant when Country Slaughter thundered across home plate, I wrapped myself around baseball. Out of my young life went the marbles and comic books and the Boy Scouts regalia; into my life came *The Sporting News* ("The Bible of Baseball"), *Sport* magazine, *The Official Rules of Baseball*, and then, not the least, a glove bought with $10 earned by helping an old truck farmer on his rounds through our neighborhood.

Eschewing girls and cars and music, I filled my adolescent and teenage years with white bread and baseball: playing ragged sandlot ball in the pre–Little League days, attending home games of the Class AA Birmingham Barons, falling asleep to Harry Caray's broadcasts of Cardinals games over KMOX in St. Louis, being the youngest person in the crowd at wintertime Hot Stove League meetings in a downtown hotel (where I actually met Harry "The Hat" Walker), going to a summer baseball camp in the scraggly hills of the Missouri Ozarks (where Ty Cobb was a guest instructor), desperately trying to strengthen my wiry frame—all of this in preparation for the day when I would try to make it in pro ball.

The time came in the spring of 1954, as soon as I had graduated from high school, when I lit out for Florida to take my shot. At the end of a month at a baseball school, where scouts checked out the eighty-odd young hopefuls working out and playing games in an old ballpark at Cocoa, I was among a batch to be signed to conditional $150-a-month contracts by the Panama City Fliers of the Class D Alabama-Florida League. When I arrived in Panama City for spring training, bushed from having ridden all night across Florida with a lumbering teenaged outfielder aptly named Ron Horsely, I found that nearly sixty teenagers had similar deals and that the contract entitled us to meal tickets and a cot on the covered roof of the Dixie-Sherman

Hotel. There were five other second basemen in camp, and I didn't make the first cut. On the third day, the harried player-manager gathered his ragtag group around the pitcher's mound and said the bus would leave at noon the next day for Tallahassee and a game against their Class B club. "Those whose names I call can go," he said. My name wasn't called.

A week later I was in Graceville, Florida, the smallest town in professional baseball, and the next five days were the headiest of my young life. I was the only second baseman in the camp of the Graceville Oilers, who played in a high school football stadium beneath the shadow of the World's Largest Peanut Sheller, a gleaming conical silo behind home plate. It looked like I might make it, until we played an exhibition game against a team from Fort Benning, Georgia, stacked with players from the higher minor leagues who were avoiding the post–Korean War draft. I turned a couple of double plays with a scrawny brown shortstop named Joaquin Toyo and threw out a runner at third base on a relay from the outfield, but I struck out all four times I came to bat against a flamethrowing left-hander. We lost 16-3, and since the lefty had rung up eight others on strikeouts I didn't feel so bad when we were called together the next morning by our manager. "How the hell y'all gonna hit ol' Onion Davis up at Dothan if you can't hit this damned *private?*" drawled Cat Milner, referring to the sly veteran left-hander whom Graceville would face in the season opener a week hence. "Jesus Christ, boys, this is a simple game. All you do is hit the ball and run like hell." After the workout my roommate and I went up to collect our daily meal money. "We got a second baseman coming in on the bus right now from Corpus Christi," Milner said, more to my roomie than to me, for killing a kid's dream was an ugly business, "so I gotta let the kid go." Within an hour I was standing beside the road with my thumb out and tears in my eyes: eighteen years old, a has-been already.

But the game stayed with me as the years wore on, in spite of my failure as a player; and even as it continued without me (except as a fan who happened to write about it now and then), I realized that baseball had became one of the few constants in my life. The game might have changed some, outwardly, in the four decades since Graceville, but between the foul lines it remained the simple exercise that Cat Milner had described in my youth. And since I still saw the opening of spring training in Florida as my New Year's Day, I always found a way to justify a trip down there to celebrate the rebirth it represented. Thus, on the first of March in 1993, having mailed off a book I had labored over since the fall, I left the bleak winter of Atlanta and hightailed it southward to get a jump on spring.

Staying at seedy motels amid the orange groves and palm trees, I would open a newspaper each morning and check out the Grapefruit League schedule for the day and, like a kid in a candy store, decide what delights I would sample that day. For a while I wasn't disappointed. At Al Lang Field in St. Petersburg I saw Stan "The Man" Musial, one of the heroes of my youth, stroll to the mound in a blue blazer and a pair of crisp gray slacks to throw out the ball that would open all of spring training. The next day I saw another Hall of Famer from the forties, Bob Feller, take to the mound at Winter Haven—wearing black horn-rimmed glasses and his No. 19 uniform, no less—and perform the same ritual to open the Cleveland Indians' spring season. All seemed right with the world, just as I had hoped.

Finally, on the last day I had budgeted for myself, I ran up the road to the Dodgers' encampment at Vero Beach. The little ballpark at Dodgertown had lost none of its charm in nearly four decades: seats hugging the foul lines, players lolling on open benches rather than in dugouts, ushers wearing name tags, and, beyond the chain-link outfield fences, the grassy slopes where entire families came early to enjoy the day. During the lull between batting practice and pregame infield, while the Dodgers and the Florida Marlins were cooling in the clubhouses down the right-field line, I bought a Coke and a hot dog and a Brooklyn Dodgers T-shirt, and then found my seat in the boxes near first base. Right on schedule there came the strains of "Hail to the Chief," the signal that it was time for the Dodgers' affable manager, Tommy Lasorda, to begin his amble toward the Dodgers bench from the clubhouse. Disjointed greetings from fans in the stands were met with a wave from Lasorda and a jaunty, "Great day for a ball game, huh?" Vero Beach, it appeared, was as homey as ever.

But then the reverie was broken. As the Dodgers trickled along in Lasorda's wake onto the field, a boy of about ten years rushed down to the first row of box seats and began waggling a new baseball as he spotted No. 33, Eric Davis. An immensely gifted power-hitting outfielder, Davis had had some moments in his nine years with the Cincinnati Reds, but lately he had come to be perceived as just another underachieving millionaire. The Dodgers had paid him $3.6 million in 1992, and he had hardly earned his keep; responding with a .228 batting average and just five home runs in a season full of mysterious ailments, he played in only seventy-six games as the club finished with the worst record in the major leagues. Nevertheless, here was this kid begging for a moment of time from a player who still appeared larger than life. "Eric, Eric," he piped, brandishing the ball, "over here, over here."

Davis scowled and mumbled, "I ain't got time, kid. I gotta get loose."

"Aw, c'mon, Eric, sign my ball. Please."

"I told you, I gotta get loose."

In the confines of such a cozy park, the exchange did not go unnoticed. Suddenly from the stands there was a threatening shout from a man in his fifties: "Sign the ball, you creep." Soon there went up a chant: "Sign the ball, sign the ball, sign the ball." Davis responded by shifting the equipment bag to his other shoulder, working his chaw of tobacco more vigorously, ducking his head, and stepping up his pace.

Say it ain't so. As a sort of consolation, the kid and the surly knot of fans saw Eric Davis flail away for the fences and strike out twice. For one of the few times in my life, I left a game before it had ended, and the long drive home was filled with disturbing thoughts. When I awoke the morning after my return, Atlanta was buried under nearly a foot of snow. Spring, with its promise of better days, had been snatched away from me in a variety of ways.

The incident at Vero Beach seemed to crystallize a sad state of affairs that had been a long time coming. For more than twenty years, as baseball became big business, there was open warfare between the owners and the players over who would get the bigger slice of pie. Now there were two baseball stories to report, one on the field and the other in the courts, and a murderous cycle had set in: tit for tat, *mano a mano*, an unseemly shouting match between billionaire owners and millionaire players. The players won free agency and the right to arbitration, and the owners increased ticket prices or simply dumped their costlier players to regain their lost profit. The innocent fan, forced to cough up an average of $123 just to take his family of four to an Atlanta Braves game, was caught in the middle.

It didn't take much prescience to see that one day there would be such an impasse that an entire season might be canceled because of the bickering. There had been some tinkering with the game in recent times—expansion, a glut of televised games, cavernous cookie-cutter stadiums, the designated hitter, divisional play—but these hadn't changed the basic nature of the game on the field. It was still sixty feet and six inches from the pitching rubber to home plate, ninety feet between the bases, three strikes and you're out, it ain't over 'til it's over. Catching some grainy film of a World Series from the days of Ty Cobb and Babe Ruth, one could draw comfort from seeing how little the game had changed—then, as now, men bunted and hit behind the runner and threw to the cutoff man and backed up bases and waylaid infielders on the double play and threw at batters' heads and even spat and scratched their crotches. But now the off-the-field shenanigans were detracting from all of that.

By the spring of '93, baseball was a mess. The average salary of major-league ballplayers had grown to $1.2 million, but they wanted more. The owners had fired yet another commissioner for indicating that his principal concern was "the best interests of the game" and hired one of their own. Now the two sides were involved in a game of chicken, to see who would be the first to blink. Said Whitey Herzog, a traditionalist from another generation, frustrated after only a year as general manager of the California Angels: "Today when you talk about trading a player, you talk about arbitration, if he has a guaranteed contract, and when is he going to be a free agent. We never talk about if he can run, hit, or throw." Said Dave Kindred, the sports columnist: "What I'd like to read is a baseball book without a dollar sign in it." My thinking was, *A curse on both their houses.* If the major-league owners and players were going to keep strutting around proclaiming themselves guardians of the national pastime, it was time they started acting like it.

And so, on a Monday in April, little more than a month after the incident at Vero Beach, I drove past Atlanta–Fulton County

Stadium, where the Braves would be playing that night before fifty thousand fans, and continued ninety miles down I-75 to attend the home opener of the Macon Braves, a Class A farm club of Atlanta. It's not that I had given up on the major-league Braves—they had, after all, won two straight National League pennants—but I was looking for the game as I had known it in more innocent times. I would check out a bunch of kids chasing their dreams in the South Atlantic League, hoping that there I might find the heart of baseball. There, at least, in a world where the average salary was about $1,000 a month, money was no distraction. There, perhaps, I might find where baseball truly lived.

Macon plays at a quaint little ballpark built in 1929, with seating for thirty-seven hundred beneath a tin roof and in precarious bleachers down the foul lines. The music of a homeboy—Otis Redding's "(Sittin' on) The Dock of the Bay"—played over the loudspeakers as 2,201 fans drifted in. One of them was a man in a Macon cap and a polo shirt and stretch Bermuda shorts who, before taking his box seat next to the visitors' dugout, went into what sounded to be his annual sermon: "This is it; this is baseball. Who wants to see a bunch of millionaires play, anyway? 'Oh, did I slide too hard? I'm sorry.' This is where it starts, folks. Pete Rose got his start right here." He sat down, to the great relief of his teenaged son. The Braves and the Charleston Rainbows lined up along the foul lines as they were introduced. The portly, graying general manager said a few words of welcome; an air force band played the National Anthem; and one of the four horses of the mounted police poised behind second base crapped on the infield, delaying the start of the game. The mayor tossed out the first ball, and the season began.

I had arrived early enough to catch Macon taking infield practice, and out of habit I checked to see who was playing second base, my position, and it was like looking at a ghost. Wearing No. 11, according to the scorecard, was a kid named Marty

Malloy, a dead ringer for me in 1954: frail and loose jointed at five ten and 160 pounds, wearing an old-fashioned crew cut, trying to sprout a mustache, hollering and slapping his glove and pirouetting out of the way of imaginary base runners as he spun on the double-play pivot. This was me with talent at the little ballpark in Graceville, Florida, on an April day nearly forty years earlier, when I was eighteen and life had not yet become complicated. My heart fairly leapt. The angst I had been feeling about baseball's present and its future was swept away almost as surely as Marty Malloy raced in and gloved his last ground ball and flicked it underhanded to the catcher.

In the ensuing weeks, as I became a regular at Luther Williams Field (I would make twenty Macon Braves games that year, but only two major-league games at Atlanta–Fulton County Stadium), I became convinced that in Marty Malloy I had found the essence of baseball. He was, for starters, the prototypical second baseman: a tough little kid who was everywhere on the field, sprawling for ground balls, lining up for the cutoff throw, backing up first base on throws from the other infielders, hanging tough against malevolent base runners intent on cutting him up on the double play; almost knock-kneed, with the quick hands and feet required to play a difficult position; the type known in the game as a dirt player. He was a left-handed batter who had always hit well but clearly had some lessons to learn as he clawed his way up through the minors. His manager and the cadre of roving instructors in the Atlanta farm system agreed that he had an outside chance to make it to the major leagues someday if he continued to work hard and the cards fell right. These were older men, of another generation, and they loved the kid. "Marty's possessed; he's on a mission," one of them told me. "Marty could be my own son," said another. There was something about the kid that took them back to their own youth, back to simpler times.

Indeed, Marty Malloy seemed to represent an America that was hardly there anymore: small-town America, with its trust in hard work and the flag and friendships that last a lifetime. He had grown up in a forgotten corner of Florida, in the piney woods along the Suwannee River on the Gulf Coast, in a county with only one traffic light. His father was the local high school coach, and the only thing he had ever wanted to do was play professional baseball. His passions, beyond that, were fishing and hunting, listening to country music, and following the stock car races. He was right out of central casting: everybody's rookie, every mother's son, a fearless kid totally without guile or pretensions, a boy entering manhood on the dusty infields of the muggy South.

Lo, just when baseball appeared to be committing suicide, here came Huck Finn to play some ball.

P.H.
December 1995

CHAPTER 1

Throughout the fall of '93 and what passes for winter in his neck of the Florida outback, the kid began most days by driving his pickup truck to a construction site thirty miles away in Gainesville, the big city in those parts, where he stood around in the predawn hour sipping coffee from a paper cup and warming himself over a bonfire of lumber scraps, in the company of men with names like Cotton and Spiderman and Curly, while they all waited for sunrise and the foreman. For those other men, poorly educated laborers whose years were measured by a time clock, this was as good as life promised to get. They would needle him from time to time about his ballplaying, about how he would probably get so rich one day that he would up and buy his own construction business just so he could boss them around, but for the most part they spoke of joists and drywall and plumbing and women. He enjoyed the camaraderie and would laugh with them as they spun their tales of other jobs and other towns, and all in all he liked the work because it paid $8 an hour and it kept him in shape and it didn't take much thinking to pour concrete. It could be better—as it was for the players who had gotten bonuses so large that they didn't have to work at all in the off-season—and it could be worse. He shivered to think of working on the floor of a sporting goods store, as his best buddy in baseball had done one winter, because, to tell the truth, he didn't much like crowds unless they were in a grandstand, cheering as he flew around the bases.

It hadn't been all work, of course. His main diversion had been the deer-hunting season. He and five of his childhood chums leased a hunting lodge, a ramshackle cabin in the hammocks of Dixie County where they kept their dogs in rickety pens ankle deep in shit, and with one more weekend remaining in the season, he was sure to reach his limit of seven deer. There had been the football and basketball seasons at Trenton High, where his father was athletic director and head coach of the football and baseball teams; at the University of Florida in Gainesville, home of his beloved Gators; and on television, by way of a dish in the backyard that delivered the sports world to their den. There had been the trips over to the high school gym every other night after dinner, where his father served as a spotter while he spent an hour lifting weights to the twangs of Hank Williams, Jr.'s "A Country Boy Can Survive" coming from a boom box on the carpeted floor. And always there had been the more somber piece of new business that hung over him like a cloud: whether to marry the young woman who had presented him with a son during the summer.

Thoughts of baseball were never far away, just on the back burner. The mail brought *Baseball America* and *Baseball Weekly* and *The Sporting News*, a shiny new black Wilson glove from somebody in the Atlanta Braves' front office, a pair of batting gloves from the agent in Clearwater he had hired "just to get the other ones off my back," and a letter from the Braves telling him when to report to spring training. There had been phone calls from Tom Waldrop, the best buddy, who was, in this off-season, working as a personal trainer at a private health club in his snowed-in hometown of Decatur, Illinois; Waldrop delivered the sobering news that their rommmate from the summer before had been released in spite of a decent show of power and speed. Paul Runge, a manager in the Braves' farm system, who lived not thirty minutes away in Williston, Florida, also called, just checking in. In December, just before Christmas, Marty was a guest instructor at a kids' baseball clinic held by Santa Fe Community College, where he had been a star before turning pro. It had taken a full month to recover from the aches and pains of his first full 140-game season, but now some internal clock was telling him it was time to get ready to go again. Would he be returned to Macon? Promoted to Durham? Leapfrogged all the way to Class AA Greenville? Much would depend on how well he prepared himself in the next two months.

On a bleak Thursday toward the end of January, even as huge chunks of ice melted and fell from the cars and vans of snowbirds from Canada and the Midwest as they fled southward on I-75, Marty Malloy decided that enough was enough of this hibernation. He had barely touched a baseball since the '93 season ended on Labor Day, except for the clinic at Santa Fe, and the off-season, that dead time referred to as "the void" by baseball's poets, was driving him nuts. Stuffing himself with food, both at his mother's table and at a workingmen's buffet near the construction site, he had added nearly ten pounds and was close to the 170-pound mark suggested by the Braves. Sticking closely to his weight lifting regimen during the winter, he had added muscle to his shoulders and thighs. He wanted to see how this new body felt, and a call the night before from the foreman on the construction job, saying the plumbers were dragging and he wouldn't be needed until the next week, had provided an opening.

Now, at two o'clock in the afternoon, wearing a pair of gray nylon wind pants and a thin T-shirt, he pounded his new glove, grabbed a couple of Louisville Sluggers, and trotted away from the brick gymnasium at Trenton High School. He tested his spikes in the end zone of the football field and continued onto the adjoining baseball diamond. Only yesterday, it seemed, this domain of the Trenton High Fighting Tigers—the gym, the stadium, the diamond—had been his world, the scene of many triumphs in all three sports. The same could be said for his father, Tommy ("Coach Malloy" in these parts), who now strolled in his son's wake; wearing jeans and a sweatshirt and sneakers, he carried an aluminum fungo bat and boxes containing three dozen new baseballs still wrapped in tissue paper, as well as a stack of mail he had brought from the post office. Sullen gray clouds from the Gulf scudded across the menacing sky, threatening more cold wind and rain, maybe enough to kill the mosquito hatch in the swamps; but for now the temperature had risen into the upper forties and was sufficiently agreeable for their purposes on this day of a new beginning.

Marty was standing near the on-deck circle doing some light stretching when his father walked up and plopped the boxes of balls and the stack of mail on the soft damp ground. Wordlessly, they surveyed the little ballpark, taking in the low rows of sagging bleachers behind the backstop, the telephone poles holding lights that looked forlorn this time of year, and the patchwork of dead, brown Bermuda grass and bright green winter rye that swept toward the chain-link outfield fences. Marty pulled on his new batting gloves and took some swings to loosen up as his father knelt and began to unwrap the baseballs.

"Too bad the cage wore out," said Tommy Malloy. "You could take some swings."

"Nobody to shag 'em, anyway," Marty said.

"Maybe the Braves have got an old cage somewhere they could let me have."

"Not a chance. It's okay. I'll just bunt and take some ground balls."

"One of my kids ought to be here when school lets out. He can take throws. Hey, I almost forgot." Tommy rummaged through the stack of mail and produced a certified letter from Atlanta. "Your contract."

"Any surprises?"

"You aren't rich yet. They've got figures for Macon, figures for Durham, figures for Greenville."

"How much for Durham?"

"Eleven hundred a month."

"The extra hundred covers Corbyn, anyway."

"It's just a start, son. That kid's expensive."

Father, son, bat, ball. Since the area around home plate was muddy, Marty took his stance on the lip of the infield grass. His father found a dry spot on the front slope of the mound, stretched his arms, gathered up a handful of the new baseballs, and began softly tossing them to his son. Marty bunted the pitches toward an imaginary spot down what passed for the third baseline. Not a word was spoken between the two of them, except for an approving "uh-huh" or "That'll work" from the father. The balls were turning green from the young rye grass, and when there was a cluster of them in a circle thirty feet away, the two would stop to collect them before beginning a new round. Soon the kid was dropping sacrifice bunts the other way, toward first base, and, finally, he began shooting bunts that were designed to skitter just past the pitcher for base hits.

All across America there were fathers who would kill for this: to have a son who played baseball, played it well enough to be regarded as a major-league prospect. The son was fortunate, too, to have a father who had played the game and knew very well the subtle joys that the boy was feeling: the smooth hardness and furled power of the bat, the ripple of the muscles, the approach of the ball; dump it, break away, hear them shout. They were in perfect synchronism, this graying father and his eager young son, embraced in a silent dance they had been performing for two-thirds of the boy's life. One could ask them independently about this and hear them stammer. "My dad played, you know; he's been there," the son would say. "Marty's had a thing for baseball from day one," was the father's feeble response. They were on the same page, more like best friends than father and son, and it was something to be savored rather than dissected and explained. Baseball and father and son were one and the same.

After nearly an hour of this, Marty tossed his bat aside, picked up his glove, and bounded out to the second-base position in his pigeon-toed trot. The school bell rang, announcing the end of classes for the day, and as the students spilled from the redbrick building, one of them, a teenaged boy carrying a first baseman's mitt, peeled away and leapt over a low fence and trotted directly to the sodden bag at first base. From a gaggle of girls drifting along beyond the right-field fence came a shout—"It's Marty. Hey, Marty!"—Marty responding with a halfhearted wave before returning to his business: smoothing the dirt with his spikes, jangling his arms and flexing his shoulders to get loose, spitting into the new glove and rubbing the pocket, then crouching to take the first ground ball of the new season. It came to him on three easy hops, slightly to his right, and he encircled the ball and gloved it and looped it to the kid at first base in one easy motion. *Thwack-scoop-toss.* Tommy, standing in the brown grass in front of home plate, took the one-hop relay from the kid, one of his American Legion team players, and sliced another one toward his son. *Thwack-scoop-toss.* Ah, to be twenty-one and undefeated! Marty moved with the ease of one who had merely taken a couple of days off, not nearly five months. Only when he flubbed a backhanded pick of a grounder far to his right did Tommy say anything—"Yeah, Tony Graffanino'd like to see *that*," a dig referring to the second baseman immediately ahead of Marty on the Braves' minor-league depth chart—but for the most part it was the same wordless dance. Marty moved to the other side of the infield and took some ground balls at shortstop and third base, his throws getting stronger as he heated up, and after an hour of this they thanked the kid at first base, gathered the balls, and headed for home.

Home was a low-slung brick three-bedroom house set on a quiet corner of the little town of Trenton, nearly obscured behind palmetto bushes, oleanders, pines, and live oaks draped with cypress moss, less than a mile away from both the school and the only traffic light in Gilchrist County. The Malloys had lived there for seven years now, ever since Tommy left the nearby town of Chiefland to take the job at Trenton High just as Marty reached high school, and by now it felt comfortable, cozy, lived in. Under a ceiling fan in the living room were a piano, a table holding a rotary phone, a formal sofa and matching chairs, and, flanking the mantel over a fireplace, framed studio portraits of Marty and his older sister, Amie. The carpeted den off the living room, dominated by a large-screen television set, a leather recliner, and a wide sofa, was the haven where the men could sprawl and watch their sports; on one wall stood a bookcase brimming with sports trophies and a set of faux-leather scrapbooks containing laminated clippings chronicling Marty's career.

Marty's bedroom was down the hallway, next to his sister's and across the way from his parents', and the narrow single bed of his childhood belied the fact that this was the room of a young man who had already played two years of professional baseball and was now a reluctant father. A hat tree held the caps of the two professional teams he had represented so far, the Braves' farm clubs at Idaho Falls and Macon, but the room was still a teenager's retreat: a poster of Deion Sanders on the door, three new bats stacked in a corner, two walls holding photographs (Marty as an eight-year-old walk-on Little Leaguer) and plaques (one from the Future Farmers of America, presented when he was twelve, for successfully fattening for market a pig named Wilbur), autographed baseballs, pennants of the Florida Gators and the Atlanta Braves, a pile of old sports tabloids and magazines. Across the hall in the master bedroom was a stark reminder that life was shifting into another gear: at the foot of his parents' bed sat a baby's playpen, for their grandson, Corbyn's, use during the long stretches when Marty was away playing ball.

Beverly Malloy was alone in the kitchen stripping kernels from ears of fresh corn when her son and husband drove up in their nearly identical Chevy pickups. She sat on a stool, wearing jeans, a handsome woman in her early fifties who ran the household and worked as an accountant for a veterinarian in Chiefland, ten miles away. Marty shuffled off to take a shower and Tommy retired to the den to read about the Florida basketball team's upset of top-ranked Kentucky the night before in Gainesville. Soon Amie got home from her job in Gainesville as a secretary in a dentist's office—reedy, twenty-four, with a squinty infectious grin, still wearing braces on her teeth from a near-fatal automobile accident a couple of years earlier—and as dark descended they all gathered at the dinner table to bow their heads and bless the bounty before plowing into Beverly's feast of fried chicken, creamed corn, mashed potatoes, sliced tomatoes, field peas, scratch biscuits, and iced tea.

At dinner, over the scraping of forks on plates, there was the muted chatter of small-town America: weather, neighbors, sports, idle comments on the small world around them. Amie pined for the day, not far away now, when her braces would come off. Beverly said the fresh vegetables kept coming in spite of the frosts, and it looked like the cold snap was about over; then added that Nikki, the young mother, had called to say she couldn't bring Corbyn tonight, but maybe this weekend. Tommy cleared his throat and said he had heard that Nikki had quit her job at the video store and was thinking about taking some classes at Santa Fe; "and how 'bout those Gators whipping up on Kentucky?" "Wait 'til you taste my strawberry pie," said Beverly. Marty flexed his shoulders and said he had used muscles today that he'd forgotten about.

"You check on the dogs this morning?" Tommy asked his son while Amie cleared the dishes and Beverly dished out the strawberry pie.

"Left 'em a whole bag of chow to fight over."

"The one with heartworm gonna make it?"

"I don't know. Hard to tell."

Beverly had been waiting to cut in. This was men's stuff, and she still didn't understand. She went ahead anyway. "Marty, why don't you just sell the things before you go?"

"They didn't cost me anything. They're for stud. Somebody gives 'em to you and you promise pups later."

"You can't feed 'em when you're gone."

"Scott and them will take care of 'em."

"But it's just something else to worry about."

"No problem. They'll be here when I get back." He grinned at his mother, hoping to close the matter. "A man's got to have his dogs."

By nine o'clock, Trenton lay in pitch black darkness. The only places still open were a convenience store and the Gilchrist County Sheriff's Department out on the beeline road to Chiefland, a whitewashed concrete-block building, where a dozen cars and pickups crouched in the brightly lighted gravel lot. Amie had gone to her room and was on the phone with a friend. The dishwasher was humming now as Beverly finished tidying up the kitchen. Tommy had rocked back in his recliner in the den and was watching a Georgetown basketball game on ESPN. Beside him, curled up like a baby on the sofa, his son slept and, no doubt, dreamed of spring training camp at West Palm Beach. Fifty more days and nights of this and he would be on his way.

CHAPTER 2

Tommy Malloy grew up in Waldo, one of the sparse cross-roads communities surrounding Gainesville in north central Florida, farming towns of about a thousand in population with names like Hawthorne and Melrose and Micanopy. His father was a truck driver for the Seaboard railroad, whose trains chugged the tracks connecting Miami and Jacksonville, and Tommy was an uncomplicated country boy whose great love was sports. He played all of them in high school, although not well enough to keep it up at a college of any size, and when he enrolled as a physical education major at the University of Florida it was to prepare himself for a lifetime as a high school coach. All along, he had been dating a Waldo girl two years younger than he—Beverly McCallister, whose family had moved there from West Virginia when she was twelve—and when he was about to graduate, in 1965, he proposed marriage to her. Lest there be any misconceptions about what lay in store, what their life together would be like, he got right to the point in his proposal: "I fish, I hunt, I coach."

After Tommy had apprenticed for a year as a junior varsity coach at Starke, just up the road from Waldo, they moved to the other side of Gainesville, to Chiefland, a farming town of less than two thousand people in what the local chamber of commerce grandly calls the Suwannee River Valley. On road maps, the area is in the armpit of Florida, 130 miles south of the state capital at Tallahassee and a like distance north of Tampa on old U.S. Highway 19, in the dense thickets less than an hour's drive west of Gainesville. The sandy soil and mild climate around the Suwannee produced peanuts, watermelons, and timber; there was a smattering of dairy farms, and those who didn't farm or raise livestock full-time or commute to salaried jobs in Gainesville were employed by the school systems or the prison outposts in Dixie, Levy, and Gilchrist counties, in one of the most economically depressed areas of the state. It was isolated country, the other Florida, a world away from anything resembling gentility and sophistication, a place where men and boys passed their time hunting deer in the scraggly forests and fishing on the picturesque Suwannee, the river of song, an eerie waterway that springs from the Okefenokee Swamp in south Georgia and is stained as black as coffee by tannic acid before it empties into the Gulf of Mexico. Beneath the front-page masthead of the weekly *Gilchrist County Journal* these days, there was this mouthful: "Now home of the World's Largest Redbelly, caught in the Suwannee River April 29, 1988, by Rick Dewees of Bell, weighing 2 pounds, 1 1/4 ounces." For the mothers who didn't stay at home there were jobs as secretaries or teachers or as domestics and waitresses at the motels and restaurants out on the highway.

Tommy had taken a job coaching junior varsity football and

varsity basketball at Chiefland High School, in the next-to-lowest classification of prep sports in the state, as the eager protégé of a legendary, barrel-chested athletic director and head football coach named Doyle McCall—"Coach Doyle" to generations of kids who had quaked in his presence—a Bear Bryant wannabe who was on his way to the Florida Sports Hall of Fame. Beverly, in the meantime, had hired on as the bookkeeper at Betts Big T Truck Stop, one of the better jobs available to women around there in those days, and they settled down to make their lives and begin a family in a simple brick house on a quiet street corner within walking distance of the school and the truck stop. Soon Amie was born, and finally, in July of 1972, there came the son Tommy had always wanted. They named him Marty Thomas Malloy. *A girl for you, a boy for me* . . . Tommy had his plans.

By the time the boy was three years old, Tommy, getting home in the late afternoon, would be met in the yard by his frail son tugging at a baseball cap that fell over his ears, wearing an old softball uniform of his father's that had been severely tailored to sort of fit, dragging a plastic bat, and yelping, "Daddy, play ball. Daddy, play ball." They would proceed to the backyard—where Tommy had already put up a low chain-link "home run fence" in anticipation of such days—to be seen and heard throughout the neighborhood tossing and batting a Wiffle ball until dark. "I told Beverly I'd never seen such hand-eye coordination at that age," Tommy said. "I never forced him to play. Didn't have to. He just seemed to have a thing for baseball from the beginning."

Tommy started a Little League program in Chiefland in 1978, when Marty was only six, and although the boy wasn't of Little League age, he was always hanging around at the little skinned-infield ballpark behind the high school, the ubiquitous walk-on, the little kid who always got stuck in right field and batted ninth when there weren't enough players available. By the time the kid was eight he had become the starting shortstop for the Scoggins Chevrolet team—"He could slide; he could catch and throw the ball; and he always made contact by then, which is something for that age"—and he had begun to watch the Atlanta Braves every night on TBS, Ted Turner's cable superstation. He loved the little guys like Brett Butler and Glenn Hubbard. (The latter was a Braves second baseman who might become Marty's manager someday as Marty worked his way up through the minor leagues in the nineties). During the 1982 season, with the Braves on their way to winning the National League West, Beverly wrote TBS and asked if they would note Marty's birthday on the air. On the night of July 6, with Marty nestled in for another night of Braves baseball on television, his face burned red when he heard the announcer, Skip Caray, wish a "happy tenth birthday to little Marty Malloy, a big Braves fan down in Chiefland, Florida." Father and son began going to Atlanta for at least one Braves game each season, on one occasion flying up on a travel package, the first time on a plane for both of them, and Tommy began sending Marty every summer to a one-week baseball camp at the University of Florida. "Others used it like baby-sitting," said Tommy, "but I sent Marty for a reason."

Just as he had brought Little League to Chiefland, when his son came of age, Tommy next began a junior varsity baseball program at Chiefland High when Marty reached the seventh grade (and, later, finagled a way to become coach of the American Legion team for which Marty would play during his teenage summers). By now the kid was obsessed with baseball, spending entire Saturdays at the high school field with his best friend, Scott Summers: "We'd take a bag of balls down there and hit grounders to each other and take batting practice all day. I always knew Marty would be a ballplayer, but I can't say he was head and shoulders above the rest of us." Said Tommy Malloy: "I thought, *He's got the skills, but he's mighty small.*" When he was a seventh-grader, there was only one boy in the whole school smaller than Marty; when he was a tenth-grader, Marty played football at 115 pounds. Said Beverly: "He might have been in the first grade when I got on him about not doing his homework and he said, 'I don't have to, Mama. I'm gonna be a ballplayer and buy you a new house, and you can quit your job.' " In due time, baseball trophies began to shove aside the first plaque he had ever won, the one for his work with Wilbur the pig.

After spending twenty years at Chiefland High, the last ten as head football coach following Coach Doyle's retirement, Tommy got into some trouble. When "the talent dried up," he had losing football seasons back-to-back, winning only four of twenty games; and a stink arose when he cut two black players who "wouldn't work in the weight room, wouldn't get with the program." A new school superintendant ("a liberal") stepped in and reinstated the two black players, not exactly a vote of confidence for Coach Malloy, and Tommy let his unhappiness be known. Almost overnight he found himself uprooting the family and moving ten miles up the road to Trenton, in neighboring Gilchrist County. It was a slightly smaller town, with a population of only eleven hundred, and the Fighting Tigers played in the state's smallest division, 1-A. Trenton was even more rural and isolated than Chiefland: off the main highway and the river, a feed-and-seed store here and a meat-and-three diner there, an inbred town of churches and sewing circles and FFA clubs, the sort of place where housewives bake pies and cool them in their open kitchen windows.

Tommy found that there was usually a pool of only a hundred

boys in the top three grades to draw from to stock the high school teams, and in his first year only sixteen players suited up for football after another racial issue arose: five black players, essentially the Trenton basketball team, quit rather than bend to Tommy's regimen. "I always thought the basketball coach put 'em up to quitting," said Tommy, but a pattern was developing in his relationship with black people. Pining for the old days of the two-handed set shot, he had squirmed out of coaching basketball when it became, in his eyes, an undisciplined game for black kids. He was the son of a truck driver from Waldo, had lived his life among north Florida Crackers, had learned his coaching from a magisterial hard-liner who had barely faced integration, and was ill-prepared to handle the cultural differences. (Although he managed to refrain from using the word "nigger," he seemed to take it personally when Marty taped a poster of the flashy black Brave Deion Sanders on his bedroom door, and "thought I'd never see the day" when he found that the beat writer covering the Macon Braves was black.) There would be no liberal school superintendent to reprimand Tommy in Trenton, so he blithely coached his maiden football season there with only five players on the bench. All of the Trenton players that year were white.

The move to Trenton coincided with Marty's entering high school, and he blossomed into a small-town hero, a feisty little fellow who starred in three sports, dated the best female athlete in school (Nikki Pugh, a high-scoring basketball player and aggressive softball shortstop), and was the idol of towheaded kids all over town. Marty would become "a pretty good little point guard" in basketball and would make first-team all-state 1-A as a quarterback and defensive back ("He'd tackle anybody, didn't matter how big they were"), but baseball was his real passion. Playing shortstop, batting second in the order, he was a terror in those boondocks, easily batting .500 in high school and during the summer's American Legion play; still, not many baseball scouts found Trenton, Florida. There was a scare during a Legion game just after he had graduated from high school, when he fell while rounding first base and tore up his left kneecap— one doctor said to forget baseball, the boy might never walk; another performed reconstructive surgery, and there have been no problems since—but his biggest problems were that he still weighed less than 150 pounds and had never been tested in anything resembling stern competition. There was no longer any doubt that Marty intended to exercise his dream to become a professional baseball player. The big question was when.

It would be difficult to exaggerate the profound impact of Marty's father on his development as a ballplayer in those crucial adolescent and teenage years. Tommy Malloy was much more than just a doting father who loved his only son and had casual dreams of watching his son climb the ladder to the major leagues. Although he hadn't been much of a player himself, Tommy knew the game inside out. He had the perfect temperament to be a coach—pensive, calm, observant, patient— and so Marty had a huge advantage over those many thousands of kids across America who harbored dreams of playing the game professionally. In a sense, the kid was enrolled in a private baseball academy every day of his young life, from sunup to lights-out.

Tommy knew that baseball is anything but a simple game, that it involves a lot more than hitting the ball and running like hell, and ever since the days of "Daddy, play ball. Daddy, play ball," he had been passing knowledge along to his son. They would be in the den, watching a major-league game on television, and Tommy would say, "Okay, he's got him set up; been working him outside; now he's gonna try to jam him." They would be seated next to each other in the dugout at the little Trenton High ball field during a game, and Tommy would point out that the opposing pitcher was telegraphing his pitches by holding his glove in one position for a fastball and in another for a curve. They would be on the field on a Sunday afternoon, just the two of them, and Tommy would demonstrate the crossover step while breaking away from first base on a steal; or the way to circle a ground ball in order to be moving toward first to make the throw; or the importance of always hitting the bag with the left (inside) foot to avoid a costly wide swing while running the bases. They would be on the Suwannee fishing, and the education would continue: about the chess game between the pitcher and the batter, about defensing the bunt, about the double-play feed, about how a smart infielder knows the next pitch and the hitter's tendencies against it and "cheats" accordingly.

Football is primarily a game of brawn, basketball a free-spirited exercise in agility, but baseball truly is the delicate game of inches that we have always called it. Baseball takes some brawn and some agility, but what separates the high school heroes from the ones who go on into pro ball is attention to the fine points that, at the higher levels of the game, make all the difference in whether a play is made, an extra base is taken, a game is won or lost. Through constant repetition in practice and then in actual game situations, ballplayers must become instinctive. Tommy Malloy knew that most young players just out of high school don't begin to learn these things until they sign and go off to rookie ball or to their first spring training camp. He had given his son a huge leg up on all of those other kids across the country, a thorough education in the basics of the game, and as soon as Marty's body caught up with his mind, they both knew, he would be ready.

• • •

Primarily because of his lack of size, Marty decided to delay his attempt at pro ball by accepting a baseball scholarship at Santa Fe Community College in Gainesville, a two-year school only a thirty-minute drive from his parents' house in Trenton. Santa Fe was a pure commuter college, with eighteen thousand students but not a dormitory in sight, a place where adults went for nighttime vocational classes and kids from the underfinanced public school systems in poor rural counties such as Gilchrist went for remedial work that might qualify them academically for the University of Florida. (Marty's sister, Amie, had attended SFCC to become a dental technician, then gone to work for the dentists who had repaired her jaw after the automobile accident.) The least of Marty Malloy's interests was book learning; he was there to play baseball. His father loaned him an old pickup, and for two years he turned east at the traffic light in Trenton and hightailed it every day for the SFCC campus, to dutifully sit through morning classes before suiting up to play in afternoon games at a trim little hilltop ballpark on the campus grounds. Most of the time there were two dozen fans and a couple of scouts lolling in the aluminum bleachers crowded behind home plate.

The state of Florida, like California and Texas, has a strong junior college baseball program, followed closely by major-league scouts and their bird dog deputies—volunteers who tip the scouts off to local prospects and are paid a tiny stipend if they pan out—and Marty began to attract attention. Moving to second base and batting in the two-hole, being coached by someone other than his father for the first time in his life, he accomplished what he had sought. He got his weight up to 160, averaged .406 in his two seasons there, and missed by one vote being named the best junior college player in the state. He had been selected in the thirty-first round of the major league draft of 1991 by the California Angels, but the money wasn't going to amount to anything, and he "didn't want to be an Angel"; he wanted to be an Atlanta Brave. First-round draft choices in those days were getting signing bonuses in the high six figures, and a tenth-round selection might fetch $50,000 or more; but those big-bucks contracts almost always went to the big muscular power hitters or pitchers whose fastballs registered better than ninety miles an hour on the radar gun. Nifty little middle in-fielders like Marty Malloy were a dime a dozen, even when they put up the numbers he had at Santa Fe. And so, wondering where his beloved Braves had been all of this time, he reluctantly accepted a two-year baseball scholarship at the University of Florida, figuring he might play one year, improve his chances, and submit himself again to the draft.

During most of Marty Malloy's lifetime, the Atlanta Braves had been the laughingstock of major-league baseball. TBS's pro-motional bleatings about the Braves' being "America's team" brought patronizing chuckles if not gales of laughter from the distant corners of the nation, where the Braves' bumblings were exposed nightly on cable television. They had won the National League's Western Division pennant in 1969, only to be blown away in the play-offs by New York's amazin' Mets, and about the only thing Atlanta fans had to cheer about during the long dark decade that followed was Henry Aaron's relentless and ulti-mately successful chase of Babe Ruth's career home run record. By late August and September of each year, when football season was cranking up and the Braves had disappeared from the race for the pennant, the front office fretted that there might not be a thousand people in the stands. "Yeah, I was wondering what time the game starts tonight," went the story about a fan calling Atlanta–Fulton County Stadium, the hopeful response being, "What time can you be here?" But finishing so poorly for so long meant that the Braves were able to pick high in the annual draft of promising high school and college players, and in 1982 they again won the division (to be swept in the play-offs once more, this time by the St. Louis Cardinals). They were headed to the top the next year, too, until a panicky late-season trade— the proven leadoff man Brett Butler and a promising young power hitter named Brook Jacoby to Cleveland for a pitcher, Len Barker, whose arm blew the moment he arrived in Atlanta— tore the heart from the club and sent the entire organization reeling again.

Now, suddenly, or at least it appeared so to the casual fan, everything had changed. During the 1991 season, bolstered again by the high draft choices that resulted from several years of poor finishes, the Braves had surged from worst to first in the division and wound up in the World Series. The citizens of Atlanta, which had come to be known as Losersville in professional sports circles, had lost their equilibrium over "the Bravos." The stadium was filled every night with fifty thousand delirious fans, who pushed political correctness aside by wearing faux–Plains Indian warbonnets, streaking their faces with war paint, brandishing foam tomahawks, and doing the relentless tomahawk chop as the Braves forged ahead on the field. They were being projected to repeat as division champions in '92 and finally were living up to their billing as America's team. Baseball people acknowledged that Atlanta looked like the team of the decade, but they knew well that it hadn't happened overnight.

The key to this new success dated back to the late eighties, when Ted Turner, the mercurial founder of TBS and Cable News Network and owner of the Braves (once, in 1977, he had relieved his manager for one day and suited up to manage the club himself, causing an amendment in the rule book outlawing such shenanigans), finally turned over the baseball operations of his broadcasting empire to baseball men. Ever since Branch

Rickey pioneered the farm system with the St. Louis Cardinals in the twenties and then fine-tuned it with the Brooklyn Dodgers following the Second World War, it has been a given that the surest and cheapest way to build an enduring organization is from the bottom up, through the nurturing and development of a club's own players, rather than going out every year and filling needs by buying expensive players or making trades. In the late eighties the Braves concentrated on just that. They jumped far ahead of the other major-league operations by hiring more scouts, operating more minor-league clubs, signing more young players, and hiring more coaches and roving instructors to tutor these kids than anybody else. To be sure, thanks to coffers overflowing with money derived from cable television revenue, they were able to fill holes on the big-league roster by going out and snatching high-priced free agents as the need arose—Terry Pendleton and Sid Bream were the principal additions in '91—but the bulk of those clubs had been homegrown, raised in a farm system now judged as the most productive in the game.

The Braves' theory was a copy of the St. Louis Cardinals' notorious "chain gang" of more than half a century earlier: sign as many kids as possible, marginal and otherwise, get 'em cheap, give 'em crash courses in the basics, and see who survives the lowest minor leagues. ("Actually, we've got *three* teams," the saying went in the dozens of small towns across America with Cardinals' farm clubs, "one coming, one going, one playing.") It was like panning for gold: the more gravel you sift, the more gold you'll find. The difference was, back in the fifties the man in charge was usually a player-manager, a former star on his last legs who had little time for teaching and nursemaiding, so a kid second baseman learned the double-play pivot the hard way, literally by the seat of his pants. Now, in the nineties, of the twenty-eight major-league organizations, only Atlanta had three rookie-league operations (seven had two, the rest one apiece); and whereas most clubs in baseball's six rookie leagues had two coaches or even only one to assist the manager, the Braves routinely assigned a third coach to help carry the load: teaching, throwing batting practice, hitting fungo, baby-sitting, sometimes pinch-hitting for the bus driver on long overnight runs. "No doubt about it," said Rod Gilbreath, a former Braves infielder now in Atlanta's minor-league office, "the toughest jump for a player isn't from triple-A to the big leagues anymore, but from rookie ball to Class A."

When it came time for the June '92 draft, there was "a lot going on," said Tommy Malloy. "Me, I wanted him to take the scholarship, be a Gator, get an education, but he'd done so badly in school that he was going to have to go to summer school just to be eligible for the scholarship at Florida. The Yankees, Braves, Angels, Rockies, they'd all indicated they would draft him. The Braves' scout in Tallahassee, Steve Givens, had asked Marty what it would take to sign him, and he'd said, 'Draft me high enough, I'll sign.' Well, he sat by the phone all day when the draft began. The first day, nothing. The second day, nothing. The Braves didn't draft him at all, and after Marty heard the thirtieth round had passed he trashed his Braves cap. Just yanked it off his head and threw it in the trash basket. The poor kid didn't know what to do, but a couple of days later he swallowed his pride and called Givens and asked if it was too late to sign. I guess I knew he'd do it, all along."

The Braves gave Marty a bonus of $15,000—half to sign, the rest a year later, plus the usual incentives for advancement ($1,000 when he made it to Class AA, $2,000 for AAA, $5,000 if he made the Braves' roster)—and before he knew it he was packing his bags for Idaho Falls, Idaho, in the rookie-level Pioneer

League. He had figured they might start him out close to home, at their rookie club in West Palm Beach, but instead he had to spread out the Rand McNally atlas on the floor in his parents' den, looking for Idaho.

CHAPTER 3

On a morning late in June, less than a week after he had signed with the Braves, Marty was driven by his parents to the little airport in Gainesville for the first leg of a long flight to what might as well have been the end of the earth for a nineteen-year-old who had lived so close to the hearth. His mother hugged him, and his father told him, "You'll be okay, son, as long as you remember where you come from." This was it, the moment he had dreamed of and worked toward, but there was a dark unknown out there and he was scared. "That was one sick boy we put on the plane to Idaho Falls," said Tommy. "He'd thought they might start him out close to home, and here he was going to the other side of the country. Most of his life had been spent within thirty miles of Trenton, and the only plane he'd ever been on was when we flew up to Atlanta to see a Braves game that time. So he called me from the Atlanta airport and then from Salt Lake, homesick already. When he finally got to Idaho Falls, it really got bad. Been living at sea level all his life, and now he's at a mile high. It was cold, too, as far he was concerned, and what they do is put you up in a hotel the first three days and then you're on your own. When he called me from the hotel, he said he was looking out the window at the Snake River. I said, 'Don't go jumping in the Snake River now, son,' and I didn't hear him laugh."

The Idaho Falls Braves of the Pioneer League were already a week into their abbreviated, seventy-six-game season, and when Marty checked in at the ballpark he found that he wasn't alone in being homesick and disoriented. All of the others on the thirty-man roster were also far away from home for the first time—one, an outfielder named Miguel Correa, was from Puerto Rico, and the others had been brought in from all over the United States— and most of them were teenagers who had been playing high school ball less than a month before. The manager was a forty-one-year-old Texan named Dave Hilton who had made it to the big leagues at twenty-two and spent four years as a utility infielder with the San Diego Padres before being struck with hepatitis. He played out his string in Japan and Mexico, became a minor-league instructor, and now had his first managing job. "The learning isn't just on the field," he said. "For the first time in your life, you're renting an apartment, doing laundry, cooking, balancing a checkbook, being away from home, taking responsibility for yourself." Marty was comforted by Hilton's relative youth and by the sounds of Southern drawls: one of the three Idaho Falls coaches was Paul Runge, the former Braves shortstop who lived in Williston, Florida; and still there, nursing the rookies through their baptism, was Bobby Dews of Albany, Georgia, a former minor-league infielder and coach for the big club who now served as field coordinator, in charge of instruction for the two-hundred-odd players in the Braves' farm system.

During the first week, the kid who had grown up at sea level could hardly breathe as he took ground balls in the mile-high altitude. His pay of $850 a month wouldn't go very far, so he crowded into a rental house with six other players. They shared the cooking, such as it was, and bummed rides to the ballpark (few had cars) and learned that somebody besides Mom has to do the laundry. Calling collect nearly every night ("*Very* late, given the time difference," said Tommy Malloy, whose monthly telephone bills were topping $200), Marty began to work it out both off the field and on. In that alien environment, twenty-four hundred miles from the Suwannee River, he had to adjust not only to the altitude but to playing every night and enduring bus rides of up to fifteen hours through the Rockies to the Canadian towns of Medicine Hat and Lethbridge. A game at Butte, Montana, in late August was called on account of a snowstorm after six innings, the first snow he had ever seen, and another, at Salt Lake City, Utah, was attended by a hostile overflow crowd of twelve-thousand. (When the Idaho Falls right fielder, Tom Waldrop, trotted out to take his position in the bottom of the first inning that night, he was greeted with a chorus of taunts by a thousand fans standing in a roped-off area in the grass. "Hey, c'mon, gimme a break, this is my first game in pro ball," he pleaded to them, and they cheered his every move for the rest of the night.)

Of all the adjustments a kid has to make upon entering pro ball, however, the toughest is one that would seem inconsequential to the layman: the move from aluminum bats to those made of wood. None of the kids in the Pioneer League had ever laid their hands on a wooden bat. For three decades or so, for the simple reason that metal bats don't break and need replacing, American baseball players from Little League through college had been brandishing featherweight aluminum models. Baseball purists were driven mad by hearing not a solid *whack* as bat met ball, only a puny *clink*, but that wasn't the most significant problem. Not only were the metal bats lighter, but their sweet spot was just about anywhere the ball met the bat. As a result, even fireballing pitchers at the highest level of college ball didn't bother trying the heater on the hands. Thus, scouts could only guess how well a high school prospect might fare against the fastball on the hands, and not until the aluminum bats were put away would they find out if a young pitcher had the guts to take a chance on maiming a batter with a ninety-mile-an-hour bullet on the inside of the plate.

But the distance between the bases is ninety feet, whether at the little ball field behind Trenton High or at McDermott Field in Idaho Falls, and Marty coped very well, indeed. Because he had started playing baseball at such a young age under the ministrations of a knowing father and in a climate that permitted baseball practically year-round, he already had many more games under his belt than most of the others in the Pioneer League. It had taken Mark Lemke, the parent Braves' current second baseman, two years to get out of rookie ball (and he averaged only .270 in those two seasons), but Marty was finding the Pioneer League relatively easy pickings. He was clearly the best defensive second baseman in the league, and with hundreds of hours in the batting cage he overcame the wooden-bat problem and wound up leading the club in hitting at .315. The rookie-level Braves finished dead last in the Pioneer League with a record of 27-49, the first losers Marty had ever been associated with, but winning didn't mean that much in rookie ball as far as the organization men were concerned. When Tommy had flown out there to spend a week during the season ("My second plane ride, and my last"), he came home convinced that his son had done the right thing in turning pro rather than taking the scholarship at Florida. Marty had joined the company of men, the brotherhood of baseball.

Bushed from playing in sixty-two professional games over a seventy-day period, Marty was welcomed home as a hero of sorts—big spread in the *Gilchrist County Journal*, a speech to the Rotary Club, lots of tales of the great beyond to share on deer-hunting escapades with his childhood pals Scott Summers and Marcus Corbin, a part-time job on Marcus's grandfather's cattle ranch outside of town—but he also made a couple of boyish mistakes. "I'd let him use this old pickup truck to go back and forth to Gainesville when he was at college," said Tommy, "and told him he could have it if he'd pick up the insurance, but *noooo* . . . He took some of his bonus money and went down to the bank and got a loan to go with it and bought this monster pickup, the kind with the big tires and the spotlights and mud flaps, and he tore up the engine two days later. It was going to cost fifteen hundred dollars to replace it, so he had to get rid of the truck. Then there was the girl."

Forever, it seemed, Marty had been dating Nikki Pugh, the pretty blonde who had been his female equivalent in sports at Trenton High. They weren't exactly childhood sweethearts in the fairy-tale sense ("They're both headstrong and fight like cats and dogs," said Tommy); rather, they were star athletes attracted to each other on that common ground. But when they graduated, their paths veered off in opposite directions. Only twice did Nikki drive over to Gainesville to watch Marty play during his two seasons at Santa Fe Community College, and when Marty embarked on his baseball career, Nikki was left behind, coping with the divorce of her parents and her mother's remarriage, minding the video store in Trenton, stuck in a patriarchal society, doubtless resenting Marty's success. Just before Christmas, after a period of several weeks when they had not even spoken to each other, Nikki called to advise Marty that she was pregnant. They had conceived within a week of his return from Idaho Falls right after Labor Day.

A child? This hadn't been a part of the plan. They were both still children themselves. Just when Marty should have been basking in the glow of his successful entry into pro ball and looking forward to his first spring training camp, when his parents should have begun fancying their son as an Atlanta Brave, a gloom settled over the Malloy household. Long nights were spent in agonizing discussions over what to do about Nikki and the baby, which was due in the middle of the upcoming season. "Do the right thing" was another of Tommy Malloy's homilies, but that presented a quandary: the right thing was for Marty to marry the girl and face up to his responsibilities, but then what would become of Marty's dream? He was in a situation that was different from that of his friends, most of whom were finding some sort of a job and would likely be spending the rest of their lives in or around Trenton. Marty had possibilities that went far beyond Gilchrist County. With the proper application and with some breaks here and there, he had a chance to earn millions of dollars as a major-league baseball player, to become a national hero of sorts, doing what he had trained himself to do since childhood. Now this. On the other side of town, of course, Nikki Pugh had a quandary of her own, one of even larger proportions: she was with child, and a child needed a father. Marty decided to sit on it and take things one day at a time.

Thus, when the time came for him to report to his first minor-league camp at West Palm Beach in March of 1993, to personally check out the competition and see how he stacked up within the organization, Marty was again "one sick boy." He had to hitch a ride to spring training with Tom Waldrop, since the debacle with the pickup had left him without wheels, and when he got there he was intimidated by the sheer number of players in the Braves' minor-league complex. There were nearly two hundred of them, being driven like cattle from one practice field to another; more than a dozen of them were second basemen. He took a close look at the one who appeared to be his main competition in the immediate future—a bigger and stronger kid named Tony Graffanino, son of a New York cop, who had batted .347 at Idaho Falls in 1991 but only .240 at Class A Macon in '92 and would likely be promoted to advanced-A Durham that year—before closing all of that out of his mind and turning to work on his own game. He got hot with the bat during the closing games of spring training, and when camp broke he and Waldrop, who had hit .311 and led Idaho Falls in runs batted in, took off again. They were Mutt and Jeff, the scrappy little second baseman and the tall power-hitting outfielder, but they shared an intensity about the game that had made them best friends. In Waldrop's gray Oldsmobile sedan with an Illinois vanity license tag representing the number he had worn in junior college— TOM W 7—they made the long haul to the next stop on their serendipitous journey toward the big leagues: Macon, Georgia, of the South Atlantic League.

When they arrived in Macon, a somnolent town in middle Georgia with a metro population of 120,000, only an hour-and-a-half drive south of Atlanta, they found that they and Miguel Correa and a Dominican catcher named Miguel Soto were the only position players of seventeen from the '92 Idaho Falls team who had been promoted to Macon's low-A roster. One from that team had remained in rookie ball, at Danville, Virginia, in the Appalachian League, and another had jumped to Durham in the Carolina League. All of their other teammates from Idaho Falls had been thanked for their efforts and released, stripped of their dreams, free to get on with their lives. The attrition had already begun, and when Marty looked around at Macon he saw no raw rookies in his midst. The first baseman was a larruping left-handed hitter named Kevin Grijak, a free spirit who had spent the second half of the '92 season at Macon. The shortstop was a slick-fielding Californian, Jason Keeline, who had divided his time between Macon and Durham the previous season but, at twenty-four, was running out of time. At third base was a genuine bonus baby with great promise, a nineteen-year-old black kid from Oakland named Bobby Smith, who had turned down college basketball scholarships (he and Jason Kidd, today a star with the Dallas Mavericks, had been the two best point guards in the state) to take $50,000 as an eleventh-round draft choice; he had batted only .235 with the rookie team at West Palm Beach but was being rushed along and was already projected as a bona fide major-league prospect. Correa and Waldrop, with solid rookie seasons behind them, appeared to be the most promising outfielders. The pitching staff, featuring a couple of hard-throwing top-round draft choices named Jamie Arnold and Matt Murray, plus several sleepers with solid rookie-league performances behind them, looked to be the best in the Sally League.

The Macon manager was Marty Malloy's kind of guy: a straight shooter from the Appalachian hill country who drove a pickup truck and had hunting and country music in his blood. Randy Ingle was an angular, rangy man (six two, 185 pounds) who had spent nine years as an infielder in the Braves' system before retiring as a player in 1986 at the ripe old age of twenty-eight. "I was having my best year, hitting three eighteen, at Richmond," he said, "when they called me in to say they were bringing up Jeff Blauser [the Braves' current shortstop] for the play-offs. They said they wanted to find out if he was ready for triple-A. 'Now the press is going to come around,' they told me, 'so we want you to tell 'em you've got a strained back or something.' The hell with that. I told 'em I wasn't going to lie for 'em, they could do that themselves." He quit in a huff and went home to Forest City, North Carolina, but found that baseball had become a way of life. "I sold fifty-eight Electrolux vacuum cleaners in three weeks, set some kind of record, but I hated it; called Hank [Aaron, then head of development] and begged to get back in." He became an organization man for the Braves—roving instructor, scout, coach—and now, at thirty-five, after three years of managing at the rookie level, he himself had made it to Class A at Macon. His work was never done: he was at the ballpark by three o'clock, on the phone to Atlanta, pitching batting practice, working with Marty and the other players on specific aspects of the game, hitting pregame infield practice, managing that night's game, then faxing a report on the game to the special line in Atlanta, finally reaching his apartment around midnight. Ingle was the classic organization soldier, a baseball rat who couldn't give up the game, one who would drive home for the off-season to paint houses or whatever while he awaited marching orders for the next year.

Ingle and his two coaches—a young, former minor-league catcher named Joe Szekely and a savvy older man, Larry Jaster, the pitching coach, who had a special niche in the Baseball Hall of Fame for having pitched five shutouts against the eventual world champion Dodgers in 1966—were Marty's immediate supervisors, as it were, but now that he had survived rookie ball and made it to Class A, he would go under the microscope. He had become a prospect, not just one of a hundred rookies learning to cope with being away from home, and from this point on in his career, every time he looked up there would likely be another roving instructor waiting for him at the ballpark. So boggling was the number of old baseball men employed by the Braves to watch over player development—scouts alone numbered fifty-seven, from the man assigned to scout the big club's next opponent to a fellow named Givanni Viceisza hunting for talent down in Curaçao—that no deed went unnoticed. If Marty got creamed on a double play or missed a bunt sign in a game against, say, the Spartanburg Phillies, everybody in the Braves family would know about it the next morning. Armed with radar guns and stopwatches and daily reports faxed to Atlanta by the manager every night, to be summarized and left on an electronic bulletin board, these men and scores of others in the organization—managers, coaches, trainers, roving instructors, even the strength and conditioning coach—were like tutors in an exclusive private school.

"Atlanta," to those in the field, meant the offices of Player Development and Scouting, located in the club level of Atlanta–Fulton County Stadium—minor-league central, as it were, the clearinghouse for all data regarding the Marty Malloys. The head man there was Chuck LaMar, thirty-six, a button-down grip-and-grin sort whose only on-field experience in baseball was as a small-time high school and college coach; he suddenly appeared in the mid-eighties as a scouting supervisor with the Cincinnati Reds, moving on to the Pittsburgh Pirates as director of minor-league operations, then coming to the Braves when they overhauled their system. His two assistants were Rod Gilbreath, a third-round draft choice of the Braves in 1970, who played for seven years in the majors but never fulfilled his promise; and another button-downer from the Pirates' front office, thirty-three-year-old Scott Proefrock, whose chief credential seemed to be his master's degree in sports management from the University of Massachusetts. LaMar and Proefrock symbolized the new baseball executive, one trained not on the field but in the office, and a certain amount of animosity was directed toward them by all of those vigorous older baseball men out there in the field, the baseball rats, who sweated and rode the buses and hit fungoes and threw batting practice to kids who could be their sons.

The quintessential baseball man on the front lines for the

Braves in the early nineties was Bobby Dews. Son of a vagabond minor-league catcher who, in nearly three decades of wandering through the minors, became a legend from Waycross, Georgia, to Billings, Montana, Bobby grew up in the rolling farmlands of south Georgia, where every pasture was a potential ball field. After starring at Georgia Tech in baseball and basketball, he signed with the St. Louis Cardinals in 1960 at the age of twenty-one. He got as high as triple-A in eleven years as a shortstop in the Cardinals' organization, then finally gave it up and joined the Braves as an instructor. In the two decades that followed, he managed in the minors (five play-off teams in eleven years), coached with the big club (four years), became director of player development, and served as a roving instructor. There were few managers and coaches in the Braves' farm system, it seemed, who had not been managed by Bobby Dews during their own playing careers.

Now, at fifty-four, with the official title of field coordinator ("responsible for supervising instruction throughout the Braves' minor league system," according to the Atlanta media guide), Dews knew more about each and every player in the Braves' organization than any person alive. His job was to keep tabs on all of them, in person, and it was a frenetic life. When he drove away from his house in Albany, Georgia, to make the opening of spring training at West Palm Beach in the middle of February each year, he knew that he couldn't expect to see much of his wife until the close of the Fall Instructional League in West Palm at the end of October. ("It's hell on a marriage, I tell you. I'm home to rest up, and they don't call me for three months, but my wife's all wired about her school teaching in the winter.") Dews lived in his car, at budget motels, and at the ballparks wherever Braves farm clubs were playing, putting on a Braves uniform to pitch batting practice, hit fungoes, take ground balls himself to demonstrate his point. And he was forever on the phone, patching into the organization's electronic bulletin board: "That's where ninety per cent of our 'high-powered meetings' take place. One man checking messages on his voice mail." What Tommy Malloy had been for one player—his son—Bobby Dews tried to be for some two hundred of them.

Marty and Tom found a player to share the rent in a three-bedroom apartment on the edge of Macon—Jay Noel, a young outfielder from Ft. Myers, Florida, who had been taken in the eighteenth round but got only thirty-four at bats with the West Palm Beach rookie club in '92—and the three of them quickly went about the business of settling into a routine: sharing the cooking, lifting weights every other day when they were in town, at a gym called Conditioning Unlimited ("Where the Macon Braves Train!" read their ad in the game program), getting to the ballpark by four o'clock each afternoon for early work in the batting cage behind the aluminum bleachers, playing the night's game before crowds that seldom surpassed a thousand, showering in the cramped quarters beneath the grandstand of the second-oldest active ballpark in professional baseball (the oldest was at Greensboro, North Carolina, in the same league), then cruising the dead streets of Macon in a futile search for delights that were not to be found, ending the long day by talking baseball over eggs or hamburgers at a Waffle House on the road to Atlanta.

Although the parent Braves regarded Macon as a perfect site for raising young ballplayers, with its charming little park and its solitude, it wasn't exactly the sort of place a twenty-year-old with galloping hormones would choose to spend the summer. The town wasn't sleepy but comatose, its better days having been in the first part of the twentieth century, when it was an overgrown textile town and a retail trading center for the farmers of the rich

Black Belt in middle Georgia, where cotton and peaches were the major crops. After the Second World War, when both textile manufacturing and farming declined, the town grew inward, becoming an isolated outpost nearly two hours from anywhere, a self-sustaining county seat with a couple of small colleges and a smattering of light industries and retail stores stuck in the oppressive humidity of the plains that undulate across Georgia's belly. But this isolation had helped make Macon a strong minor-league baseball town from the start, in 1904, and through the years a lot of players stopped there on their way to the majors; the first home run hit at Luther Williams Field in 1929 was by Paul Richards, and Pete Rose was indeed among the future stars of Cincinnati's Big Red Machine who matriculated with the Macon Peaches in the early sixties.

There were fourteen clubs in the Sally League, from the Albany Polecats in south Georgia to the Hagerstown Suns in Maryland, each with a twenty-five-man roster and a manager in his thirties who, at best, had tasted the proverbial cup of coffee in the big leagues. Most of the players in the league were like Marty Malloy: twenty years old, survivors of rookie ball, now fully engaged in a full-blown, 140-game schedule, being closely monitored by their parent organization, still learning to cope with the travel and the poor lighting and the daily grind made worse by the oppressive Southern heat. For the first time in their embryonic careers they were going up every night against players who had *all* been stars in their own hometowns. "That's probably the hardest adjustment they have to make," said Randy Ingle. "In rookie ball, there were a lot of pitchers who weren't going to make it. They got weeded out pretty fast. But in the Sally League, in A ball, every night now they're seeing pitchers they used to see once a week."

In the early going, it looked like Marty hadn't gotten that message. He tore out of the gate like a spooked horse. In that home opener against Charleston he went four-for-five—his only out coming on a sensational belly-flopping catch of a liner headed toward the gap in left center—and neatly turned the pivot on two double plays. With his reckless enthusiasm—sliding headfirst, diving for ground balls, backing up bases, screaming for the relay throw—he reminded the older patrons of young Pete Rose, "Charlie Hustle." Since Atlanta didn't want to see Marty's confidence jangled, Ingle was holding him out of games against left-handed pitchers—replacing him at second base with a young switch-hitter named Nelson Paulino, latest in a long line of little middle infielders from the town of San Pedro de Macoris in the Dominican Republic—and that partly accounted for Marty's maintaining a .350 batting average as the season entered the summer months.

Clearly, this batch of kids who had played only seventy games or so in the short-season rookie leagues found the daily grind of a long Class A season catching up with them. The Macon Braves had enjoyed only two off-days in the first forty-five days of the schedule ("Yeah, and when they do get an off-day," said Dews, "they spend it chasing women"), and when their old recycled Greyhound bus returned them to Luther Williams Field after an eight-game odyssey to Charlestown, West Virginia, and Hickory, North Carolina, near the end of May, they were whipped, and ahead of them still lay the endless muggy summer of the Deep South.

Willie Stargell was waiting for them when they returned from that trip. Pops, as he was known during his twenty years as not just a prodigious slugger but also the spiritual leader of Pittsburgh Pirate clubs that came to be called "the family," was serving the Braves these days less as a roving batting instructor than as a father confessor. There was plenty he could teach these kids about hitting—he finished his major-league career with a .282 batting average and 475 homers, making the Hall of Fame in his first year of eligibility—but it was his good-natured sagacity and reverence for the game, the traits that had led to his nickname, that made him particularly valuable to the organization. To be sure, he would often fly from his home on the Atlantic Ocean at Wilmington, North Carolina, to spend a week at a time with the high-classification clubs at Richmond and Greenville, fine-tuning the mechanics of blue-chip prospects like Ryan Klesko and Javier Lopez and Chipper Jones. But at fifty-two, Stargell's real value was as a surrogate uncle to twenty-year-old kids in the lowest classifications: the voice of another generation, a wise old owl, the ghost of baseball past.

Around four o'clock in the afternoon on the last Wednesday in May, three hours before the Braves would wind up a brief home stand (to head out afterwards on *another* eight-day road trip), not a dozen Macon players had drifted onto the field. Both the temperature and the humidity were abnormally high, and nobody was stepping lively. While Randy Ingle slapped ground balls to Marty, mainly to check out the knee he had twisted when taken out on a double play a few days earlier, the other Braves shagged balls in the outfield. In the batting cage for some special tutoring was Terrell Buckley—another superb athlete, like Deion Sanders and Bo Jackson, trying to double up in pro football and baseball. (Buckley, then with the Green Bay Packers, had been a defensive back with Sanders at Florida State University.) Standing outside the cage, counseling him and watching every move, was Stargell. "Line drives, all I want to see is line drives and ground balls," Stargell was saying sotto voce as the batting-practice lobs kept coming from the young coach, Joe Szekely. "That's it, that's it. Go with the pitch. You got wheels, son. The whole idea is to use 'em." There was desperation in Buckley's eyes; he was hitting .184 so far, and in spite of his blazing speed had stolen only six bases in ten attempts.

Stargell, who had put on considerable weight during his ten-year retirement, was dressed like a fan who had talked his way onto the field: white Atlanta Braves spring training cap, dirty jogging shoes, wrinkled olive trousers, a hideous rayon shirt featuring red stock cars beneath green pine boughs. "If you ask me," he said to Buckley when their session at the batting cage was finished, "I say the kitchen staff at the Ritz-Carlton could beat the Green Bay Packers any day, *Christmas* Day, you name it." Buckley was trying to compose a rejoinder, but Stargell had already sauntered away, headed for the batting cage behind the right-field bleachers. Soon he was kneeling in the mud and flipping balls to Tom Waldrop, who was struggling at .211 so far this year, with only three homers, in a training exercise known as soft toss. For fifteen minutes Stargell tossed baseballs up to Waldrop, who faced him and caught each ball with his bat and slashed it down the length of the cage; the lesson of the day was to snap the bat rather than drag it through the strike zone.

Later, when the full complement of Macon players had shown up and batting practice began in earnest, Stargell sat alone in the cool of the dugout. He was sweating profusely, wiping his glistening forehead with a bandanna, and the knees of his trousers were soaked from kneeling on ground still soggy from an all-night rain. For the next half hour, between needling the young players who passed and sending them for Diet Cokes, he spoke softly about baseball not as a diversion but as a way of life. "I spend a lot of time in spring training with the kids, the ones they've just signed, sitting around with 'em, talking baseball," he said. "I think they ought to know about the history of the game, ought to know what they're becoming a part of. I remember one day this spring asking a bunch of 'em if they knew the names Koufax and Gibson. Well, they just looked at each other when I said 'Koufax,' and somebody said, 'Isn't Gibson the guy that played outfield for the Dodgers?' Sandy Koufax and Bob Gibson, and they never heard of 'em. Then I said, 'Well, I *know* you've heard of Custer's Last Stand.' Sure, they knew about Custer; got that in history class. 'Well, boys, something you probably don't know is that on the day Custer made his last stand out at Little Bighorn, there was an afternoon baseball game being played in Chicago.' That got their attention." That year, 1876, was indeed the first year of major-league baseball as we know it.

He recalled an incident from his first year in the minors, in 1959, as a nineteen-year-old outfielder with San Angelo in the high desert of west Texas and New Mexico, in the Class D Sophomore League, where a dozen players would hit thirty or more homers every year in the high altitude, and elephantine earned-run averages of 6.00 were not uncommon. "One day we were playing in Roswell, New Mexico, and they told us this old guy who used to be a hero in those parts wanted to come out and take some batting practice with us," he was saying as the Macon players retired to the clubhouse and the Capitol City players wandered onto the field, in bright orange practice jerseys, to loosen up. "I didn't know who Joe Bauman was, but I learned pretty quick that he was a hometown boy and he'd hit seventy-two homers there one year. Anyway, here was this old guy in one of those thick old wool uniforms from another era, and when he went into the cages he began to hit shots I couldn't believe. It was amazing. Here was this guy who seemed ancient to me at the time, and he just couldn't quit. He must have been in his forties, and he was laughing and pounding the ball like he was just another rookie. I didn't understand the feeling for a long time, but somewhere in there, your passion for the game becomes a way of life."

Talk soon got around to the days, thirty and forty years earlier, when there were fewer major-league franchises and less television and the big leagues seemed almost unattainable to a kid toiling in the obscurity of the lowliest minor leagues. "I didn't spend but three and a half years in the minors, which wasn't much in those days, and by the time I got to the majors those guys were like gods to me. I mean, places like San Angelo, the Pioneer League, Asheville, and Columbus, that's a long way from Pittsburgh. You didn't see 'em on TV all the time like kids do now. The big-leaguers, they were just a *rumor*, something you read about in *The Sporting News*, you know. I don't know why, but I still remember the fancy way Vada Pinson dressed, good-looking jackets and slacks, two-tone shoes, smooth face. And my first game up with Pittsburgh we were playing the Braves at Forbes Field, and when Bob Friend busted Hank Aaron on the hands, Aaron inside-outed the ball for a homer off that iron gate out in right center. I was thinking, *Im a left-hander and I haven't hit that gate yet. I better go back to San Angelo where I belong.* Inside-outed it. Scared me to death, just to watch."

On the second day of June they were in Augusta, Georgia, to open a four-game series with the Pirates' farm club there. The Braves had played forty-three games in forty-five days, and their bats were dragging. Several factors were conspiring against Marty—the relentless season, the humidity, the book being kept on him by Sally pitchers and managers, his having to sit out five games with the busted knee—and he had lost thirty points on his batting average, down to .307. Still, he had been named to play in the league all-star game and was back to strength, resting through a rare off-day created by a rainout; he was lying up in his room at a LaQuinta motel in Augusta, nearly one year from the day he had signed with the Braves, when the phone rang. Nikki was going into labor. He flew home to witness the birth of Corbyn, was driven to Macon three days later by his sister, and entered the Braves clubhouse with a box of cigars. He told the Macon *Telegraph* that he planned to marry Nikki when he got home at the end of the season, but in truth, he was far from sure about that. For the first time, a month away from his twenty-first birthday, Marty Malloy's life was getting complicated.

As it often happens in the low minors when young players begin to tire, June was the cruelest month. Doubleheaders began to stack up because of the torrential late-afternoon thunderstorms in the South. Terrell Buckley had thrown in the towel, giving up baseball after batting just .196 with thirty strikeouts in only 107 at bats. Macon had finished second in the first half, but its best pitchers had been promoted to Durham and Greenville, so things didn't look promising for the club in the second half. Pitcher Ken Giard had walked into Randy Ingle's office one day to say he thought he had a drinking problem, at the age of twenty, and was whisked away to a clinic in Atlanta for twenty-eight days. Marty tried to keep a stiff upper lip—"I can cope; having a baby tells me there's more important things in life than baseball"—but the season was beginning to wear on him. He had inexplicably begun flailing for the fences, striking out too often, and his batting average plummeted. He had been hurt again, this time tearing up his shoulder on a headfirst slide, losing three more games on the bench. He had been fined $100 for a brawl precipitated when an Augusta pitcher threw behind Jason Keeline's head ("Gotta stand up for my shortstop"). None of this was lost on Bobby Dews as he traveled the Braves' minor-league circuit.

Checking his voice mail from the phone in his room at the Red Roof Inn in Durham, where he was spending the first week of July with the Durham Bulls, Dews heard an S.O.S. from Randy Ingle, whose Braves were only fifty miles away in Greensboro, playing the Yankees' farm club there. "Bobby, Randy. Marty's going to get killed out there if you don't come help him some more with the pivot. He's still hitting pretty fly balls to the track, too. Poor kid's below three-hundred and his butt's dragging. We'll be home for a while, starting Monday. Hope to see you this week." Dews checked his *Baseball America* directory—a pocket guide listing complete schedules and everything else anyone might need to know about the minor leagues—and saw that Macon would be back at Luther Williams Field for an eight-game home stand beginning July 5. *There goes another Fourth of July.* He tried to placate his wife, in Albany, booked himself into the Comfort Inn in Macon for the coming week, loaded up the car, and headed south again.

Wrinkled, scarred, red faced, wiping his face with a bandanna, Dews stood in the shade next to the box seats behind the batting cage in Macon two days later, his uniform soaked with sweat in the 103-degree sauna. "Can you believe a fifty-three-year-old pitching fifteen minutes of BP in this heat?" he said after finishing his stint on the mound. Ingle was throwing batting practice now, soon to be relieved by pitching coach Larry Jaster. Everybody was wearing shorts, making regular trips to the relative cool of the dugout, where a bucket of ice shavings and chunks of watermelon were laid out on the bench. The bosses were here tonight, Dews said—Chuck LaMar had just left for dinner before that night's game against the Albany Polecats, an Orioles' farm club, with a couple of scouts—and it seemed that he was about to tear into these new white-collar baseball executives, in the manner of a grunt on the assembly line grumbling about the CEO, when he saw Marty motioning to him from second base. Dews took a position beside the batting cage, fished a ball from his hip pocket, hefted his fungo, and began whacking ground balls to the kid.

"Marty'd take a thousand grounders in this heat if I let him," Dews said as we watched the kid gobble the ball like a vacuum cleaner and toss it back on one hop. "At this age, they don't save anything. They're undefeated; they'll never die. I guess we're to blame for part of that. We teach 'em not to be afraid, not to hold back, not to be afraid to commit even if they make a mistake." There was the familiar *thwack-scoop-toss*. "They're a year older and smarter up here, and there's just so much I can do with him during the season," Dews said. "I'd like to get my hands on him in the Instructional League this fall. He's got a hell of a lot to work on. Those fly balls to the fence are a lot of fun, make him feel good, but in Richmond they'd just be a can of corn; they'd be caught. I've got a 'Confucius say' about that: 'Little man, big swing, short career.' I don't want to see anything but line drives and ground balls from Marty. He's gotta learn to bunt and take more pitches, too, if he's gonna hit second, or else he'll just be another eight-hole hitter with slightly better than average speed." He sliced his hand across his throat, signaling to Malloy that he'd had enough ground balls for the day. "And the pivot. There are seven ways to make it. Marty knows all of 'em, but he's still getting hit out there. In the big leagues, those runners know how to hurt you without even cutting you. I tell 'em they've got to be like fighter pilots, zip in and zip out before these big destroyers can get 'em. He's got to learn how to see 'em coming out of the corner of one eye, see which way they're going to come at him, before he commits. That takes a lot of practice, a lot of games, and if he doesn't learn it he's going to get hurt bad. The kid's problem is, he thinks it's macho to hang in there against the big guys. Sometimes he's too tough for his own good."

Everyone agrees that the catcher has the most demanding position on the field, Yogi Berra's reference to the "tools of ignorance" notwithstanding. He must have the physical strength to withstand the constant crouching and to stand up to onrushing base runners. He must be agile enough, even while laden with all of that protective gear, not only to receive pitches thrown into the dirt or over his head but also to throw to any base with accuracy and without any wasted motion, to make the play on bunts in front of the plate, and to corral twisting foul balls popped into the lights and in the treacherous no-man's-land between the plate and the box seats. Most important, though, since he is directly involved in every single pitch of every game and is the only infielder with a full view of the entire playing field laid out in front of him, he must be the quarterback: calling pitches, signaling defensive alignments, barking directions to the infielders when a play is in motion. He is the boss on the field, and there is little wonder why former catchers, traditionally, have made the best managers.

The second toughest position is shortstop, followed closely by second base. "I always thought short was harder than second because of the range and the long throws," said Randy Ingle, who, like Bobby Dews, had been primarily a shortstop but occasionally was moved over to second base in his declining years. "At third base, the big thing is to stop the ball, no matter how ugly it might get, because you've usually got time to recover and make the throw. At second base, most of the time, you've got a little leeway to catch the ball and then make that little snap throw. There's less margin for error at shortstop—you can't bobble the ball; you've got to come up firing; and the throw's got to be right on the money—but at least everything is in front of you. The toughest thing about second is that almost everything is *behind* you, and most of the time you're throwing across your body. That's what the double-play pivot is all about, and if you don't make the pivot you don't belong at second base."

Those seven ways of making the pivot at second base, as prescribed by Bobby Dews, can be taught in ten minutes. If the feed from short or third is expected on the right (outfield) side, the second baseman tags the bag with his left foot and steps with his right foot in one of three directions to make the throw to first: backwards, toward the right fielder; at a ninety-degree angle, toward the left fielder; or straight ahead, toward third base. If the feed is a lead throw, on the first-base side, he tags the bag with his right foot and steps backwards or directly toward first or toward home plate. The seventh pivot involves getting to the bag early, straddling it, and making the tag and throw from a stationary position. All of these moves are learned easily enough in practice, at half speed, but in a game situation there are two complicating factors: the second baseman doesn't know in advance where the feed will come, or whether the runner is sliding to the inside or the outside or directly into the bag. It's happening in a split second, and it's a bitch.

"The ideal is to get a slight lead throw, chest high, so you can throw it first and then get out of there," said Ingle. The double play is one of the prettiest sights in the game aesthetically, is known in baseball lore as the pitcher's best friend, and this pivot, Ingle's ideal, is the one that looks like ballet: the second baseman sweeping across the bag and in one fluid motion taking the feed at the letters and dragging his toe across the bag and planting his left foot and throwing to first just in time to pirouette out of danger in an airborne cartwheel. "Two things," said Ingle. "You can't be afraid you're going to get hurt, and you've always got to hang loose and expect the worst feed."

Although from time to time scouts have been dispatched in search of lanky second basemen with greater range, like the Chicago Cubs' Ryne Sandberg (even he was a converted shortstop), the quintessential second baseman has traditionally been the little guy like Nellie Fox or Eddie Stanky of older times, or the Braves' own Glenn Hubbard or Mark Lemke. "The short guys are likely to have quicker movements, fewer moving parts," said Ingle. "Marty's like that. A little guy like that doesn't have to wind up to make his throw to first. You can only guess most of the time which way the runner's coming at you, so you take 'em one at a time: determine where the feed's coming from, tag the bag accordingly, make the throw, and get the hell out of there. It can take four or five years of doing it in games before it becomes instinctive." Ingle laughed at a memory. "In my last couple of years as a player, just messing around in the afternoon, I'd bet the guys I could make the throw without looking. I'd focus on some pretty girl sitting in the box seats behind third base, straddle the bag, take the feed, and make a perfect throw to first, all of it without looking at anything but the girl in the seats. Never tried it in a game, but I'd been at it long enough to prove it could be done."

And so the season wore on through the stultifying heat of July and August in middle Georgia toward its conclusion. Ken Giard returned from the alcoholism rehabilitation clinic in Atlanta and began pitching out of the bull pen like a new man. The lone groundskeeper, an employee of the city parks department, took to giving parched Luther Williams Field its first of six waterings every day at daybreak. Randy Ingle lured Marty to a sports bar to celebrate his twenty-first birthday, in July, and a few beers led to shots of tequila and a fierce morning after ("my first hard liquor and my last"). Beverly and Tommy Malloy kept making the six-hour drive up from Trenton to watch their son play—Beverly bringing an iron, collecting Marty's shirts, and pressing them on the bureau in their motel room—and on most weekends when the Braves were at home, there would be visits from Marty's friends or cousins. Marty kept a Polaroid shot of his infant son, Corbyn, in the narrow plywood cubicle that was his locker in the clubhouse. Often it seemed like there were more scouts than fans in the stands. Finally, when Tom Waldrop was promoted to Durham with less than two weeks left on the schedule—he had gotten his average up to .246, with eleven home runs, and Atlanta wanted to give him a taste of Carolina League pitching—Marty and Jay Noel had the phone at their apartment disconnected to save money.

Stripped of their pitching in the second half, the Macon Braves finished in the middle of the pack overall, some twenty games behind Savannah. But it had been a satisfactory season for Marty. His batting average of .293 was only three percentage points behind Kevin Grijak's, and he led the club in bases on balls and stolen bases (twenty-four in thirty-one attempts). Randy Ingle liked what he had seen. "It's great if you can win pennants," he was saying one day with less than a week to go, "but my job is to see these kids develop. Just the other night, Marty turned a perfect double play, made a move we'd been working on, and when he got back to the dugout there was a big smile on his face, and I said, 'See there, what'd I tell you?' I'd say he's right on schedule to move up to Durham next year. All in all, I think he's got a better than average chance to make it to the Braves one day. He's hardheaded, but he knows what he's got to do. He's got to retool himself at the plate, learn to bunt, forget about going for the fences, cut down on strikeouts and work for more walks, and learn to hit lefties. I don't think he had two dozen at bats against left-handers, and next year they aren't going to sit him down against 'em anymore. The kid's got a good arm and great range in the field. He's got great instincts, hustle, and work habits. I love him."

Even though his football team was already into its season at Trenton, Tommy Malloy drove to Savannah for the Macon Braves' final game on the day before Labor Day, to fetch his son and take him home for the off-season. One of Marty's cousins, meanwhile, had driven to Macon and loaded up his pickup with Marty's belongings. Marty heard through Randy Ingle, who had gotten word over the Braves' wire, that Tom Waldrop had hit .441 with a homer in his eleven games with the Durham Bulls. On the long drive home with his father, from Savannah to Gilchrist County, Marty sorted out his priorities. For starters, he would see about Nikki and their child. Then he would get some wheels with the rest of his bonus money, pour concrete with a construction gang in Gainesville, try to get himself up to 170 pounds, and maintain a regimen of weight training at the high school gym to further strengthen himself. But for now, as he and his father crossed the state line and were welcomed home again to Florida, he would sleep and he would dream.

CHAPTER 4

From that day in late January when he had ventured onto the ball field behind the high school in Trenton to drop bunts and take some ground balls from his father, marking the unofficial beginning of his third season in pro ball, Marty began to gather steam like a locomotive. He continued his work with weights every other night at the school gym, and soon he cut back on his hours at the construction site in Gainesville, knocking off at lunch every day so he could be on the field by two o'clock. When he had returned home from the season at Macon he had given some thought to teaching himself to bat right-handed, to become a switch-hitter—on orders from Atlanta, he had been allowed to bat only twenty times against left-handers, managing to eke out five base hits on bunts and squibbed ground balls to the opposite side of the infield—but after a few hours of hitting off a tee, all alone at the little ball field, he found that he was so dominantly left-handed that he gave up the idea. His main project for the coming season, then, would be to learn how to cope with left-handed pitching, to "retool himself at the plate" as Randy Ingle had put it, so he wouldn't be benched every time a lefty was on the mound.

Little had been resolved between him and Nikki, and the issue continued to hover like a black cloud over the Malloys' house. Immediately upon Corbyn's birth during the previous summer, Marty had begun writing a check to Nikki for $100 each month, plus paying for health insurance premiums and taking care of whatever medical costs that weren't covered, and Beverly and Tommy had kicked in by buying groceries and Pampers and baby clothes whenever the need arose. These arrangements, in the beginning, were meant to be temporary until some sort of resolution could be reached. When Marty had first returned from Macon, Tommy had thought his son might marry Nikki, grudgingly "do the right thing," but that possibility had been dashed as it became clear that there was no apparent love between them, only a child they had incautiously brought into the world, and the situation was fraught with all of the anger and frustrations of a bitter divorce. And ultimately there was an aching sadness, expressed by Tommy when he mused upon his own marriage. "I was lucky," he said. "I found a woman who lets me live my life, and I love her." The "temporary" financial arrangements became permanent, and Nikki didn't like it one bit.

But beyond the welfare of the child lay what was probably the root of Nikki's anger toward Marty. It was she who had carried the baby, slumping around town for nine months, getting bigger by the day, while he was off hearing the roar of the crowd; it was she, a young woman with dreams of her own, who had seen her life get interrupted; it was she who saw Marty's success intrude upon any hopes for her own. There was little future for her or any other young person in Trenton, but as long as there was a baby to be nursed and fed there was little opportunity for her to take up studies at Santa Fe Community College or to spend full workdays at a job in Gainesville. She was stuck right there in Trenton; and to make matters worse, her new stepfather had his own resentments toward Marty and wouldn't even let him through the door to visit the baby. Marty and Nikki were at an impasse that threatened to go on for a very long time. Throughout the fall and winter, they fought in a tug-of-war over such basic matters as who would keep Corbyn for the night. They were children themselves, obliged to raise a child.

At least Marty could immerse himself in thoughts of baseball, and this year he was in a much better frame of mind as he looked ahead to spring training at the Braves' minor-league complex. This time he had been smarter about buying a vehicle—with some of the remaining $7,500 of his signing bonus he had bought a pickup from a friend he could trust, a two-year-old Chevy S-10 with twenty thousand miles on it, the same as his father's except that it had smoked windows, a "fuzz-buster," four-wheel drive, and a powerful speaker system—and, more important, he had more of a sense of where he stood with the Braves after two successful seasons in the organization. Every day from that beginning in late January, he and his father could be seen working out at the high school field beside the football stadium from three o'clock until dusk.

Life began to quicken toward the day he was to report to West Palm Beach in early March. He got his legal limit of deer, and then some, on the last weekend of the hunting season. One day he went by the hunting lodge in the woods of Dixie County, found his ailing dog dead of heartworm disease, and had to shovel a hole and bury him beneath the pines. Hunting season over, he washed a winter's worth of mud from the pickup. On the first weekend of February he drove it down to Williston, where Paul Runge was holding a kids' baseball clinic; among the major-league players who had stopped by to help out, en route to spring training themselves, was none other than Brett Butler, the premier bunter in baseball, and Marty was buoyed not so much by the chats he had with him about bunting and baserunning as by the fact that the star center fielder of the Los Angeles Dodgers was actually smaller than he, by about an inch and ten pounds. When the first week of March rolled around, he had said farewell to the construction crew, driven over for some Florida Gators baseball games (he would have been playing his second and final year for them if he hadn't turned pro), taken up an aluminum bat and poled three home runs in an exhibition game between current and former Trenton High Fighting Tigers, and even coached third base as his father's team won its first five games. Finally, on March 11, he hugged everybody good-bye and roared away for the three-hundred-mile drive downstate to West Palm Beach, the real Florida, with its palm trees and white beaches and blistering sun.

Marty's mandate for the coming season was clear and simple—learn to handle left-handed pitching—and the long drive to spring training gave him plenty of time to think about it. Even though he needed more refinement in the field, especially on the double play, he probably was already capable of holding his own as a second baseman at the double-A or even triple-A level. He had been, after all, the best fielding second baseman in the league during his first two seasons in the lowest minor leagues. But baseball history was littered with dandy little middle infielders who couldn't buy a base hit and were relegated to the eighth-hole in the batting order. "Any club that needs hitting from its shortstop or second baseman is in trouble," said Sonny Jackson, a light-hitting shortstop for the Braves during the late sixties and now a Braves minor-league coach, but the organization's poo-bahs didn't exactly agree. They fancied Marty as a smart little two-hole hitter who could bunt and draw bases on balls and slash ground ball hits against anybody. No longer would he be coddled against left-handed pitchers.

Since the beginning of baseball, there has been a premium on signing left-handed pitchers, and many otherwise ordinary pitchers have made it to the major leagues simply because they threw with their left hand. They have a large advantage over right-handed pitchers, for two reasons: they seem genetically incapable of throwing a ball straight, and they are a rarity. (Usually, on a twelve-man pitching staff, no more than three of them will be lefties, even though teams actively seek them.) They are particularly murderous against left-handed batters when they learn to drop their delivery to three-quarters, or sidearm, because in doing so they can make the ball appear as if it is being thrown from the first-base coach's box. Right-handed batters *love* to see a lefty on the mound, because their delivery comes into them and is clear to see. But the same delivery is coming out of nowhere to a left-handed batter, and when the ball isn't curving away from them, it is tailing in on their hands at the last split second. And then, of course, because most of the people who pitch batting practice are former infielders and catchers—right-handers—batters seldom hit against lefties except in game situations.

Aggressive left-handed hitters with big swings have been pushed to the point of madness by left-handed pitchers. There is an apocryphal story about a legendary left-handed long-ball hitter in the high-altitude Class C West Texas–New Mexico League of the fifties, Big John something-or-other, who averaged nearly .500 against right-handers but less than .100 against lefties. There was an item once in *The Sporting News* about Big

John strolling the sidewalks of Clovis, New Mexico, the morning after being humiliated in four at bats by a lefty. Seeing a blind man with a tin cup, Big John gave the panhandler a quarter and was continuing his stroll, feeling sanctimonious, when he saw the man reach into the cup and pull out the quarter with his left hand. Big John retraced his steps and wrestled the quarter away. "You sonofabitch," he said, "no goddam left-hander is getting *my* money."

Willie Stargell had played in that league as a kid on the way up, and he knew the feeling. "How many kids throw left-handed on the sandlots?" he said. "Not until you get to pro ball are you going to start seeing lefties, and it can be a shock. On top of that, with the kids these days, they've been able to get around on stuff on the hands because of the aluminum bats all the way through high school. The answer for lefties against lefties, especially with these little guys like Marty, is to lower your expectations; bunt, or go the other way [to the left side]." Said a left-handed slugger named Bob Montag, a legendary home run hitter with the Atlanta Crackers ("the Yankees of the minor leagues") in the fifties, "Lefties had my full attention. I concentrated more when a lefty was on the mound, really bore down against 'em and tried to hit the ball up the middle or to left. I got where it didn't make any difference to me, righty or lefty, but it didn't happen overnight."

As he maneuvered his pickup down Florida's Turnpike toward West Palm, Marty tried to change his mind-set, his whole idea of himself as a hitter. Visions of left-handers swirled in his head as he talked to himself: *head down, tuck the right shoulder, pick up the ball, inside-out swing, ground ball to the left side.* It wouldn't be easy for an aggressive kid like Marty to lower his expectations, to concentrate on simply making contact, but that's what he would have to do this year if he didn't want to wind up in the inconsequential eight-hole. He would have to leave the home runs to

Tom Waldrop, the doubles to the gaps to Bobby Smith. His job was to get on base and move the runners along from the two-hole, and this would mean, in a way, remaking his personality: becoming patient, hitting 'em where they ain't, slapping the ball and running like hell.

During his first spring training at the Braves' sprawling minor-league complex at West Palm, Marty had felt hopelessly lost in the swirl of frantic preparations and weaning of nearly two hundred rookies that takes place in three weeks of intense work. In spite of his solid rookie-league season, which should have inspired self-confidence, he had no sense of place, little feel for exactly where he stood within the organization, and much paranoia that one fuckup at the wrong time—an embarrassing at bat, a foolish play in the field, missing a sign, showing up late and at the wrong field—might set the gallery of coaches and instructors to shaking their heads and clucking and writing something bad about him on the clipboards they toted from field to field like drill instructors at Parris Island. "Don't be afraid," Bobby Dews was always telling the young ones, but the advice was difficult to follow when everybody knew that a major aim in spring training was to get all of the players together in one place at the same time to find out who could play and who couldn't. That first time around, he had known only Dews and the coaches who had been at Idaho Falls, he wasn't into the special rhythm of spring training, and he didn't even have his own car to take him from the motel to the playing fields. When he finally met Glenn Hubbard—the sawed-off second baseman whom he had idolized from those Braves teams of the early eighties, now a coach for the organization—he stammered and called him "sir" as Hubbard shook his hand and proceeded to demonstrate some variations on the double-play pivot.

This time, though, he was ready. He had learned the routine during that first camp; knew all of the coaches by name and reputation (Hubbard had become "Hubbie"); knew it was okay to go back through the line for seconds at the Ramada dining hall; knew that all he had to do to get in some extra licks at the TATC (the Tommie Aaron Training Center—named for Hank's deceased brother—a steel shed the size of an airplane hangar that contained the indoor batting cages and weight-training facilities) was to ask Jay Ward or some other batting instructor if they could meet there at seven-thirty in the morning; knew the names and locations of each of the five practice fields. Most important, now that he had nearly two hundred games of pro ball under his belt, Marty had confidence in himself. He understood that these older instructors roving the fields were his friends and believers, not his enemies, and that made all the difference. Now he could proceed at his own pace without fear of being released, work on things like bunting and hitting lefties, prepare for the long season ahead no matter where it would be spent; he knew to take it slow at first to avoid injuries, to time it so that he would be on a roll when camp broke and he was off to begin another season. Now, in short, he felt like a part of the Braves' family.

Arriving in West Palm around noon, Marty checked into the Braves minor-leaguers' motel and found he would be rooming with John Knott, a first baseman–third baseman who had led Macon with fourteen home runs in '93, his first year in pro ball. In the years before the Braves got serious about their minor-league operation, the kids were scrunched up three to a room in a pair of notorious fleabags in seedy downtown West Palm, the Alma Hotel and the Dixie Courts Motel, but now they were ensconced at a glitzy high-rise Ramada Inn, whence they could look across rippled Clear Lake and see the lights of Municipal Stadium, spring home of the Braves, about two miles away. This Ramada had housed the big club until they were moved to even fancier digs, the Palm Beach Gardens Marriott, and Marty had never seen such a place: spacious soaring atrium in the lobby, swimming pools everywhere, room service, lively nightclub, bar with a big-screen television for watching sports, airy convention halls at every turn, and on the ground floor the huge restaurant-cum-dining-hall where nearly two hundred players would be taking their meals. The place was reserved for baseball people for the month of March—even for umpires, as evidenced by a vanity license plate out in the parking lot: YER OUT.

Marty tossed his stuff inside the door of his room and then drove around the lake to the ballpark, where he underwent a cursory physical examination and was fitted with a uniform (he would wear No. 19 during spring camp); then he returned to the motel. He showered, walked through the buffet line at the dining hall, caught up on the news with teammates from his Macon and Idaho days, called his parents collect in Trenton, then turned in early so he would be rested up for what he saw as the first day of the rest of his life.

When baseball fans think of West Palm Beach, they picture Municipal Stadium, where the Braves and the Montreal Expos shared accommodations and played their home spring training games. It was the usual chummy spring training ballpark, where seventy-two hundred fans could sit near the playing field for close-up views of their heroes while palm trees swayed like hula dancers in the background, and when the Braves and the Expos became contenders during the early nineties, it became a major destination on the Grapefruit League map. But few fans as much as noticed the small billboard off to one side of the parking lot—WELCOME TO BRAVES MINOR LEAGUE COMPLEX—or ventured down a rippled asphalt walk barely wide enough for two golf carts to pass, where another sign warned the hopeful but uninvited, NO TRYOUTS DURING SPRING TRAINING. Blocking the view of what lay beyond were two buses, one of them an old converted Blue Bird school bus spray-painted blue and bearing the Braves' tomahawk, the other the aging Greyhound that had been lugging the Macon Braves around the Sally League for years, and then the horizon opened to reveal what would be home for Marty Malloy and all of the other Braves farmhands during the next three-and-a-half weeks.

This was what Branch Rickey had in mind when he concocted Dodgertown in Vero Beach right after the end of the Second World War to bring uniformity to the education of the Dodgers' young players. The Braves' minor-league complex was concentrated on three ball fields that fanned out from a concrete-block rest room and a set of five-row aluminum bleachers. Except for the occasional parents and pals and girlfriends with cameras, hardly anybody ever sat in the bleachers; watching young men go over the fundamentals of baseball step by step, day by day, over and over and over again is not a spectator sport. The action was on the three ball fields, each named for a Brave from the past (Henry Aaron, Eddie Mathews, and the late Bill Lucas, major-league baseball's first black executive), and all of them were identical: blue concrete-block dugouts, rubber-tired state-of-the-art batting cages, pitching machines, chain-link fences with oleanders and palm trees as a backdrop, portable screens scattered here and there to protect fielders during batting practice. There were two other fields out there in the distance somewhere, Outback and Spahn, but these three were the center ring of what was anything but a circus.

The daily labors there resembled basic training in the military. Group work would begin each morning at exactly ten o'-clock on the Eddie Mathews field, when Bobby Dews, wearing his white home Braves uniform with the number 5 and his name across the back, would stand on the mound and gather his charges to outline the day's work. Pitchers wore red jerseys, position players blue, the numbers on their backs ranging from 1 (a rookie outfielder named Anthony Ruff) to 99 (the Macon relief pitcher Leo Ramirez). Every morning during that first week of camp they began with the same routine: pickoff throws and rundown situations. With a pitcher or an outfielder on first base—no sliding; running only at three-quarters speed—and a full complement of infielders, the runner would break for second and let himself get caught in a rundown. It was quiet, except for Dews: "Remember, never let him get between you and home plate; always run him back." Every ten minutes the drill expanded until, finally, with the bases full, there was a triple steal. At ten-thirty everybody dispersed to the other fields—rookies on the Aaron field, Class A players on Mathews, the AA and AAA players on Lucas—to stretch, then throw, then play pepper, the ancient exercise wherein a batter taps tosses back to three or four fielders arrayed in front of him. At eleven o'clock there was more work on pickoffs and rundowns. Finally, at eleven-thirty, pitchers were running along the outfield fences, infielders were fielding ground balls, and outfielders were taking balls shot from cannons manned by coaches down the foul lines. Just before noon, with the sun blazing through the high cirrus clouds and pushing temperatures into the eighties, the infielders and outfielders began working on relays from the outfield.

There was an irony in all of this regimentation: it tended to produce joyless robots, cool machines, automatons who moved on the field like members of a precision drill team. These same drills were occurring on minor-league fields throughout the spring training camps, in Florida and Arizona alike, in some ways taking the joy and adventure out of the game; this was the precise purpose of the daily repetitions. "By the time I'd made it [to the big leagues] I'd been in the Baltimore system for four years, and I really knew the game," Merv Rettenmund, an outfielder for the Orioles in the late sixties and seventies, once told Roger Angell of *The New Yorker:* "We were a boring club to watch, because on the routine plays—the cutoffs, the relays, the rundowns—everyone did it right. No exceptions. Nowadays, the routine infield pop-up is no longer routine on some occasions— it's an adventure." During that era, every young player who joined the Dodgers organization was handed a paperback that became his bible—*The Dodger Way of Baseball*—to ensure that everyone in the system, from top to bottom, did everything the same way, from leading off of first base to working the wheel coverage in a bunt situation. "We don't want any surprises," said Bobby Dews. "That's what you get in a sandlot game. First you catch the ball, then you throw it. If you make the basic plays, the odds are that you won't need the sensational catch to save two runs, because there won't be two runners in scoring position in the first place."

Watching over the whole process were the minor-league su- pervisors Chuck LaMar and Rod Gilbreath, bumping along from field to field on canopied golf carts, and on one of those mornings, Hank Aaron himself, now a front-office executive, clad in gray slacks and a rayon shirt and sneakers. Silently, all business, the players endured the morning routine because they knew the fun—batting practice—would be their reward in the afternoon. At noon they began drifting in from the fields like cows answering the distant clanging of a dinner bell, heading for the clubhouse for what passed for lunch. "We try to vary the menu," said Dews. "Ham-and-cheese sandwiches on Monday, cheese-and-ham on Tuesday." With their paper plates holding sandwiches, fruit, and a cookie, paper cups holding iced tea, they hunkered over picnic tables in the clubhouse or drifted outside to the shadow cast by the TATC shed. While they ate in silence, cooling down and thinking their private thoughts, they could hear the organ playing and then the public address announcer giving out the starting lineups for that afternoon's Atlanta or Montreal game on the main stage of Municipal Stadium.

Energized by lunch and the prospects of batting practice, they smiled for the first time when they returned to the fields for the afternoon. The earnest crack of bats meeting balls rang over the complex as they swung away at the pitching from the coaches and, eventually, when there were no more fresh arms left, the pitching machines. "Hey, Eddie, how you holding up?" somebody shouted to Eddie Watt, a potbellied soldier who would serve this season as pitching coach for the rookie-level Gulf Coast League Braves at West Palm. "Hell, they're *lovin'* it," he croaked as the rookies teed off on his soft lobs, pulling everything. "Hey, we ain't using but half the field here." Now and then a soft "dammit" or "shit" was heard from players still rusty from the winter's layoff, but mostly there were the sounds of ringing line drives and the rippling of the mesh in the batting cages on foul tips. From the stadium nearby there would be a sudden roar from the crowd—a David Justice home run? a great stop by Jeff Blauser? a strikeout from Greg Maddux?—but the young players had their own games to worry about and paid it little attention. Their day officially ended around three o'clock, although some would hang back for some special tutoring (bunting tips from Sonny Jackson, advice on gripping the curveball from Larry Jaster, the pivot from Glenn Hubbard), and by four in the afternoon the fields were deserted except for groundskeepers watering and dragging the infields in preparation for the next day's work.

Quickly showered and dressed in the cramped clubhouse, as crowded as Grand Central, the players raced for dinner at the Ramada and then trudged to the motel's convention rooms for nightly lectures on everything from venereal diseases to health insurance programs. One night Willie Stargell got the rawest rookies together for his annual fireside chat about baseball and

Custer's Last Stand, and every other night the thirty-odd Latin players came together for English lessons taught by someone from the local school system. Milling around in the hotel lobby afterward, they would talk about matters beyond their control: the NCAA basketball tournament (Marty's Gators were headed into the Final Four), Michael Jordan's desperate attempts to learn baseball overnight in spring training with the Chicago White Sox over in Sarasota (most of them loved Jordan as a basketball player but didn't approve of his knocking some full-time prospect out of a job), the rumblings that the major-league players might strike during the season (they had only a vague awareness that the union's position might help them if they ever made it to the big leagues). Only late at night, as they slumped off to their rooms, did they wrestle privately with what loomed largest on their minds: would they be moved up this year, be held back, or—the unspeakable—be unconditionally released?

Marty, full of himself this second time around, was going about his business. He had begun most days by being first in line for a six-thirty breakfast at the buffet table downstairs, then hustling over for work at the indoor batting cages in TATC, followed by some weight lifting. He would hassle the former infielders, Hubbard and Runge, for some private work on things like the pivot or feed on the double play, or collar Sonny Jackson for tips on bunting for a base hit, then go through the full-squad workout, ending the day with more individual work ("See there, it's like money in the bank," Dews was telling him late one afternoon as Marty dropped bunts down the third baseline). His hands were blistered with what looked like rope burns from the accumulated hours of batting practice, and his legs felt so dead that he was saving the leg work portion of his work in the weight room for the very end of the day, when he wouldn't need the legs anymore. On a Friday morning, March 18, after a week of this, he was ready for games, itching for some live action. "After a while you get tired of just talking about it, getting all this advice from the coaches," he said as the other players drifted out from the clubhouse to begin another day of repetitions. His forehead was blistered below the cap line from exposure to the wind and sun. Tony Graffanino, who was now being touted by the press as the Braves' latest second baseman of the future, had just been sent back to the minor-league camp after getting some at bats and some chances in the field with the big club, but Marty tried not to think about that. "I'm ready to play some games so I can try some of this stuff I've been working on. I can't worry about him [Graffanino] or anybody else. It's gonna be a long season, wherever it is, and I've got to be ready for it. Last year I got off to a slow start in games here but got hot in the last few days. That's what you want to do, come flying out of spring training on a roll."

That night, at the Ramada cafeteria, there were hamburgers and potato salad on the buffet line. While Marty, Tom Waldrop, and John Knott hunkered down over their plates in a distant corner of the room, Bobby Dews, Dave Hilton, and Glenn Hubbard manned a round table near the entrance. Hilton, Marty's manager at Idaho Falls, was in charge of checking off the names of the players as they drifted in, their hair still wet from showers, and Dews served as a greeter. "*Bway-nose know-chaize*, Julio, or is it *tar-daize* this time of day?" he would say in his painful south Georgia drawl, trying to make the Latin players feel at home. Hilton spoke again of how much fun it is to see young players, away from home for the first time in their lives, learning how to take care of themselves. Nearby, the young coach, Joe Szekely, joyfully tossed his new baby in the air, making the older fathers wince. Hubbard continued with a story from his first year as a coach in the organization: "It was against Bluefield, I remember, in the Appalachian League, and our pitcher had his best stuff, but they were killing him. It must have been about the fifth inning when I found out why. Our second baseman wasn't giving the sign to our shortstop about who'd cover second, except when a fastball had been called, so the other guys knew exactly what was coming on every pitch . . ." Dews told about a gifted but flaky outfielder named Joe Patterson and the day they flew into the Phoenix airport with the Tulsa Oilers in triple-A: "There was this big sign that said, 'Welcome to Phoenix,' and Joe said, 'Well, here we are, Bobby, we finally made it to the big time. The Big F' " Dews was in his thirty-fifth spring training camp now, but there had been a moment of hesitation during the off-season when his name was mentioned for the baseball coaching job at his alma mater, Georgia Tech. It would have paid $165,000 plus considerable perquisites, quite a raise over the $65,000 he got from the Braves, and he lusted for the chance to come in from the cold, but he was passed over for a college coach twenty years his junior.

The moment the players had been waiting for came the next morning, a Saturday, the eighth day of spring training, when they reached the clubhouse. In each locker there was a printout listing the tentative assignments for the '94 season of every player in the organization. Not surprising, most of the players from the 1993 Macon team, including Marty and Tom Waldrop, were headed for the Durham Bulls of the advanced-A Carolina League. At ten o'clock they gathered as usual around the mound on the Mathews field. Nearby, on the Lucas field, a complement of Braves players not making the big club's trip to Port St. Lucie for a game with the Mets—Fred McGriff, Jeff Blauser, David Justice, Terry Pendleton—took some batting practice. Marty and Tom and the others paid scant attention, though, focusing instead on Chuck LaMar as he stood on the mound and addressed the assemblage: "We've posted the rosters for Richmond, Greenville, Durham, and so forth, but it doesn't mean you'll break camp with that club. Ten or fifteen of you will move up or down, according to how you play in the games beginning Tuesday. If you're pissed off, that's all right. Now. When we start playing these games, I don't want you to forget these fundamentals we've been working on . . ."

So the waiting was over for Marty, not that there had been much of a question about where he would be playing. He and Waldrop had been standing beside each other on the lip of the mound, and now they looked at each other and grinned. For them, right on schedule in their third year of pro ball, it would be the Durham Bulls and Durham Athletic Park, made famous by the movie *Bull Durham*. Intracamp games would begin that afternoon, LaMar said. They all stepped livelier as they dispersed to the various fields for the morning's work on fundamentals. Had he bothered to check it out, Marty would have found that, of the 106 in his rookie class of '92, only forty-nine were still in the Braves' organization.

That afternoon, as organ music drifted over from Municipal Stadium, the Durham Bulls came together for the first time. Marty's manager at Durham would be a startling change from the down-home Randy Ingle of Macon—Matt West, a handsome and articulate thirty-four-year-old whose pitching career had been shortened when he took a line drive in the face. West had a degree in political science from Long Beach State and drove a Mercedes instead of a pickup; hitting infield practice before that first intracamp game, West mused, "Nicely done, nicely done," every time Marty turned a double play or the third baseman Bobby Smith backhanded a grounder and gunned it to Kevin Grijak at first base.

Once the first game of the spring began, the Durham Bulls against the Macon Braves, there was a vibrancy in the air that had not been felt before. Chuck LaMar and Rod Gilbreath edged closer to the backstop at Lucas Field in their golf carts, and those players not assigned to play sat on a single aluminum bench or stood and hooked their fingers through the chain-link backstop to yell encouragement. A pitch chart was being kept by a pitcher who wouldn't work that day, Chris Seelbach of the Greenville Braves, and a local umpire called balls and strikes while another pitcher worked the bases. (The nurturing of the young pitchers' arms had begun. The maximum number of innings each pitcher would be allowed to throw all year, including spring and Instructional League games, was his age multiplied by ten.) The game got under way with all of the buoyancy of a grudge match on the sandlots. "Whaddya care, Bobby, whaddya care?" one of the coaches shouted when Bobby Smith glowered at the umpire over a called strike; Smith shot the next pitch into the gap in right center for a belly-flopping triple and was greeted by Matt West, coaching third base, with a "nicely done, nicely done."

Marty, on his first at bat of the new year, got a dubious hit off of an infielder's glove and lit out for second base on the next pitch, plowing headfirst into the bag for a stolen base. When the dust cleared, he could be seen standing on the bag, wincing and kneading his left shoulder, the one he had hurt at Macon the year before, which had forced him to sit out four games. The field grew quiet as a trainer raced out to second base like a medical corpsman during battle, his fanny pack full of first-aid supplies jiggling as he ran, but Marty shrugged him off. "Let's check it out later, okay?" he said, dismissing the trainer, dusting off and taking his lead off the bag. By "later" Marty meant at the end of the season; not right now, not during the first game of spring camp. He did not suffer being benched gladly, and his managers had learned to dispatch an injured Marty Malloy to the bull pen so he wouldn't drive them nuts in the dugout, begging to get into the game. The trainer, Jay Williams, who would serve the

Durham Bulls that season, insisted on wrapping the shoulder with an elaborate ice bag immediately after the game and every afternoon for the next week. "The kid's going to be fine if he doesn't kill himself first," said Bobby Dews, smiling and shaking his head, about to give up trying to convince him to slide feet-first. "No sweat," Marty said. "I'll just play through it. We can check it out in September."

The pace began to roll toward the day they would break camp and drive to their destinations to begin the new season. (Those assigned to the three rookie-league clubs, whose seasons wouldn't begin until June, would be held back in extended spring training.) On the Tuesday following Marty's mishap in the first camp game, the Durham club took the old Macon bus up the road to Vero Beach for a game against the Dodgers' advanced-A Bakersfield club in the California League, and Marty played all nine innings, going 2-for-4 (including a triple off of a left-hander), turning the pivot on two double plays. They began playing home-and-home games against other Class A clubs in the area, and Marty was off to a fine start; in that first week's games he was 5-for-14, with the triple and a double and a bunt single coming against lefties. Then, on the Saturday that ended the first week of games, with Durham on the road playing the Mets' club at Port St. Lucie, he was held back at West Palm so the brass could have a look at Nelson Paulino at second base. Marty had worked out that morning with the rookies on the Aaron field, taking infield and batting practice, and was ready to knock off for the afternoon when Dews came to him at lunch and told him to keep his uniform on, that he was "going to get [his] feet wet." Marty dutifully hung around the fields, intently watching as both Greenville and Richmond played outside clubs, when suddenly Dews called for him and threw him in at second base for triple-A Richmond against the Ottawa Lynx, Montreal's club in the International League, one step from the majors. "I had butterflies," he would say later. "I figured in triple-A they threw the ball a hundred miles an hour, but what I found out was, they get it over the plate." He flied to center field in his only at bat and handled a couple of chances without incident in the three innings he played. He should have found out the name of the Ottawa pitcher he had batted against, he said, so maybe they would have something to talk about if they both made it to the majors someday.

Chuck LaMar's caveat on the morning the tentative rosters were announced—that "ten or fifteen of you will move up or down, according to how you play in the games"—was coming to pass now. At least that many players were shuffled about as the final rosters for the four top minor-league clubs were fine-tuned. Durham was being assigned several great pitching prospects who had been at Macon the year before, including the high-round draft choices Jamie Arnold and Matt Murray. Jason Keeline, none too pleased, had failed to make the move up to AA Greenville and again would be Marty's double-play partner. Tom Waldrop was having an awful spring at the plate but would go to Durham as a platooning right fielder and designated hitter. The reliever Leo Ramirez, a sidearming right-hander who had saved seventeen games and had his moments in '93 at Macon, was released outright on the grounds that he was already twenty-five years old, after only that one season in pro ball. Terrell Buckley, the Green Bay Packers' defensive back, had been cajoled into trying baseball one more time; he, too, was released. John Knott, Marty's spring roommate at the Ramada, was being held back at Macon to give some experience to a club overstocked with green young players. The best news from Marty's standpoint was that the leadoff man at Durham would be a scrappy little dirt player along the lines of Lenny Dykstra, the Philadelphia Phillies' tobacco-chewing center fielder: Mike

Warner, who had batted .319 at Durham in '93 but was being returned to the Bulls as a DH until his throwing arm healed from arthroscopic surgery. Marty was back in the two-hole now, and twice already in spring games he had slashed singles past drawn-in third basemen to score the speedy Warner, who had singled and stolen second.

On the last weekend of spring training, Marty got a call from his mother with the news that Corbyn had taken his first steps on the day he turned ten months old. Beverly Malloy had also helped Marty find an apartment for him and Tom Waldrop to share in Durham—a married couple from Trenton, now living in Durham, had sent her some brochures for rentals in the area—so that chore was out of the way. Everything was on course now. The shoulder was okay, the blisters on his hands had turned to calluses, he had gotten his second wind, and he was nailing the ball. One of the coaches for Durham would be Rick Albert, a man in his forties who had been a spray-hitting second baseman during his own playing career, and Albert had set a goal for Marty during the upcoming season: twenty bunts for base hits. Indeed, Marty, who had tracked down Brett Butler one day before the Dodgers played an exhibition against the Braves at Muncipal Stadium and had another conversation with him about bunting and baserunning, was showing bunt on every at bat; to his glee, he was also slicing singles and doubles past drawn-in third basemen. There were final tune-up games against Macon on that last weekend, and after a morning game on Monday they would break camp and drive away to Durham. There was talk that the Bulls' home opener at Durham Athletic Park might attract upwards of nine thousand fans, nearly twice the capacity of the legendary little ballpark that had been there for more than half a century. "You'll never really understand why you love this game," Marty was told by one of the older instructors, "until you've played at the DAP."

CHAPTER 5

The day for breaking camp would be a long one, covering 550 miles, with a layover for dinner in Trenton, and Marty was eager to get going. He gobbled his last breakfast at the Ramada, tossed his belongings into the pickup, stopped on the way to the playing fields to check the oil and fill up with gas, and was in uniform by ten o'clock for a final camp game against the young Macon club. It was a listless exercise with nothing on the line, and noon couldn't come soon enough for players whose minds were already on Macon and Durham. They were in and out of the showers in a flash, soon part of a caravan on Florida's Turnpike, headed north to the next adventure.

Marty arrived in Trenton at dusk to find that Nikki had left Corbyn at his parents' house. Tom Waldrop had peeled off the interstate at Gainesville for a quick visit with an aunt and uncle who lived there, then found his way to the Malloys' for dinner. It was Beverly Malloy's usual country feast. Marty was miffed that Nikki hadn't stuck around—further evidence of the standoff between them, he reckoned—but he made the best of the last hours he would spend with his son until the season ended in September. While his mother washed his clothes and ironed his shirts, Marty played with Corbyn, bouncing him on his knee and marveling as the boy gurgled and waddled toward him like a colt learning to walk. He and Tom said good-bye and left in tandem around nine o'clock, Marty leading the way over backroads until they picked up the interstate around Jacksonville, and at one in the morning they arrived at the motel in Savannah where the Bulls had been booked for the midpoint in their journey.

They left Savannah at daybreak Tuesday for the 360-mile push to Durham on interstates, pausing for diversion at a gaudy state-line tourist stop called South of the Border (fireworks, trinkets, eats), reached the city limits of Durham around one o'clock, and drove straight to the apartment they had leased sight unseen. It was in the Willowdale Apartments, a complex favored by young divorcees and blue-collar workers, only ten minutes from the DAP in downtown Durham and next door to a shopping center where they would have free privileges at a fitness center called the Spa. Their roommates were already there: a rangy blond left-handed reliever named John Simmons, who had been with them at Macon the year before; and Mike Warner, at least until his arm healed and (he hoped) he was promoted to play center field at Greenville. The apartment was okay, a furnished three-bedroom renting for $750 a month, an improvement over the hovel Marty and Tom had shared in Macon and a long way from the old house six of them had called home in Idaho Falls during their rookie year.

They barely had time to agree on living arrangements (Warner would sleep on the sofa until he found another place) before it was time to go downtown and make their first official appearances as Durham Bulls. It was Meet the Bulls Night at the Hilton Hotel, and upwards of two hundred fans were there to have a look at them, get autographs, eat barbecue, and hear a few words from Matt West about the club's prospects. The young players, fit and tanned from a month beneath Florida's bright skies, brought the promise of spring to fans still ashen from a winter spent indoors. Basketball still dominated the sports pages at that time of year—the Duke Blue Devils, of Durham, were in the NCAA's Final Four tournament just under way in Charlotte (as were Marty's Florida Gators)—but this was heady stuff, this turnout just to meet the players, a pleasant omen for the season ahead of them. At midafternoon of the next day, after being fitted for uniforms (Marty would wear the number 10) and shown their way around the ballpark, the 1994 Durham Bulls drifted onto the field for their first look at the DAP and a workout that ran into the early evening, and about one hundred fans showed up for that, too. They would open the season with seven games on the road, in Virginia, before making their home debut on Friday night, April 15.

No other state in America can match North Carolina's tradition in baseball at the grassroots level, and there was a time, before California's population explosion during the Second World War, when none supplied so many players per capita for the professional leagues. This goes back to the decades between the two world wars, when the state's economy was driven by textiles, tobacco, and furniture making. Whole towns sprang up around company-owned mill villages from one end of the state to the other, inbred enclaves whose unlettered residents ("lintheads" was the working pejorative for those in the textile mill towns) owed their souls to the company store. The paternalistic mill owners controlled nearly every aspect of life in those ragged little communities—they had built the houses, the schools, the churches, the stores, the infirmaries, even the greenhouses— and one way they had of diverting the residents' attention from their dreary labor in those huge windowless sweatshops, to stave off mutiny, was to sponsor mill-town baseball teams. They built ball fields, encouraged the young men to take up this healthy pursuit, outfitted them with uniforms and equipment, and made it seem a patriotic duty for the mill-towners to go out and support the local club. Fierce rivalries sprang up between these mill towns, some of them only ten miles apart, and soon it became a point of civic pride when, say, the team from little Tarboro rode over on a Sunday afternoon and kicked the shit out of lordly Rocky Mount.

It didn't take long for a healthy young man to figure out that one way out of the mill village was to excel at baseball, get good enough at it that he could hire himself out to the professional teams in the larger towns. That was precisely the background of Enos "Country" Slaughter, a Roxboro boy who went on to become one of the stars of the St. Louis Cardinals of the late thirties and forties. Except for Charlotte, the only real city the state has ever had, North Carolina was largely rural with midsized towns, regional trading centers spaced every fifty to a hundred miles. Thus, when the Second World War had ended and people fled the mill towns and the tobacco fields for a better life, there was a strong base of baseball fans in towns now grown large enough to support a professional team in the low minor leagues. Indeed, in 1949, minor-league baseball's high-water point in terms of numbers (fifty-nine leagues, 448 teams, nearly eight thousand players, an all-time attendance record of nearly 40 million), North Carolina had more professional teams than any other state: forty-four in seven leagues, from the Charlotte Hornets in Class B to the High Point–Thomasville Hi-Toms in

Class D. The sprawling state of Texas was second, with thirty-seven teams, followed by Georgia, with twenty-four, and California, with twenty-two.

Durham was among those mid-sized towns with a population quite sufficient to support a club in the low minors. Primarily a tobacco-processing center, as well known as the home of Bull Durham tobacco as for Duke University, Durham had been in professional ball since the twenties, when the Durham Bulls of the Piedmont League played at city-owned El Toro Stadium in the shadows of a cluster of redbrick warehouses near downtown. Country-come-to-town baseball fanatics filled the little ballpark's rickety wooden stands to cheer the Bulls as they played rivals from such nearby towns as Raleigh and Greensboro and Burlington, in an era known for civic hatreds that spilled over onto the playing field. When El Toro Stadium's stands burned to the ground in 1939, a covered grandstand was built of brick and steel, and it was renamed Durham Athletic Park. Then, in 1945, just as the boys began trickling home from the war and baseball was on the verge of entering its Golden Era—when there were only sixteen major-league cities and no television to speak of and it seemed as though every town of any size in America had its own minor-league club—Durham became a charter member of the Carolina League.

The league's fortunes would fluctuate wildly over the next three decades, as would happen throughout professional baseball, but the Carolina League endured. Overall attendance doubled from 536,000 (an average of about one thousand per game) in that first year, 1945, to more than a million in '47. Except for the St. Louis Cardinals, who wholly owned the club in Winston-Salem as part of their far-flung chain gang (the Cardinals' farm system once consisted of thirty-three teams, compared to today's norm of six), the major-league front offices had not yet adopted the full-scale practice of using the minor leagues for player development; most rosters were filled with local boys, career minor-leaguers who spent years with the same club. One of those was Leo "Muscle" Shoals, who hit fifty-five home runs in '49 for the Reidsville Luckies (many of the teams had tobacco-related nicknames, like Bulls, Tobs, Tars, Leafs). Another was Durham pitcher Eddie Neville, who was 25-10 that same year and had a career won-lost record of 75-38 in the league. And there was Willie Duke (one of many to go off to the war as a prospect and come back a has-been), who averaged .331 in fifteen years in the minors; and Woody Fair, another war veteran, who batted .348, scored 161 runs, and drove in another 161 for the '46 Bulls. Still other hometown heroes, like "Teapot" Frye and "Crash" Davis, were best remembered for their monickers. Then, as the minor leagues became farm system incubators during the fifties and sixties, the Carolina League every year began churning out players headed not only for the major leagues but for the Hall of Fame: Willie McCovey, Carl Yastrzemski, Joe Morgan, Johnny Bench, Rod Carew, ad infinitum. Arguably, the Carolina League had become the jewel of the low minors as far as sending players to the majors was concerned.

But the advent of television and air-conditioning began taking its toll from a business standpoint in the fifties and sixties, and minor-league franchises started dying like mosquitoes at first frost. There were better things to do now in those small towns all across America, like stay home under the air conditioner and watch televised major-league games for free, and the minor-league franchises that survived did so only through heavy subsidy from their parent organizations. Overall attendance in the Carolina League plummeted from 1 million in '49 to less than one-third of that in '59. There was a resurgence of interest in the early sixties, when the league was expanded to ten members and a newcomer, the old tobacco town of Kinston, averaged better than two thousand fans a game. But then, in 1972, the unthinkable happened: the Durham Bulls, a fixture in the minor leagues for half a century, folded for lack of interest. Three years later, there were only four teams left in the league—Rocky Mount and Winston-Salem in North Carolina, Salem and Lynchburg over the line in Virginia—and the all-star teams featured such forgettable names as Frank Grundler and Elijah Bonaparte. Durham Athletic Park, the beloved DAP, lay dormant and forlorn, a widow before her time.

Then, during the winter preceding the 1980 season, when minor-league baseball seemed to be on the verge of another resurgence—due, in part, to the fans' distaste over another round of squabbling between the owners and the players at the major-league level—a young entrepreneur from Greensboro figured it was a propitious time to bring baseball back to Durham. Miles Wolff was only thirty-four, regarded as a wunderkind after some years of dabbling with minor-league franchises in those parts, and he had just given birth to a baseball tabloid, *Baseball America*, based in Durham, which soon would replace *The Sporting News* as the bible of baseball. As a local boy, Wolff didn't have to spring for any marketing research to know that the area called the Research Triangle was ripe for baseball if the idea was presented properly. The Triangle was formed by the intertwined towns of Durham, Raleigh, and Chapel Hill, whose populations totaled nearly half a million people, and its diversified economy made it one of the most stable urban areas in the country. For Wolff's purposes, the Triangle held a solid core of baseball fans with money to spend: an interesting stew of the retired old-timers left over from the tobacco days of the forties and fifties and the academics and students representing the three major universities in the area (Duke, North Carolina State, and North Carolina). The key was to put together a class act: a winning club, in the charming old DAP, pitched as "the Triangle's team."

Wolff wrote a check for $2,417 to the Carolina League for

franchise rights, paid out $80,000 to upgrade the DAP, signed a player development contract with the Atlanta Braves, and opened the gates for the 1980 season. He had hoped to average close to a thousand fans a game, and he could hardly believe his eyes when watching the Durham Bulls play at the DAP became second only to Atlantic Coast Conference basketball as the hottest ticket in the Triangle. The parent Braves were the Triangle's favorite big-league club, thanks to their proximity, TBS's broadcasts, and their revitalization on the field, and they assigned a bevy of promising young prospects from their refurbished farm system to the new Bulls. With a bombastic career minor-leaguer named "Dirty Al" Gallagher as manager and such future Braves as Milt Thompson and Gerald Perry as the leading men, the Bulls were an exciting team, based on speed and brash. They finished that season with a record of 84-56. More important, to Wolff, were the gate receipts. The Bulls led the Carolina League in attendance that year with 175,000 paid (an average of twenty-five hundred per game), more than the entire league had drawn during any of the bleak seasons between 1975 and 1977, more than any individual club in the league had drawn since 1947. Carolina League attendance had tripled, from the two hundred thousand of the year before, when there were only six clubs, to six hundred thousand. The Durham Bulls—and the Carolina League—were back.

It got better every year during the eighties, especially when the 1981 major-league season was virtually destroyed by a full-blown players' strike. As the Braves strengthened their farm system through high draft choices and a commitment to scouting and player development, the Bulls, as their top Class A club, were a prime beneficiary. Now there was a steady stream of bona fide major-league prospects passing through on their way up. Nearly half of the players who would make the Braves major-league baseball's team of the nineties—stars like Mark Lemke,

Jeff Blauser, David Justice, and Steve Avery—matriculated at Durham during the mid- and late eighties. Now it wasn't uncommon to see overflow crowds at the DAP, whose ancient confines could hold five thousand fans if they scrunched up and spilled over onto the grassy banks beyond the outfield fences. With the release in 1989 of a feature movie called *Bull Durham*, the tale of a fictional Bulls team and its comic perambulations through a season at the DAP, the Bulls became America's favorite minor-league team. Baseball fans from all over the country began building vacation trips around a visit to Durham to catch the Bulls, now beginning to outdraw much larger cities like Memphis in AA and Phoenix in AAA, and the sale of such Bulls memorabilia as T-shirts and caps (with the fanciful logo of a snorting bull jumping through an ornate *D*) became a booming cottage industry. As further proof of his perspicacity, Miles Wolff sold the Bulls to a broadcasting corporation in the Triangle following the 1990 season. Against his investment of $82,417 in 1980 (the franchise fee plus the cost of upgrading the DAP), he walked away with $4 million.

Most of the players who would make up the 1994 Durham Bulls had seen the movie when they were still in high school, and although they might not be interested in Miles Wolff's financial windfall, they were excited about the prospect of playing at the DAP before crowds nearly five times as large as they had seen in rookie ball and at Macon. This was to have been the season the Bulls moved out of the decaying old ballpark and into new digs, a "new old" edifice under construction less than a mile away on the other side of downtown Durham, but a series of snafus would delay the move until '95. That was all right for Marty and the other Bulls as they settled into town and prepared for the new season. "The new park sounds like it's going to be something else," Marty said, "but to tell the truth I'd like to be able to say I played where the movie got made." Tom Waldrop had gotten a taste of the DAP during his late-season call-up the year before, and he had mixed feelings: "Those fences in right field have got some angles you wouldn't believe, and the playing field is kind of waffled, but it's great. It's like playing in a museum."

Their opener at the DAP would come later, after they started the season with series at Prince William and Lynchburg. For now, Matt West and his coaches—Rick Albert, a stocky forty-three-year-old in his seventeenth year as a manager and coach in the Braves' system, and white-haired Bill Slack, the winningest manager in the history of the Carolina League, now sixty-one and giving himself three more years before retirement—were busy sorting out the players they had drawn from the deep pool of talent in the Braves' system. Of the twenty-five-man roster, sixteen had played at Macon the year before, four had been sent down from AA Greenville of the Southern League so they could get in more playing time, and the others were being jumped from the rookie leagues to advanced-A. Four of these 1994 Bulls were seen by the organization as genuine blue-chip prospects: the pitchers Jamie Arnold and Matt Murray, the young third baseman Bobby Smith, and the outfielder Damon Hollins. All had been high draft choices and, except for Murray, were nineteen going on twenty. (Murray was twenty-three, had been the second pitcher drafted behind Steve Avery in 1988, but had been delayed by a series of injuries.) Of all the others on the roster, for those who liked to dope the horses and give odds, Marty appeared to be the best bet to make the major leagues somewhere in the future—after, say, three or four more full seasons in the minors. The others were long shots, but as West would say, "That's why we play the games." A history of the Carolina League had just been published, with the title *Separating the Men from the Boys*, and that was what this season promised for those players on the Bulls' roster.

When Marty checked out his partners around the infield, it

looked like a reprise of the '93 season at Macon. Once again he would be given all the playing time he could stand at second base and would be backed up by Nelson Paulino, another of those middle infielders who seemed to come off a production line in the steamy little Dominican town of San Pedro de Macoris; a switch-hitter, Paulino had tied Marty for the lead in stolen bases at Macon with twenty-four but had batted a meek .231 and didn't appear to have much of a future with the Braves. Shortstop would be shared for the time being by Jason Keeline, the broad-chested, slick fielder whose age and inability to hit were working against him (he would turn twenty-five in the first week of the season and was the club's elder), and a raw Mexican teenager named Julio Trapaga, with shoulders so broad that it appeared he had left a coat hanger in his shirt. Trapaga had hit .148 in only fifty-four at bats in the AAA Mexican League in '93 before the Braves thought they saw something and signed him as a free agent (at a cut in pay from $2,400 a month to half of that). At first base would be another Dominican, the brooding Raymond Apolinar Nunez, who had some possibilities as a power hitter but sometimes found his defensive obligations as mysterious as the English language. He would be platooned with the rakish left-handed slugger Kevin Grijak, whose adventures around the bag and in the outfield, where he would sometimes be used in a pinch, cried out "designated hitter." At third would be the stately Bobby Smith; a gleam in the Braves' eyes, a superb athlete just beginning to learn baseball after being taken in the eleventh round in '92; caramel skinned, still growing at six three and 190 pounds, cool as his pencil-thin mustache, characterized by one instructor as "a man among boys, the guy everybody wants to room with."

Most of the catching would be handled by Brad Rippelmeyer, who had hit nineteen homers for Durham in '92, but then batted only .191 at Greenville the next season, and now, twenty-four and one of six married Bulls, was being returned to the DAP for one last look by the Braves' organization. (He was the son of Ray Rippelmeyer, who had pitched in thirty-nine undistinguished innings for the Washington Senators in 1962.) Rippelmeyer's principal backup would be David Toth, who had batted .246 as Macon's starting catcher in '93, his second straight year with that club. The third catcher on the roster was Adrian Garcia, a stocky bilingual kid from New Jersey, whose destiny seemed to be to handle the grunt work in the bull pen—he had gotten into only 125 games in four years as a pro—and to serve as a translator for the three Latins on the club, with whom he shared an apartment.

In the outfield there were as many question marks as there was promise: a proven commodity with a broken wing, a teenaged can't-miss prospect who might or might not be ready for the Carolina League, and two feast-or-famine left-handed swingers capable of big home run numbers if they ever discovered the strike zone and, thus, their groove. The proven commodity was Mike Warner, the gritty little outfielder reminiscent of Lenny Dykstra; he had hit .319 with the Bulls in '93, with a good on-base percentage and twenty-nine stolen bases, and would be with Greenville if not for the arm surgery. The phenom was nineteen-year-old Damon Hollins, a powerfully built Californian who would play center field and bat cleanup after a sensational rookie year at Danville in the Appalachian League; one of those rare ones who throws left but bats right, he was regarded after that one season as one of the top prospects in the low minors. The organization was still waiting for a breakthrough year from Juan Williams, the twenty-one-year-old son of a California preacher, who seemed to light up their eyes with another moon shot just when they were about ready to give up on him (he had hit a five-hundred-footer during spring training that caused a work stoppage on the Mathews field when it bounced once and made it to a golf course across Congress Boulevard); he had spent all of '93 with the Bulls, mashing eleven homers but striking out 120 times in 403 at bats. And the Braves were waiting for Tom Waldrop, who had hit .441 with a homer in his late-season call-up from Macon in '93 but was getting along in years (he had turned twenty-four during the winter); he, like Williams, was prone to strikeouts, but his twenty-one homers in 183 games in the low minors were sufficient evidence to inspire the Braves to keep him around for a while longer.

Of the eleven pitchers, the right-handers Matt Murray and Jamie Arnold would be the most closely watched throughout the organization. Both had been high draft choices, fetching half-a-million-dollar signing bonuses, and they could light up radar guns with their fastballs. Murray was a massive specimen, six six and 235 pounds, a thick-necked blond from Massachusetts, and everything had been going according to schedule until he tore up his elbow while pitching a shutout on opening day at the DAP in 1991. He sat out the rest of that season and all of the next but came back to pitch extremely well for Macon in '93 (7-3, 1.83 ERA, seventy-seven strikeouts in eighty-three innings). Now he was taking up valuable space on the big club's forty-man roster, the top priority list of untouchables, and this was to be the make-or-break year for him. The situation wasn't quite as critical for Arnold, the son of a truck driver and a trailer-park manager in Kissimmee, Florida, but the promise was the same: he had gotten $420,000 as the Braves' first pick in the '91 draft, pitched well at Macon in his first full season (3.12 ERA, 124 strikeouts against fifty-six walks in '93), and was coming along nicely. They would be joined in the starting rotation by a pair of right-handers who were on different career paths: Mike D'Andrea and Blase Sparma. D'Andrea had been signed as a free agent choice from the un-baseball state of Maine, and he was looking like a bargain; built like a bull, armed with a will of iron and a heavy fastball (it didn't break ninety miles an hour, but it popped mitts and induced ground balls), he attacked hitters and had gotten 156 strikeouts in only 136 innings at Macon in '93. Sparma, a third-round pick in '91 and son of the late ex–Tiger pitcher Joe Sparma, had been a disappointment in '93 at Greenville (5-12, 4.85, a frightening 238 base runners in 150 innings) and was back at the DAP in search of himself.

The fifth starter was a six-five, two-hundred-pound right-hander named Jeff Bock, and therein lay a sweet story that was getting much play in the Triangle. The ashes of his grandfather, an old Bulls pitcher named Buck Weaver, had been raked into the mound at the DAP upon his death in 1962. Then his father, Pete Bock, had become the general manager of the Bulls when Miles Wolff rescuscitated the franchise in '80 (and had a bit part in *Bull Durham*). Next, Jeff himself, who had been a batboy when his father was GM, had been discovered by the Braves in a tryout camp at the DAP; and now, having performed capably in a rookie year that saw him pass through Idaho Falls, Danville, and Macon, here he was at what he rightfully could call the old family stomping grounds. Durham fans, then, would have a vested interest every time Jeff Bock took to a mound that was, to him, hallowed ground. And there was interest, too, in the fortunes of another right-hander on the staff, for those who knew of his travails. Ken Giard, the kid who had turned to Alcoholics Anonymous during the season at Macon in '93, had finished with an embarrassing 1-7 won-lost record, but he had come back strong from his rehabilitation, recording a 3.84 ERA for the season, and when he learned on his twenty-first birthday that he was headed to Durham for the '94 season, he had every reason to feel that he had been shot at and missed.

Of the others on Matt West's pitching staff, on the basis on prior performance, the best appeared to be Marty's other roommate, John Simmons. A lanky (six six, 220 pounds) left-hander who, incidentally, had scored 1250 on his Scholastic Aptitute Test, graduated from college cum laude in English, and was sailing toward an MBA at St. Xavier University, near Chicago, Simmons had been a dependable reliever at Macon in '93, with a 2.66 ERA and only forty-nine hits allowed in sixty-eight innings. ("My kind of reliever," Randy Ingle had said. "All hell breaks loose, John strolls in from the pen, and pretty soon people are falling asleep in the stands.") There were three other lefties on the staff: Carl Schutz, a squat Louisianan with only thirty-six innings as a pro; Tony Stoecklin, an Illinois kid who had finally put it together after two straight years at Idaho Falls (2.42 and fifty-one strikeouts against fourteen walks in '93); and Jason Butler, one of five players on the roster from Illinois, who had completed two so-so seasons at Macon. Rounding out the staff was a young right-hander from Michigan, Matt Byrd, who had done well in his rookie season at Danville (5-2, 1.96, fifty-seven strikeouts and only seventeen walks) but had pitched just forty-one innings of pro ball.

All of the Bulls were on a fairly rigid timetable, a calendar for advancement, and in a perfect world a kid who had signed right out of high school would make his first spring camp with the big club at the age of twenty-three after five full seasons in the minors. He would have progressed steadily upward through the system, from rookie ball to triple-A, and if he stuck he could expect a major-league career of at least ten years that would qualify him for one of the fattest pension plans in America. But things can happen to severely after the timetable. The most common is a serious injury, of the sort that had already cost Matt Murray a full two years. For another, the needs of the big club can drastically change over a five-year period; a gaping hole at shortstop, for instance, could be filled through a trade at the big-league level; or, less common, a new manager at the top or even a new type of ballpark might create an entirely different philosophy (from one, say, emphasizing speed and defense to one depending on the three-run homer) from what was in place when the kid was originally signed.

The meter runs faster for some players than for others, depending on the position. Catchers are granted more time to develop than any of the position players, for two reasons: there is a shortage of them because catching means work, and it simply takes longer to develop all the necessary skills. Organizations tend to be more patient with pitchers, too—especially those like Murray and Arnold who are blessed with great stuff—because it can take half a dozen seasons for a young one with a live arm to learn the *art* of pitching. The thinking about middle infielders, like Marty, is that they will have peaked after about five years in the minors. The shortest timetable is for hitters—outfielders and corner infielders—who are likely to be released if they haven't come around by their fourth season of pro ball. Predicting a young prospect's rate of development is not a science by any means, and the baseball chronicles are full of tales about can't-miss prospects who missed (of the twenty-four first-round draft choices in 1975, only the catcher Rick Cerone truly made it) and late bloomers who put in a long apprenticeship (the shortstop and base-stealer Maury Wills made it, at age twenty-seven, after ten seasons in the minors). "What's the old line?" said Bobby Dews. "The race may not always go to the swiftest, but that's the way to bet."

For the kids in the minors, the ultimate show of faith is to be placed on the parent organization's forty-man roster: the big club's twenty-five, plus fifteen prospects they dare not expose to various drafts. Unlike in the tyrannical days of Branch Rickey's sprawling Cardinals chain gang, when a player had no recourse but to spend his entire career stuck in one organization unless he got traded, today there is some protection. The big club is allowed to option a player on the forty-man roster three times before the player is out of options and thus left exposed in an open draft. Then there is the complicated Rule 5 draft, held during major-league baseball's annual winter meetings, which is designed to free minor-league prospects hung up in talent-rich organizations. The Rule 5 draft is keyed to a player's age at first signing and his number of years in the minors, and Marty was quite aware that he could become rule-fived after this, only his third year of pro ball. The rub was that the drafting club would have to pay the Braves $50,000 to get Malloy, and if he didn't stay on their twenty-five-man roster for the entire season, they would have to offer him back to the Braves for $25,000. It's called "rent-a-prospect," and when it works the prospect becomes George Bell or Dave Hollins, two very successful Rule 5 alumni. When it doesn't, it's a waste of $25,000 and a year in a young player's life.

Matt West, in his first year as a manager anywhere, was also under the microscope. His career as a player had been an interesting one. He had been on a tennis scholarship at Long Beach State in California, where he was majoring in political science, when he attended a baseball tryout camp on a dare. He had been a three-sport star in high school but had played softball representing a bar where he worked and had pitched only one-third of an inning for Long Beach State. He practiced pitching, he said, for a full week before the tryout—he was big (six four, 195 pounds) and he could, in the vernacular, "bring it"—and the scouts were impressed. "They said, 'Where'd you come from? We don't even have your name anywhere on our scouting sheets,' " said West. "I signed for nothing, and a week later I was pitching in rookie ball for the Braves in Florida." During his third year in pro ball he took a line drive in the face in a game at Savannah, requiring considerable surgery, and three times he underwent arthroscopic surgery for rotator-cuff injuries. He retired after eight so-so years in the Braves' and Seattle Mariners' organizations (he was with Durham in 1983, when the manager was Bobby Dews), having made it as far as Seattle's AAA club, and now he was in his sixth year as a Braves minor-league instructor, the past two spent as pitching coach at Durham. He had lobbied hard for the job as manager of the Bulls, and he knew he was being closely watched. "I know the thinking is that middle infielders and catchers make the best managers, and I was just a pitcher," he said. "But I know this game, and [managing] is all about communication, anyway. I played under Bobby Dews for three years, and he was the best manager I ever had, because he could communicate. Stop me if I ever go a day without speaking to every one of my players, even if it's just to say, 'How's it going?' I went ahead and got my degree in political science, and I could be making a lot of money doing any number of other things with my life, but I love this. I've made the right choice."

Marty Malloy had never seen a human being quite like West. For the first eighteen years of his life, until he played the two seasons at Santa Fe Community College in Gainesville, his only mentor had been his father. Then, in rookie ball at Idaho Falls, there had been the boyish manager, Dave Hilton, and the coach Paul Runge of Williston, a short hop down a country road from Trenton. At Macon, of course, there had been Randy Ingle: a good old boy from a tiny North Carolina town, a former infielder, a pickup truck kind of guy. Always around had been Bobby Dews of Albany, in deep southwest Georgia, the laidback sort who could talk dogs and hunting and country music with anybody. But now there was this: Matt West, an intense

Californian with piercing blue eyes and a penchant for double entendre, the abstract, the clever rejoinder. One day during batting practice before the season began, when Bobby Smith left the cage after lining several pitches from West into the deepest corners of the DAP, West jubilantly shouted, "Mister Smith goes to Atlanta!!" Bobby got the message and grinned. But Marty, jumping into the cage to take his own licks, gave no sign that he had ever heard of the Jimmy Stewart movie *Mister Smith Goes to Washington*. He already missed Randy Ingle, who would say, "See there, nailed the sonofabitch, didn't you?" when he took a left-hander to the gap in left center. He didn't quite know what to make of someone who said, "Nicely done."

Early on the morning of April 7, Marty and the Bulls piled onto a bus leased from a transportation company in Raleigh, its destination scroll reading DURHAM BULLS, for the four-hour drive to Woodbridge, Virginia, a southern suburb of Washington, to open the season against the Prince William Cannons. "You can't get anything done on the road," Randy Ingle had said the year before, a common complaint of managers who are paid to develop players more than to win games. "They're either watering the field, or the home club's using it." But for the Bulls, it would be enough to finally get down to business after more than a month of messing around with fundamentals and batting practice and running in the outfield. They checked into a Days Inn, grabbed some lunch, made fitful attempts to nap, and were gathered around the bus in front of the motel well ahead of the appointed hour for the short ride to the ballpark, home of the Chicago White Sox' Carolina League farm team. Quickly dressed at the clubhouse in thick sweatshirts and turtlenecks for the chill of a lingering winter—the temperature that night would drop into the thirties—they went through a gleeful round of batting practice and pregame infield, ever glancing at the Cannons players, some of whom they remembered from the '93 Hickory Crawdads of the Sally League.

Marty was astonished when he checked the starting lineups, taped to the wall of the dugout by Matt West, and found that he was batting eighth in the order. He knew that Prince William's eleven-man pitching staff was stacked with seven left-handers and that their starter that night was a lefty named Scott Christman, who had been the White Sox' first-round draft choice less than a year before. But *eighth?* The last time Marty had batted anywhere but in the two-hole was as a runt walk-on right fielder with the Scoggins Chevrolet Little League team in Chiefland. He read down the lineup again: Mike Warner was leading off, the way it ought to be, but what was Damon Hollins, an RBI guy, doing in the two-hole, where he, Marty, was supposed to be? *What the hell is this?* All during the winter he had envisioned himself in the two-hole: bunting, taking lefties to the left side, moving the runners along if it meant giving himself up with a ground ball to the right side of the infield. All during spring training that was what everybody had pounded into his head and what he had worked on. Now this, batting eighth, just ahead of Julio Trapaga, who couldn't hit for shit. *Eighth*, for God's sake, where former prospects go to die. He was in there, anyway, and against a lefty who was one of the top young prospects in baseball, so he would make the best of it. West could have gone at second base with Nelson Paulino, the switch-hitting third middle infielder some regarded as Marty's caddy, but he hadn't.

And so the season began. In the cold night air of early April, only 2,527 fans showed up to watch a game that wasn't decided until the bottom of the ninth inning. Christman and the Bulls' starter, the bulldoggish Mike D'Andrea, had kept the offenses at bay in the early innings before turning it over to relievers who were even more effective. Durham led 2-1, and victory seemed at hand until the Cannons' first baseman doubled deep to right center with two out in the ninth. On came a speedy Panamanian, Geovany Miranda, to pinch-run. The next batter lashed a ground ball to Bobby Smith at third, who threw in the dirt to Raymond Nunez at first, too late to get the runner, but when Nunez smothered the errant throw and saw Miranda flying around third and dashing for home, he surprised everybody by firing a strike to his catcher, Brad Rippelmeyer, who tagged Miranda for the out that sealed the game. Marty was hitless in three at bats, grounding out to second with men on first and third to end one inning, but then none of the Bulls had hit the ball well; they were outhit 8-3, and one of their runs had scored on a balk.

West was ecstatic about winning his first game as a manager, even by such a tenuous thread, but the series at Prince William went downhill after that. The Bulls lost the second game 9-1 because of a nightmarish third inning by Jamie Arnold, who gave up eight runs on five hits, three walks, three wild pitches, a hit batsman, and an error of his own. Marty was collared again in four at bats, all against left-handers, and West was thrown out of the game after arguing a call at home plate. Marty sat in game three, against another heralded lefty, Mike Bertotti, who would strike out eleven Bulls in a 5-0 shutout. In the final game of the series, on a rainy and cold Sunday afternoon with only 1,639 fans huddling in the stands, the Bulls got their offense going but lost a toe-to-toe twenty-four-hit slugfest 7-6 in eleven innings. Marty was still batting eighth in the order, even against right-handers, but this time he broke the ice by getting two hits in four at bats, one of them his first bunt hit of the season.

They boarded the bus and headed back to Durham immediately after the game to work on some things at the DAP on their off-day, Monday, and on Tuesday they headed off again, this time for the two-hour ride to Lynchburg for a three-game set against the Red Sox' farm club there. D'Andrea pitched a 6-0 shutout in the opener (he was now 2-0 and had given up only five hits and one earned run in ten innings), and Marty went 2-for-4 and scored his first run of the year. There were more firsts for him on the next night—he was inserted in the two-hole, doubled, stole a base, and made an error—but the Bulls lost 6-3 before a gathering of only 956 hardy fans in chilly weather. Marty sat again on Thursday night, when West chose to go with Paulino's right-handed bat at leadoff against another lefty, and it turned out to be another unpleasant evening for the Bulls; they were only one out away from a win when a pinch hitter put the ball into the brisk air for a windblown three-run homer that won the game for Lynchburg 6-5.

Marty skulked onto the bus afterward feeling none too cocky after the first week of the season. Losing depressed him, and being benched was worse. Commandeering two seats for himself in the middle of the bus, slipping a Hank Jr. tape into his Walkman, he stretched out and began trying to figure the pluses and minuses. He felt he was hitting the ball well, although nothing was falling for him, and he was somewhat buoyed by the fact that he had run through some choice left-handed pitching and struck out only once in nineteen at bats. Still, this batting deep in the order, except for that one game, rankled him, and he hadn't gotten the answer he wanted about that. One day on the road, he and Bobby Smith had gone to Matt West to discuss the situation—Bobby seemed to be suited for the heart of the order but was batting seventh—and West's answer didn't appease them. "Look, don't worry," West had told them. "It's a long season. The at bats, that's what counts, no matter where you're hitting." *Yeah, right,* Marty was thinking as the bus rolled toward Durham and the next night's home opener at the DAP.

A small band of the Bulls' faithful, unwilling to wait for their first look at the club in action, had driven up to Lynchburg to catch part of the series there. They were strung out behind the team bus now as it rumbled down the road leading back to Durham, and one of them was Matt West's striking young blonde wife, Juliana, following in a Mercedes that had seen its best days. Around eleven o'clock, as the caravan reached the North Carolina line, the bus driver saw headlights frantically blinking behind him. He conferred with West, then pulled the bus to the side of the road. West leapt off and trotted to his wife's rescue. The Mercedes had finally conked, and they would have to make arrangements and come back for it later. In a few minutes West reboarded with his wife and she joined him in the shotgun seat. *Woman on the bus!* The cardplaying and general revelry suddenly stopped and the bus went silent, as when a hunter enters the forest and the cicadas cease their chirring.

The driver had closed the door and was looking to rejoin the traffic when suddenly a flat Southern voice twanged from the tomblike darkness: "It wouldn't o' happened if you'd been drivin' an American car."

There was muffled laughter, tentative and uneasy. Juliana whispered to her husband, "Who was that?"

"What?" West was deadpanning it. "That was just the bus starting up."

"No, somebody joked about my car."

"Oh, *that*. That was just Marty."

"Which one's he? I don't know the players yet."

"Marty Malloy," West said. "He's a Chevy man himself. You'll get to know Marty before it's over."

CHAPTER 6

On the next night, a Friday, with Prince William and then Lynchburg returning their visits for a seven-game home stand, the Bulls were to open the final season at the DAP. The deadline for mailing income tax returns was midnight that night, and as a courtesy the Bulls had arranged for the post office to dispatch a clerk to collect returns in a cardboard box set up in the concourse. By five-thirty, thirty minutes before the gates would open and a full two hours before the first pitch was scheduled, several dozen fans were already milling about the funky little turreted ticket window, most of them wearing Bulls caps bought across the street at a souvenir outlet called Ballpark Corner, idly talking baseball, rising tiptoed and squinting through the chain-link fence for a glimpse of any signs of life on the emerald diamond below. This was being billed as the "*final*

final season at the DAP," commemorated by T-shirts saying as much, a subtle dig at the delays over construction of the new, seventy-five-hundred-seat ballpark that at last was going up just on the other side of downtown Durham.

Although it was clear to most that the DAP had outlived its time, that it was truly a relic now, the people of Durham still regarded the old ballpark as a civic treasure. If it ain't broke, why fix it? In two bond referendums, to prove their point, the voters had soundly rejected plans to finance a $16 million state-of-the-art ballpark to replace it, touching off endless lively debates on the editorial pages of the Durham *Herald-Sun*, and finally the conglomerate that had bought the franchise from Miles Wolff following the 1990 season—Capitol Broadcasting, based in Raleigh, whose WDNC carried all 140 of the Bulls' games—came up with the financing through private certificates of participation. They had heavily promoted the '93 season as the last fling at the DAP, and the Bulls drew a record 305,692 fans in sixty-nine home dates (4,430 per game in a park seating 5,000), enough to outdraw a dozen cities across America with populations more than ten times greater than Durham's. A full house had shown up for what was to have been the last game ever at the DAP, on the day before Labor Day in 1993, but rain forced a cancellation before they could complete an inning. There was a particular poignance now in the notation scrawled in indelible ink on the top row of the bleachers in centerfield—THE DIAMOND DOLLS WERE HERE 9-3-93—for there were more delays, from a foul-up over the letting of construction bids to unusually raw winter weather, and it became necessary to play one more season at the DAP.

Nobody doubted that the new park, as yet unnamed, was going to be a piece of work, a more than adequate replacement. It had been designed by the same architectural firm that had drawn up Oriole Park at Camden Yards in Baltimore and the other new venues in Cleveland and Texas; "new old" parks, as it were, retaining the old brick-and-steel charm of ballparks past but eliminating such aggravations as narrow seats, views obstructed by posts, inadequate parking, rank rest rooms, and cramped dressing rooms.

The DAP had all of those drawbacks and more. It lay in a graveyard of old brick tobacco warehouses and water tanks, a playground in a pile of rubble, left to its own devices. For parking, one simply created a space on any of the narrow streets surrounding the ballpark and hoofed it for five blocks or more. Rest rooms were scant, their toilets and urinals reeking and overflowing by the fourth inning, and lines there were as long as at the concessions stands. Once they had paid their respects to the "special charm" of the DAP, the players, managers, coaches, and trainers would begin the litany of its failings: cramped clubhouses with room for only five men to shower at a time (most visiting clubs chose to dress and shower at their motel), a training room with the spartan amenities of a first-aid station, no tunnel leading directly from the clubhouses to the dugouts, poor lighting, drainage so poor that the slightest downpour threatened a rainout, and an undulating outfield surface as rough and uneven as a country pasture.

Still, the DAP beckoned. For a fan who had fallen in love with the game during the forties and fifties, watching the Bulls play there was enough to bring tears. Dressed in the royal-blue-and-bronze ("Texas tan") colors of the Bulls, ringed by tiers of warped wooden outfield fences adorned with bright advertising, the DAP was cramped, hot, and boisterous in a delightful way, brimming with an egalitarian stew: snot-nosed urchins stomping out plastic cups in the precarious aluminum bleachers; old codgers, black and white, keeping scorecards and rolling their own cigarettes in the shade of the grandstand roof; teenaged girls blinking their lashes at the players from box seats near the dugouts;

and the university crowd, frat boys and professors alike, wearing
their khaki twill Duck Head trousers and Reeboks and Bulls regalia, sniffily heading straight for the bleachers or the grassy picnic area beyond the left-field fence. They loved the DAP in spite
of its shortcomings, and the debate over whether to abandon the
old place for a sleek new venue was not unlike the one that had
raged in Nashville twenty-five years earlier when the operators
of the Grand Ole Opry wanted to move out of historic old Ryman Auditorium, with its ghost of Hank Williams, hard wooden
pews, and insufferable heat, to a cavernous air-conditioned
palace with plush red carpeting and swivel seats. As with Ryman,
the purists had lost to the moneymen.

Presiding over the acolytes from his seat in the press box, a
concrete pillbox burrowed under the box seats behind home
plate, was a droll public-address announcer named Bob Guy,
whose delivery was remindful of Garrison Keillor, the home-
spun Minnesota monologist of National Public Radio's *Prairie
Home Companion*. Guy, whose day job was with a magazine dis-
tribution firm in town, carried on an unobtrusive commentary
with the fans and was a treasure in his own right. It wasn't
enough for him to announce that someone had left his headlights on; rather, he would drawl, "There's a blue Honda testing
its battery. Now we know that a Honda is below the dignity of
many of you, but just the same . . ." At most minor-league ballparks, some local singer warbled "The Star-Spangled Banner"
night after night, but the fans did it themselves at the DAP. "And
now we ask you to please stand and *honor America* by singing the
National Anthem," Bob Guy would intone, and many an umpire
on his first trip to Durham, standing at attention with the crowd
at his back, had been startled to hear five thousand voices actually singing every word in earnest. On this night the American
flag hung at half-mast in center field in memory of three North
Carolina soldiers who had been killed by friendly fire over Iraq;

and later in the spring, reflecting Durham's conservative roots, the flag would be lowered for a full month to observe the death of the disgraced ex-president Richard Nixon.

The young Bulls had been on the field since three-thirty, dressed in their royal blue practice jerseys and white pants, going about their business as though it were another day at camp in West Palm Beach. Like any manager who hopes to keep his job in an organization, Matt West understood his mandate: "Every day is broken into two parts. For the first three hours, we work on individual stuff. At seven o'clock we put those skills to work as a team and try to kick the shit out of the other guys." They had taken a right turn out of the clubhouse and headed for right field, where all twenty-five of them went through stretching exercises under the scrutiny of West and the trainer, Jay Williams. Then, while the pitchers got in some light running along the outfield fences and the outfielders shagged fly balls, the infielders—one more time, at three-quarters speed—went through simulated rundown situations involving runners on the move from first and third bases. Finally, at four o'clock, the batting cage and protective screens were rolled into place and batting practice began. Since Prince William would be pitching another of its left-handers that night, the bulk of BP would be thrown by a coach named Jerry Nyman, a left-hander, who would be the pitching coach at Danville once the short-season rookie leagues began play but had been called to fill in for Bill Slack when Slack was felled by kidney stones on the season's eve.

Marty would be batting at the bottom of the order again, and he tried not to show disappointment as he waited his turn outside the batting cage. "It doesn't show, but I'm hitting the shit out of the ball," he said. After the opening series at Prince William and Lynchburg, in nineteen at bats he was averaging

.267. He had doubled against a lefty, had gotten that first bunt hit, "but the best news is, I've only struck out once." He appeared jaunty, tanned, rearing to go as he jumped into the cage and dug in. It was a rare opportunity for him to swing against a lefty other than in game conditions, and he and Nyman made the most of it. Nyman dropped his delivery almost to sidearm and began sweeping his throws over the outside corner. "That's it, that's it, opposite field," Nyman said, expressing displeasure ("Naw, naw, we don't need *that*") every time Marty tried to drive the ball toward the inviting right-field porch only three hundred feet down the line. Marty was being double-teamed, couldn't get away with anything. "They all hear that porch out there singing to 'em," said West, leaning against the cage like an overseer, "but the good ones don't listen."

The heavy leaden skies opened up before they could complete the first round of batting practice, and the tarpaulin was rolled onto the field for the first time that day at four-thirty. The weather didn't look promising as the Prince William players, having dressed at the Red Roof Inn, drifted off their bus and onto the field, heading for their dugout. The tarp came off at six, just as the gates opened and the first fans began finding their seats, but the Bulls had barely begun their round of pregame infield practice when they had to abort; the grounds crew scrambled and covered the field once more. Up in the radio booth, Bill Miller, the chief of the grounds crew, sat at a color computer screen that monitored the cloud patterns. "We're in a sea of tranquility, surrounded by hell," he said. Those predictions Marty had heard, at West Palm, of an overflow crowd of nine thousand for the home opener had been over the mark (it would be announced as 4,437); but in spite of the threat of rain, the fans kept coming, bustling under the protection of the grandstand roof, randy with anticipation. The players, meanwhile, had retreated to the clubhouse to sip juice and snack on orange slices, slip into their white game shirts, and wait out the weather.

"The Lord wants the Bulls to get this one in," somebody said around six-thirty, and sure enough, soon the little ballpark was rocking with the oompah music of a makeshift brass ensemble, the twenty-piece Durham Community Band. At seven-fifteen, with his announcement that the game would be delayed only fifteen minutes, Bob Guy soothed the masses: "Welcome to the first game of the *final* final season at the DAP." Hoots, cheers, applause. "Thanks to the politicians and the money people who saw to it that the new park wouldn't be ready, we can now enjoy one more year in this . . . this *palace* . . ." To the taped strains of "Wooly Bully," out pranced the Bulls' mascot, Wool E. Bull, actually a local actor known only as Jef stuffed into a Bulls uniform—horns, tail, the number 00—brandishing a white *D* battle flag as he clumped madly back and forth between the dugouts to the cheers of the crowd. The makers of the movie *Bull Durham* had left behind a huge mechanical bull atop the right-field fences, with a legend reading HIT BULL WIN STEAK, and when the 1994 Durham Bulls were introduced for the first time the bull's eyes began blinking red, its tail wagged, and bursts of smoke snorted from its nostrils.

As would happen before every game, a Little League team had been selected to accompany the Bulls onto the field during the introductions—this night the Field of Dreams Team was from nearby Carrboro—and a tyke named Brady Herman, their second baseman, clung to Marty. "At second base for the Bulls, batting ninth, Marty Malloy, accompanied by Brady Herman," said Bob Guy. It was hard to tell who was more pumped up: Marty or the ten-year-old beside him. The only time his adrenalin had ever flowed like it did at that moment was on those Friday nights when the Trenton High Fighting Tigers burst under the goalposts at the little football stadium back home. "And now we ask you to please stand and *honor America* . . ."

• • •

Pitching for the Bulls was the bony right-hander Blase Sparma, now in his fourth year of pro ball after playing for Ohio State, a kid so skinny that his uniform belt served the practical purpose of holding his britches up. Sparma had something to prove this year, having spent the entire '93 season at Greenville none too auspiciously, and he had every reason to think the Braves might already be running out of patience with him. He began the game ominously by walking the Cannons' frisky lead-off man, Essex "Gas" Burton, a muscled switch-hitting second baseman who had led all of the minor leagues with seventy-four stolen bases the year before at South Bend in the Midwest League and was the fastest man in all of baseball. The crowd, knowing its baseball, sat back and groaned. This guy *looked* like trouble—indeed, Rick Albert had put a stopwatch on him during the opening series at Prince William and found that he could take a lead and hit second base in an astonishing 2.8 seconds, one-tenth of a second faster than anyone in recent baseball history—and his presence on first base created tension all around the Bulls' infield. But the fans were up and cheering when Sparma caught Burton leaning, too eager to be on his way to second, and promptly picked him off first before he had thrown a pitch to the next batter.

On the mound for Prince William was Mike Bertotti again, but this time Durham crawled all over him from the start. Two doubles, two singles, a Prince William error, and a walk by Bertotti made it 4-0, Durham, and the crowd was on its feet again wanting more. Even when Bobby Smith struck out, swinging, for the second out, their hopes were alive as Marty stepped in with runners at first and third. He had been held out of that game in Virginia, with the lefty Bertotti on the mound, and that alone gave the Cannons a notion: little guy, left-handed; gotta be a reason he's batting ninth; pitch him away. With the catcher setting up on the outside corner, they got him easily; Marty was late getting around on the first pitch, a fastball off the plate, fouling it into the third-base bleachers; he took a sweeping curve on the outside corner for a strike; and then, on another fastball on the outside corner, he weakly bounced into a force at short-stop. Once Bertotti had departed and was replaced by a right-hander, Marty would single off the shortstop's glove, extending a modest hitting streak to four games, and later hit a liner to center field that might have been a double, scoring Smith from first, but instead was caught and turned into a double play when Bobby couldn't get back to the bag in time. Sparma and two relievers shut the gate on the Cannons, and Durham won its home opener 6-2.

So they had been baptized at the DAP, and they were feeling good about themelves when they showed up at midafternoon on Saturday. West would throw most of BP, since a right-hander was going for the Cannons that night, and for Marty the lessons continued. His first pitch from West was neck high, but Marty swung and fouled it into the netting.

"Would you have swung at that in a game?" West yelled.

"Probably," said Marty.

"Well, hey, look, that's *my* strike zone, not yours."

The next pitch came, in the same place, and Marty let it pass. "Good, that's it," said West. Marty began rifling shots to all corners of the field, going with the pitch, ignoring, for the time being, the short porch in right.

Willie Stargell had driven up unannounced from his home on the North Carolina coast and had chosen to spend Friday night observing from the stands. Now he stood behind the cage, still dressed like a fan who had wandered onto the field, kibitzing with the players. "Hey, Jack, a funny thing happened last night," he said to Kevin Grijak, who had hit his third home run of the young season the night before, with his parents visiting from their suburb in Michigan. "I met some really nice people, and I couldn't believe it when they said they were your parents." He whispered to Tom Waldrop, who had only two hits in fifteen at bats: "Head down now, Tommy, and don't move your feet so much. It's like the wheels of a car. If you don't have good balance, the whole thing'll fall apart. Front end, transmission, engine, everything." To anybody who might be listening: "You're born with bat speed, but confidence can be learned. It's mental attitude. The guy with the great set of nuts will be the great hitter. A season comes in three parts: one, they can't get you out; two, you can't buy a hit; the third part can go either way—it's what you make of it. The guy with the great nuts makes something good out of it." The players hadn't seen Stargell since spring training, and even as they awaited their turn in the cage they had an ear cocked his way to glean whatever they could. "I grew up in some mean streets, in Oakland, and when I was just a little kid I learned that there was a bear out there and he could eat you up. But I got where I liked it. I learned to get back out there the next day, looking for the bear . . ." He was interrupted when a fan who had talked his way onto the field came over and asked Stargell to autograph his Bulls program, "for my little boy."

Kevin Grijak's parents would have more to cheer about that night. He tied the game at 3-3 in the eighth with a towering home run over everything in right—no bloop DAP Special here—and scored the run that won it in the eleventh for the Bulls, 4-3, drilling a double down the right-field line and galloping home when Brad Rippelmeyer, unsuccessful on two attempts to bunt him to third, got a hanging curve and strung a clothesline single to left. Bob Guy's custom was to play a song called "I Need a Hero" in tight situations, and it was becoming Grijak's personal anthem. His career to date had prepared no one for this. A big raffish kid (six two, 195 pounds, and growing) who could, Marty said, "walk into a room full of women and take his pick," Grijak had hit only seven home runs with fifty-eight RBIs at Macon the year before, in his third full season of pro ball. The Braves didn't know where to hide him defensively, but at the plate he had a good feel for the strike zone and a killer's instinct (the "good nuts" Willie Stargell had talked about) no matter who was pitching. Back home, he and his father had a pitching machine that could be rigged to simulate a left-hander's curveball, so lefties presented him with no mysteries. Now it was all coming together for him, it appeared. In only twenty-eight at bats, he was batting .393, with a gaudy slugging percentage of .857, and his four homers already led the league. An overflow crowd of 5,238 had spilled over into the center-field bleachers, on a cool night that found Duke playing its annual spring training football intrasquad game less than five miles away, and they had found their hero for the nonce.

While Grijak's pyrotechnics were getting all of the attention in the stands, Marty was quietly learning some lessons. All of the repetitions in the world can't fully prepare a player for certain situations that develop in the heat of a game, and on this night he would experience two defining moments, one on the positive side, the other not. The first occurred while he was batting third in the fifth inning and, with Bobby Smith on first, no outs, and the Bulls down 2-1, he squared around to show bunt. The ploy brought a full-bore charge from the Cannons' third baseman, who had not forgotten that Marty had bunted on him for a base hit a week earlier at Prince William. The pitch was called a strike, but that was of no matter to Marty. He squared to bunt again on the next pitch, and this time he shot a hard bunt past the charging third baseman for a base hit that died in the infield dirt. The rally ended when Mike Warner grounded into a double play, erasing Marty, and Julio Trapaga struck out; but Brett Butler would have been proud of the number Marty had done on the overly aggressive Prince William third baseman.

Bobby Dews would not have been proud of Marty, though, when he was charged with two errors on one play in the eighth inning. By that time, Prince William was up, 3-1, and had a runner on first with two outs. It was a steal or hit-and-run situation, and the runner was off on the first pitch. With a right-hander at bat, it was Marty's mission to cover second on the steal, and as he raced to cover the bag, a nightmare unfolded: the batter swung and hit a twisting two-hopper through the box, causing the ball, the runner, and Marty to converge on second base in the same instant. It was one of those situations that cannot be covered in practice, and Marty was momentarily flustered. His options were to catch the ball and step on the bag for a force play, or forget the runner and simply field the ball and toss it to first to nail the batter. But the ball came to him on the dreaded in-between hop and caromed off the heel of the glove and hit him in the chest—there went one error—and when he scrambled for the ball (which had bounced in front of him onto the infield grass) and threw wildly toward first for a second error, the runners wound up at second and third. There was no harm done, since the next batter lined to right to end the inning, but as Marty trudged to the dugout he was already replaying the situation and filing it away. He estimated that he had played in more than five hundred games, from Little League to the pros, and this was the first time he had been involved in a play exactly like that. Experience meant learning, and he intended to remember this one.

Bobby Dews was in Macon that week, nursemaiding the overmatched young low-A Braves through their skittish debut in the Sally League, and he wanted to know more about the play Marty had failed to make.

"It would have been a hell of a play if he'd made it," he was told.

"I'm sure," Dews said.

"He got screened by the pitcher, too, when it went through the box."

"Of course." Dews—Doctor Dews—hadn't had to be there to size it up. "First, you catch the ball. Then you make the play. When Chipper Jones was starting out, he made more errors at short than Marty Malloy will make in his lifetime, and it was due to one thing: he always tried to turn each routine ground ball into the greatest play ever made. It isn't necessary to throw a guy out by five steps when a half step will do the job. An out's an out. You look at Chipper now, on the verge of playing in the major leagues; he's cool. He knows who's running and how much time he's got, because he's seen this play before, so he does what he's paid to do. He catches the ball, and then he throws it. Piece of cake."

Dews recalled a day during spring training, only weeks earlier, when he held back a couple of rookie-level shortstops for some extra work in the late afternoon. "I took my fungo and gave 'em a first baseman and starting hitting ground balls to their right so they had to backhand the ball and make the throw to first. I hit 'em twenty-five apiece, and each kid kicked five of 'em. Then I dismissed the first baseman and told 'em just to make the backhand, toss the ball aside, forget the throw, and they missed just one pickup between 'em of the next fifty I hit. The lesson was to concentrate on catching the ball first."

"Yeah, well, but that was just practice. It's different when the crowd's up and the game's on."

"I know that. I must have led the league in errors each of my first five years. That's about how long it takes to figure it out. You've got to remember that [Mark] Lemke didn't really start to come around until he got to Durham, and that was his fifth year in pro ball. Marty's got to see that play a few more times to get it right. We'll know he's got it when the play develops and he says to himself, *Hey, no sweat, I've seen this one before.* It's one day at a time. One *out* at a time."

On Sunday, less than an hour's drive from the DAP, twenty miles east of Raleigh in the little town of Zebulon, a noisy crowd that would total eight thousand was straining to get into the ballpark of the Class AA Carolina Mudcats for that afternoon's game against the Birmingham Barons. They were there to see the Barons' thirty-one-year-old rookie right fielder, Michael Jordan, one of the greatest basketball players of all time, who had retired from the Chicago Bulls and now was having a much-publicized fling at baseball. Marty and most of the other Durham players were big basketball fans and had kept up with Jordan's attempts during spring training—indeed, it was impossible not to do so, since every newspaper in America was publishing daily reports on his progress or lack of it—and they had mixed feelings. "It takes a lot of guts to do what he's doing," Marty had said one day in West Palm Beach, "but I keep wondering about the prospect who had to go back to A ball, the guy whose life is baseball, to make room for Michael." Jordan was a hell of a story, and no doubt many fans who might have been at the DAP for that afternoon's final game of the Prince William series had found it impossible not to run over to Zebulon to see the Michael Jordan show. He was struggling to keep his batting average at .200, striking out at an embarrassing pace, and spending a lot of time turning tail to chase down balls that had gone through his wicket; but, hey, this was a chance to see Michael Jordan. There had been standing room only everywhere the Barons and Jordan played.

Still, there was Bulls baseball at the DAP, and not even the sideshow in Zebulon would keep the faithful away. Sunday broke bright, cool, and windy over Durham, and there would be a crowd of 3,266 to watch the Bulls and Cannons go at it again. Among them was a chatty little coterie of season-ticket holders in the box seats directly behind home plate that included Matt West's wife, Juliana, and his parents. "I still can't believe my parents are living right here in Durham," West said, and therein lay a tale. He had grown up in California, but after serving the Bulls as pitching coach for two seasons he fell in love with Durham and decided to make it his home. He had met Juliana while working as a tennis pro at a California country club during his off-seasons, and when they married he brought her to Durham, where they began buying a house. Juliana found a job as nanny for the three young children of a well-heeled Durham couple, while Matt began working in the off-season as a salesman (tickets, billboard space, radio ads) for the Bulls. In the meantime, his parents were thinking of retiring back home in Ojai, California, but when a recession struck the state they saw their savings being swallowed up at an alarming rate. Matt implored them to leave and come to the Research Triangle, with its virtually recession-proof economy, and they sold their house (at a great loss) to move into a modest condominium in Durham. His mother, Caroline, found work in a job placement office for temporary workers; his stepfather, Dave Lincoln, came out of retirement to become a real estate salesman. They were graceful people, knowledgeable about baseball, happy to be there. "No telling where the Braves will send me next year and the year after that," said Matt. "I know I can't manage the Bulls forever, because it doesn't work like that, but Durham is probably the best place in America to be living right now. There's a lot of opportunity here." Matt West's opportunities included staging kids' baseball clinics in the area—three-day affairs at the DAP, with Matt paying Marty and a number of other Bulls $50 apiece to help out as coaches—and after expenses he could earn as much as $10,000 for himself over the summer, quite a supplement to the $30,000 he got for managing the Bulls.

"Well, I see where my namesake learned a thing or two last night." This was Martie Byron, a forty-six-year-old nurse at the Duke University medical complex, known around the Bulls' clubhouse for years as the lady who bakes cakes. She knew their birth dates from the program, and none passed without a cake delivered to the clubhouse by Martie. Plump and lively, married only to baseball, Martie missed nothing from her season's box seat behind the plate. She wore a Bulls cap festooned with a pound's worth of souvenir medals from all over the baseball world; diligently kept score at every game, listening on her Walkman to WDNC's broadcaster Steve Barnes, not thirty feet behind her up in the radio booth; often got permission for one or two Bulls to ride with her, rather than on the team bus, to games in nearby Winston-Salem or Kinston; relentlessly tracked down autographs from the scouts and players and even visiting writers who happened to sit near her; and missed games only when she was away on baseball junkets to places like Baltimore, Philadelphia, New York, and the Hall of Fame, at Cooperstown. She could have been called the Bulls' number one fan if not for Tinker Parnell, "Tinkerbell," a grandfather in his sixties who had his own metal nameplate permanently attached to the first row of the bleachers behind first base and was there in his Bulls cap and shorts and sneakers every night, greeting the players by name as they came out of the clubhouse to the dugout, giving the umpires hell, chain-smoking Winstons, wiping his face with a towel as the proceedings heated up, helping his grandchildren get autographs from notables like Willie Stargell. "Tinkerbell and I are on the same page," said Martie. "We're old enough to be these kids' parents. I don't know what I'd do without the DAP and baseball. Cats, maybe? No, sir, uh-uh, thank you very much."

Completing this tight little knot of the Bulls faithful gathered nightly in the box seats were Bill and Retta Law. He was retired now, having spent his working life in a dull management job with the county, arranging work schedules for maintenance crews, and life had begun in his sixties when he became president of the Raleigh Hot Stove League. As such, he had come to know every old ballplayer in the area, men like "Country" Slaughter, and once surprised even himself when he got Ted Williams to come all the way from Florida for a winter meeting. He also had a part-time job now, with Capitol Broadcasting's WRAL television station, which required him to arrive at the DAP early for every game, scouting out likely prospects for a Bulls Fan of the Day, exhorting them to scream and carry on for a roving cameraman for a promotional spot the station would carry the next day. His wife, Retta, was a piece of work: flaming red hair, jangling bracelets, incandescent smile, full of chatter about Ted Williams ("Ted said, 'Honey, you're my kind of woman' "), Richard Nixon ("I just don't get it, how people pick on him"), and her cameo appearance in *Bull Durham*: "I mean, it was October when they were filming, honey, and it took all night just to show Kevin [Costner, the star] coming to the backstop for a pop-up. That's the scene I'm in, you know, behind the backstop, screaming for the ball. I told Kevin I was wearing two sets of long johns that night and he said, 'Naw, you *weren't*,' and I told him I sure was, I'd do anything to be a star . . ." Her husband spied a trio of college frat boys, perfect for the Bulls fans spot, and made a move for them with his cameraman in tow. "Here's the deal, now, boys . . . ," he began.

With yet another left-hander pitching for Prince William, Marty was benched in favor of Jason Keeline, the shortstop, who had seen only thirteen at bats in the nine games, but he entered at second and Keeline moved over to third when Bobby Smith got hurt while making a belly-flopping catch of a foul pop in the fifth inning. He had another embarrassing moment when he led off the sixth with a sharp ground ball that looked to him—the last thing he saw before ducking his head and flying away from the plate—like a sure double into the left-field corner. When he got no sign to the contrary from Rick Albert, coaching at first, he assumed the ball had gone through, and swung wide of the bag and was smoking for second when he heard the umpire call him out; the third baseman had made a great backhanded stab of the ball and gunned him down. There were some guffaws from the crowd ("The kid's pumped up, ain't he?"), and Marty shot a hostile look at Albert as he scurried to the dugout. His hitting streak ended at five games when, in the eighth, he took three balls and then three strikes, the last a wicked curve that hooked across the outside corner. Kevin Grijak poleaxed a pair of two-run homers, which gave him five in six games against Prince William, and as far as the Cannons' pitchers were concerned, enough was enough—one of them plunked him in the helmet with a fastball, the deathly sound bringing a hush over the crowd. There were no protests from the Bulls' dugout, for, as they say, that's baseball. The Cannons' pitchers hoped it was a farewell gesture before the Braves promoted Grijak the hell out of there so the Southern League could worry about him. Mike D'Andrea got raked over for the first time, giving up eleven hits and eight runs, and the Bulls lost 9-7.

After only ten games with Durham, Marty had discovered that this wasn't going to be easy. He had been able to do what came naturally during his shakedown season in rookie ball at Idaho Falls, changing nothing about his style at the plate and batting .315 with relative ease against skittish pitchers much less experienced than he. There had been some adjustments to be made at Macon, the severest being learning to pace himself for a full season of 140 games, but his being held out against left-handed pitching had enabled him to make the Sally League all-star team without a drastic makeover. Now, though, he was feeling overmatched at times. If these guys intended to throw a fastball on the black, at the knees, they could do it more often than not. The Carolina League was, indeed, a place where the men would be separated from the boys. No longer being coddled against lefties, being thrown in there against players who had spent as much as four and five years in the minor leagues, playing for a manager he still couldn't figure out, he wasn't finding baseball such a simple game to play after all.

That Sunday night following the 9-7 loss to Prince William, he sat at a booth in Honey's, a twenty-four-hour restaurant a mile or so from his apartment, gulping a platter of country-fried steak and mashed potatoes while trying to sort out his season thus far. He was embarrassed, more than anything, about batting at the bottom of the order, he said, and he still didn't feel that Matt West had given him a sensible explanation for it. He was still smarting from that and from Rick Albert's failure, that afternoon, to signal that the ball he hit to third hadn't gone down the line for a double, but he knew he could play second base in this league—forget the two errors on one play—and if there was a word to describe his mood, it would be "defiant." He was batting .241 after only twenty-nine at bats, too early to prove anything either way, but he had seen enough to be confident. Stirring the gravy into the mashed potatoes, he narrowed his eyes and said, "I'm gonna hit three hundred here. I'm gonna play in the major leagues."

The Bulls tried not to pay attention to the spectacle on the field before Monday's game with Lynchburg, in town for a four-game set that would close the first home stand of the season, when television people not heretofore seen circled around the Red Sox as they took batting practice. They were interviewing and filming a young phenom named Trot Nixon, a strapping outfielder (six two, two hundred pounds) who less than a year earlier had been leading his Wilmington team to the North Carolina Class 4-A high school championship. Nixon had become the Boston Red Sox' first pick in the 1993 draft, fetching a signing bonus of half a million dollars, and now here he was, a week after his twentieth birthday, batting .353 with three homers after only a week and a half in advanced-A ball. "It's a big change from high school," he said as the cameras whined, "but I'm here to do whatever it takes to win ball games." He went hitless that night against another first-round pick, the right-hander Jamie Arnold; more heroics from Kevin Grijak—his seventh homer matched his entire total at Macon in '93, and he added a sacrifice fly—nailed it for the Bulls 6-1.

And then, finally, without a word from West, Marty checked the lineup card posted in the dugout and found that he had been moved to the leadoff position in the batting order for Tuesday night's game. There was a palpable strut in his stride now, as though justice had been served, when he tossed aside the lead doughnut ring in the on-deck circle and marched purposefully toward the batter's box. He would go 0-for-3 with a walk (only his second of the year) that night, be dropped to the two-hole and get two hits on Wednesday, and go hitless with another base on balls on Thursday. The Bulls dropped those three remaining games in the Lynchburg series, but it was early in the season and Marty tried not to let it get him down. He was up there where he was supposed to be now, at the top of the order, where he could make things happen, and that was what he intended to do when the Bulls got back on the bus Friday morning for a week on the road at Salem and Winston-Salem.

CHAPTER 7

They traveled in a comfortable air-conditioned bus, not some old converted Blue Bird given up for dead by a county school system, and the distances between stops in the Carolina League weren't near as killing as the fifteen-hour haul from Idaho Falls to Canada in the Pioneer League (the Bulls' longest trip was 386 miles, to Wilmington, Delaware). Even so, traveling could become an ordeal after a while, and they learned how to cope in ways of their own design. The chartered bus the Bulls rode was always split into three camps: the Latins in the rear, the cardplayers in the middle, the sleepers up front just behind Matt West, Jay Williams, and the two coaches. Marty was in the last group, and he would develop a system, as the season wore on, that worked particularly well on the six-hour run to Wilmington. Staying up until as late as three o'clock in the morning to ensure that he would sleep through the riotous card games behind him, he would board the bus at daybreak with a pillow and his Walkman, commandeer two seats, and proceed to sleep through three states.

And then there was the matter of food. Until the season with Macon, Marty had loved pizza as much as any other American kid. The fourteen clubs in the South Atlantic League were spread out over a broad area, from Albany, in deepest southwest Georgia, to Hagerstown, Maryland, near the Pennsylvania line, and most of the stops were in small towns with few amenities late at night. Players in Class A received meal money of $15 a day, which wouldn't buy many hamburgers for a growing boy, but it was sometimes difficult to spend even that pittance. It would be well past ten o'clock at night before the Macon Braves, having played their game and taken their showers, would get back to their motel on the edge of, say, Columbia, South Carolina. And there they were: tired and famished from five hours on the field, without wheels, stuck in a budget motel with no dining room, miles away from any restaurant still open at that time of day. The only answer was to have pizzas delivered to a room at the motel, where twenty-five players would converge like dogs fighting over a bone. "After a while, I got where I'd gag just thinking about it," Marty said. The Bulls' trainer, Jay Williams, had a theory after working in the minors for more than a decade: "The American pizza industry is supported by minor-league baseball."

The unavailability of food wasn't the only bad part of being on the road, where minor-leaguers spend half of the season. The ballpark was unavailable to them, too, since first dibs went to the groundskeepers and the home team, so the visitors slept late and tried to concoct ways to while away the day. At midmorning of every other day on the road, the Bulls could board the bus for the ride to a nearby fitness center, where Jay Williams would oversee their work on Nautilus machines, and often they would proceed from there to a strip of fast-food joints for lunch of a sort. But that was about the extent of the teaching that took place on the road. There was a time, in the days of train travel in the major leagues, when rookies could learn a lot of baseball on the long haul between, say, New York and Chicago, simply by hanging out in the club car while the veterans talked about the game. But this was a different breed of ballplayers, the MTV generation, kids too impatient to sit around a lobby while old guys talked about the art of stealing signs. It didn't have to be that way—one would think that an eager protégé like Marty Malloy would buttonhole Rick Albert and beg for his patient ministrations on bunting and turning the double play as the bus droned on toward the next town—but that's the way it was.

This road trip to Salem, Virginia, and Winston-Salem, North Carolina, appeared to be a relatively easy one. The ride to Salem was only 136 miles from Durham, and after the three-game set there over the weekend, they had only to ride an hour southward, back toward home, to reach Winston-Salem for four more games. It was all new to them at this point, seeing the towns and the ballparks for the first time on their maiden swing through the league, and they were still working out bus protocol as they headed for Salem on that Friday morning. Matt West might have been sitting up there in the shotgun seat, the muscles in his jaw working vigorously so that nobody dared to joke with him—they were 5-9 now, following the three straight losses to Lynchburg at the DAP, and his pitchers were leading the league in home runs allowed—but these were kids and this was an adventure. They knew they would be seeing players many of them had known the year before in the Sally League (Salem's roster was loaded with graduates of the Augusta Pirates, Winston-Salem's with those who had moved up from the Reds' farm club at Charleston, West Virginia), so this would be a chance to check out *their* progress, much in the catty way that beauty-pageant contestants ogle each other. It hadn't been fun, losing nine of their first fourteen games, but the season was young. And, hey, it could have been worse; word had already reached them that the Macon Braves, the kids a step behind them in the Braves' heirarchy, had won only one of their first ten games. "I could see it coming in spring training," Marty said with a huff. "They were a bunch of hotshot rookies talking about how they were going to tear up the Sally League. Well, there was a couple of things they still don't know about: Macon in July and the one-forty [games]."

The players would later vote Salem as the worst stop in the Carolina League because of the scant dining options at a no-frills motel in nearby Roanoke and a ballpark so inadequate that the parent Pittsburgh Pirates were threatening to pull out at the end of the season if it wasn't replaced; it didn't help their spirits when only 887 fans showed up for the opening game of the series on a Friday night. The losing streak reached four games when Salem won that night, 7-2, with Marty ensconced in the two-hole and getting a single in four at bats. They ended the streak by taking the second game 6-2, and then broke loose on Sunday afternoon, winning 11-4, with Marty going 2-for-6 and Tom Waldrop, getting a rare start in a season that wasn't going well at all, mashing a grand-slam homer.

Moving on to Winston-Salem, they had their first encounter with the Spirits, a Cincinnati farm club loaded with power hitters and playing in a neat little refurbished park where the wind seemed always at the hitters' backs. The two clubs split the series, but in those four games Winston-Salem wrecked the Bulls' pitching staff, outscoring Durham 35-23, and came out of it with a home run total nearly double that of the nearest club in the league. To worsen matters for the Bulls, Kevin Grijak, in the midst of his superhuman hitting streak, felt spasms in his back after a play at first base and had to be benched indefinitely. It came almost as a consolation prize, then, when Tom Waldrop, beginning to find his range, sailed another grand slam out of the park.

If nothing else, they had learned on that trip how the other half lives—how much more invigorating it was to play at the DAP. Twice they had played games before fewer than a thousand spectators, and the average attendance for the seven games at Salem and Winston-Salem was slightly better than fifteen hundred. On the other hand, the average attendance for the Bulls' first seven games at home was 3,698, thanks to a couple of boisterous overflow crowds, and they couldn't wait to get back to the DAP. Marty had gone 9-for-28 on the trip, making his move on .300 now since being penciled in at the front of the batting order, and he was as eager as anybody to get back to Durham and show the home folks what he could do. Awaiting them were the streaking Wilmington Blue Rocks of the Kansas City Royals' farm system and, for the first time in the season, some of the front-office brass from Atlanta.

They were welcomed back home to the DAP with open arms, no matter how shakily they had performed. The college basketball season was history; spring football practice had ended at Duke, North Carolina, and North Carolina State; and now a glorious summer of Bulls baseball lay spread out before the Durham fans. The weeklong home stand against Wilmington and Winston-Salem would turn out to be a dizzying swirl of highs and lows—one fraught with home runs, more heroics from Kevin Grijak, the first roster moves of the young season, extremes in weather that would bring the biggest and then the smallest crowds of the year, and, alas, the beginning of another losing streak. It was exciting stuff for the fans, even when the

Bulls lost, but it was driving Matt West to distraction in his first year as a manager. Earlier in the schedule, in his comments to the *Herald-Sun* following a game, he had pulled from the bag of baseball clichés ("Even though we came up short, we saw some good things out there today") no matter the horrors he had seen, but now he was becoming snappish. "The time has come to quit relying on promise, on how good we were at four o'clock, and put it to work in a game," he said after another of his pitchers had carelessly given up yet another homer on an 0-2 pitch.

Marty was feeling coltish now, certain that nothing could stop him, not even an ingrown toenail. "The ball's coming up there looking like a watermelon," he said in the clubhouse before the opening game of the series that Friday against Wilmington. He was stretched out on the padded table in the training room, yowling while Jay Williams gouged at the toenail, dropping his voice to wonder how in the world Grijak could sit with mere spasms right in the middle of a hitting streak like he had going. Williams tied a string around the toe, and Marty went out to have his biggest night of the season: 3-for-4, with a run and an RBI, suddenly bringing his batting average to .293. Carefree and intrepid, he had even gotten into a shouting match with an umpire that required West's rushing out and stepping between them to avoid his ejection and an automatic $100 fine. ("Let's see the ball," the umpire had said after a ground single had skidded on the wet outfield grass, and when Marty took the relay from Tom Waldrop and inadvertently flipped it on a short hop, the umpire got officious with him—"Nice fuckin' throw, kid"—and Marty returned the sentiment.) The Bulls lost 8-4 before a near-full house of 4,654, in a game called after eight innings because of a sudden thunderstorm; but as the paper would point out in the next day's headline, the real thunder had come on three more home run balls given up by Durham pitchers.

Not lost on the players was the fact that two of the head men

from the Braves' front office were in town for the weekend series: Rod Gilbreath, the former Braves infielder who was now
assistant director of player development, and his right-hand
man, Scott Proefrock. Long before the Saturday game began,
while the players took batting practice and the DAP filled up
with what would be the biggest crowd of the season, they had
settled beside each other in the box seats behind homeplate and
were meticulously scribbling in their notebooks. Of particular
interest would be Sunday's start by a promising young left-hander named Darrell May, who had gone a combined 15-6 with
Macon and Durham in 1993 (with 158 strikeouts and only thirty-
nine walks in 156 innings) but had just joined Durham after
coming down with tendinitis in spring training. They were cha-
grined over Friday night's performance by Matt Murray, the
towering right-hander who now had given up nine homers in
only twenty-five innings, and they were disappointed that they
wouldn't be able to check out Grijak's amazing run. And now,
said Gilbreath, looking like anything but visiting brass in his casual Dockers shoes, khaki trousers, and green polo shirt, some
problems had already developed at AA Greenville and low-A
Macon.

"Bennie [Bruce Benedict, the Greenville manager] is screaming for a bat at shortstop, and then there's Macon," Gilbreath
said. Hector Roa, a muscular little shortstop at Greenville whose
star was fading fast, had sprained his thumb in a rundown on the
base paths, and the overmatched Macon Braves had made national headlines by winning only one of their first twenty games.
Gilbreath would have a look at the Durham shortstops, Julio
Trapaga and Jason Keeline, even though neither was hitting
.200, but not much could be done about Macon. "We knew we
had too many kids down there, while some of the other clubs
like Savannah would have the best A players in their organizations," Gilbreath said. "They lost their opener eighteen-to-one,

and it got worse after that. They got the idea they might never win a ball game." He turned to Proefrock and said, "What's for dinner? Hot dog or pizza?"

Seated near them, straining to hear if they would say anything about his son, was Bud Waldrop. A chunky man built along the lines of a bulldog, with jiggling jowls and a silver crew cut beneath his new-bought Bulls cap, Tom's father was co-owner of a used-car lot in Decatur, Illinois. He had knocked off work at exactly five o'clock on Friday afternoon and driven the 885 miles like a bat out of hell, all through the night, and arrived at Tom and Marty's apartment at nine-thirty, Eastern time, Saturday morning. Too anxious to talk to the boys, to see how things were going, he hadn't taken time to stretch out for a nap. He looked like a man who had, indeed, driven fifteen and a half hours without a rest, but that was of no concern to a father who hadn't seen his ballplaying son since his departure for spring training. "His mom got to see him at West Palm, and now it's my turn," he said. "I'll probably take him out for a big steak or something after the game, so we can—" He stopped short when he saw a commotion two boxes away and heard the name of the man at the center of it, fumbled for a pen and his scorecard, and excused himself so he could join the crowd.

The real "Crash" Davis was there, holding court and signing autographs for Retta Law and Martie Byron and some other fans and, now, Bud Waldrop. Lawrence Davis, a North Carolina boy who had been nicknamed after a comic-strip character, had spent two years playing second base with the Philadelphia Athletics but came back from the Second World War a has-been, resigned to playing out his career in the minors. He starred in the Carolina League in the late forties and early fifties—was a Durham Bull, in fact, in '48—and then retired to a job in Greensboro with Burlington Industries, the textile giant. When the screenwriter and director Ron Shelton was putting together a movie called *Bull Durham*, he came across that name, Crash Davis, and knew he had to have it for the character played by Kevin Costner. He called Davis, got permission to use his name, and made something of a star of him. And now here he was, a royal blue Bulls cap covering his bald head, vibrant and beaming, receiving his fans in the front row of box seats. "Aw, it's been a lot of fun, the attention and the notoriety," he was saying between autographs. He spoke to civic clubs and got interviewed now and then, and had just come back from Hollywood. "Ron figured he owed me, I guess, for using my name in *Bull Durham*, so he gave me a part in this picture he's making about Ty Cobb. I play Wahoo Sam Crawford in that one. When I was out there the other day, we were filming a scene that had a bunch of us at the Hall of Fame, and when I got up and started running at the mouth, Ron jumped up and said, 'Cut, cut! Crash, you're not running for office; you're just an old ballplayer taking a bow. Now, let's do it again.' " As he spoke, *Bull Durham* was being shown nightly five blocks away at the Carolina Theater, a restored old movie house where the movie's world premiere had been held in 1988. Durham people were proud of the movie; indeed, a caption beneath a photo on the sports pages of the *Herald-Sun* showing a conference on the mound borrowed a favorite line from the film: "Candlesticks always make a nice gift."

Shirtsleeve weather had followed the stormy night, and the biggest gathering of the season (5,758) shoehorned into the DAP to watch the Bulls blast the lordly Blue Rocks 10-3. Marty was the only man in the Durham lineup not to get a hit, although he did walk and steal second and later score, but his roomie Tom Waldrop upheld the honor of 707 Willowdale Apartments. Bud Waldrop wouldn't have to spring for steaks, as it turned out, for in the sixth inning his son came to bat with two men on base and promptly drilled a homer off the HIT BULL WIN STEAK sign atop the tier of fences in right. Tom's average after the first twelve games of the season had been only .074, but now he was on a tear rivaling that of the absent Grijak; over the last seven games he had hit three homers, including the two grand slams on the road, with sixteen runs batted in. Father and son went out that night and hunkered down over a freebie at the Lone Star Steak House, wondering what the singles hitters were up to.

Marty gave an answer to that the next day when a right-hander brought a fastball into his wheelhouse and he propelled it onto the roof of one of the buildings in right center for his first homer of the year—only to be upstaged two innings later when Waldrop clubbed another three-run homer. (Bud Waldrop had been headed for his car to begin the long drive home to Illinois but had shuffled back to the runway between the dugout and the bleachers just in time to see this one.) The heroics of Marty and Tom were soon erased when Wilmington jumped all over the Durham relievers for eleven runs in the sixth inning and five more in the ninth, giving the visitors a 17-6 victory. Rod Gilbreath and Scott Proefrock hustled to the Bulls clubhouse after the game to visit with Darrell May—not Marty and Tom—because May had shown them what they came to see. He had spent an extra month in the sunshine at West Palm Beach, resting his arm in extended spring training, and in his first start he had shown he might be ready to move on to Greenville. Smartly working the corners, snapping a fastball when he had to, he had given up six harmless hits and struck out five before being pulled after reaching his limit of seventy-five pitches.

When Marty got back to the apartment after the game he couldn't wait to call home and tell his folks about the homer. His mother, Beverly, said Corbyn was saying "cat" now, and she wanted to know if Marty was eating his vegetables. Amie got on the line to say she was now seriously dating Scott Guthrie, an old ballplaying buddy of his, and marriage was a possibility. Then his father, Tommy, took the phone and listened patiently while Marty described the pitch he had taken to right center for the home run.

When Marty was done, his father said, "Maybe I'll be seeing you before the summer."

"But you've got spring football."

"Not anymore. I quit."

"What? You quit coaching football?"

"Twenty-nine years is enough, son. It's just athletic director and baseball coach now."

"You better give me a minute." Marty could hardly believe it. He knew how his father felt about basketball, now that it had become a black man's game, and he guessed he could understand that. But now, not even fifty-five years old, Tommy was giving up football. "What is this? It sounds like you're going to spend your time following my career."

"So?" said Tommy Malloy. "You got a problem with that?"

The first of a series of roster shufflings came immediately after the next night's game—won single-handedly by Grijak when he returned from the disabled list and hammered two gargantuan home runs, the second in the bottom of the ninth, for a 2-1 Bulls victory—when Jason Keeline was told to report to Greenville. Keeline was a good-looking blue-eyed Californian, tall and broad across the chest, a triple-A shortstop with a rookie-league bat. "Jason will never hit," Randy Ingle had said of him the year before at Macon, "but every organization can use a good shortstop like that." He had signed with the Braves for virtually nothing after two years at Cal Poly ("They were into winning, and I never got to hit away on a two-oh or a three-one count, hitter's pitches, so I could put up numbers for the scouts"), had hit poorly but fielded superbly during three years in the minors, including a sixty-nine-game stint at Durham in the second half of the '92 season, when he batted .235, and he felt like this might be his last great opportunity. He had almost made the Greenville club in spring training this year but at the last minute was assigned to Durham. Now, having turned twenty-five during the first week of the season, he had appeared in only fourteen of the Bulls' twenty-five games, sharing shortstop with the young Mexican, Trapaga, and was batting .154 in just thirty-nine at bats. He couldn't load up his car fast enough for the 250-mile drive south and west on I-85 to Greenville to replace the injured Hector Roa and perhaps, once and for all, show the Braves he could play. "I'm gonna miss him," said Marty. "Jason can flat play shortstop. I don't think I've gotten the same [double-play] feed twice from Trapaga."

Ideally, the second baseman and the shortstop would be identical twins; that's how important it is that they instinctively know each other's moves. (Indeed, for a brief period in the eighties, the brothers Cal and Billy Ripken formed the Baltimore Orioles' double-play combination.) "They have to think like twins, anyway," said Randy Ingle. "They're like links in a bicycle chain, and if they're not in synch the chain breaks. After eleven years together at Detroit, longer than any double-play combination in the history of the majors as far as I know, Lou Whitaker and Alan Trammell worked together like pistons in a fine car." In the old days—personal friendships be damned—the shortstop and the second basemen were routinely assigned to room with each other on the road, on the chance that they would eventually begin to fill the long empty hours with talk of the pivot and the feed on the double play. Except for the pitcher-catcher relationship, nowhere on the field is it more important that two players know each other's every move.

For more hours than either could compute, through two

spring camps and the season at Macon, Marty Malloy and Jason Keeline had been a team. Side by side, with the second-base bag as their common ground, they had taken thousands of ground balls and worked on the feed and the pivot on the double play, learning each other's particular rhythms and preferences and tendencies until they had become thoroughly symbiotic, like ballet dancers, almost like lovers. (There had even been a novel, *The Dreyfus Affair*, in which the second baseman fell into homosexual love with his shortstop.) This need for the shortstop and the second baseman to work as one extended beyond the double play. As guardians of the entire middle of the playing field, in the center of the action on nearly every play, each had to know where the other would be in a myriad of situations: bunt coverage, steal attempts, pickoff throws, relays and cutoffs from the outfield. They would work out silent signals between them, such as the universal open mouth/closed mouth sign to indicate who would cover second on a steal, but for the most part they developed this oneness by hours of working together.

Marty had never been able to get into a rhythm with Julio Trapaga. The angular teenaged Mexican, like most Latin infielders, favored the dazzling snap throw, often delivered from the underhanded position, which causes the ball to sink like the delivery from a submarine pitcher. "The hand should always be above the elbow at release, so you don't get that sinking throw," said Ingle. Marty would be approaching the bag looking for a chest-high feed but suddenly would have to break stride when he received a herky-jerky submarine feed at the knees, too late, more often than not, to recover and complete the double play. Worse, Trapaga struggled with his English and rarely showed up early at the ballpark to work things out with Marty. With Keeline gone, it promised to be a lonesome year around the bag for Marty.

• • •

Wintry weather struck the Triangle on the first Tuesday of May, forcing a rainout, and the season reached a nadir on many counts when management scheduled a doubleheader for the next night. With the temperature near freezing, only 285 fans showed up—the smallest crowd in the history of the DAP, as far as anyone could recall—to watch the Bulls lose both games on cheap DAP Special home runs, over the short porch in right field, by the muscular Winston-Salem Spirits. It was a particularly dispiriting night for West, the former pitcher, when both Jamie Arnold and Matt Murray again gave up gopher balls: one by Arnold in the first game, and four by Murray in a second-game stint that saw him fail to make it through the fifth inning. Marty sat out the first game, and when he got into the second one he pinched a nerve in his back while twisting to make a double-play feed—an injury that would cause him to miss the next four games. Durham lost to Winston-Salem again on the next night, on a grand-slam homer in the seventh inning, and they managed to win only one of three on a quick weekend road trip to Kinston.

Kevin Grijak, to nobody's surprise, finally got the call to Greenville when they returned home. In his three previous years of pro ball, he had hit a total of twenty-two home runs in 779 at bats—nothing to prepare the parent Braves for this tear he was on at Durham. Now, after only sixty-eight at bats with the Bulls, he had become a monster: eleven homers and twenty-two RBIs in as many games, a batting average of .368 with only six strike-outs. He had suddenly become a factor in the Braves' planning for the future, and they intended to throw him in at first base on a full-time basis with the Greenville Braves. (The DH wasn't employed in AA and AAA when two National League farm clubs played each other.) He had much to learn around the bag, but there would always be a demand for a left-handed power hitter who didn't care who was on the mound. So he drove away from

Durham, as did the left-handed pitcher Darrell May, who had shown the parent club after only ten innings with the Bulls that his arm had healed. When Bob Guy announced their promotions over the PA system upon the club's return to the DAP—"Hopefully, in a couple of years, we'll be seeing them on TBS"—the crowd broke out in sustained applause.

When the smoke had cleared from all of the roster moves, Marty found that he was leading the club in hitting at .281 and Tom Waldrop was second at .262. The Bulls, after losing five of six games in early May, were dead last in the league with a 12-19 record (although their average home attendance of 3,366 was second only to Wilmington), and it was killing Marty the way he and his teammates would scratch away, night after night, only to be done in by home run balls. The Bulls' pitching staff was giving up homers at a frightening rate. The allowable percentage is one home run per ten innings, but Durham's pitchers were giving up more than one every *five* innings (the worst offender being Matt Murray, with thirteen in thirty-one). Marty's competitive nature wouldn't allow him to focus on his own performance, but to dwell on the club's losses. "I played against Jon Nunnally [of the Kinston Indians] in junior college," he said one day after Nunnally, who had beaten out Marty by one vote as Florida's junior college player of the year in '92, had launched a pair of two-run homers against Jamie Arnold. "So I know him, right? I figured he must be hitting four hundred, but I saw where it wasn't but two-thirty-two. Well, a lot of guys are having careers off our pitching. Anyway, before the game I told our pitchers, 'No fastballs on the first pitch to this guy.' So what happens? Two fastballs on the first pitch, two home runs."

CHAPTER 8

It had taken only one month for Marty to surface as the spiritual leader of the Bulls; the unofficial team captain, the proverbial coach on the field, Matt West's tenth man. "No doubt about it," said West, "the kid's got great work habits and instincts. He's a ballplayer." Marty wouldn't turn twenty-two until July, but already he was approaching the six-hundredth game of his lifetime, from the first days in Little League through the first month of his third year in pro ball—a remarkable number of innings. As a consequence, nobody on the Bulls except the manager and the coaches was so attuned to the nuances of what was happening on the field at any given moment—the pitch count, the tendencies of both the pitcher and the batter, where everybody was positioned, even which way the flags were snapping in the wind—and this kept him a step ahead of the others, prepared him for every eventuality. As he had done the year before at Macon with the crafty pitching coach Larry Jaster, he nestled down beside Bill Slack in the dugout during Bulls' at bats to discuss what the opposing pitcher was up to as the half inning progressed: what pitches were working, what pattern he was using, whether he was telegraphing anything. Arriving at ballparks on the first swing around the league, he would spend considerable time inspecting the field to discern how balls would carom off the fences, how much foul territory he had to cover, the thickness of the grass, how well the second-base bag was anchored; then he would share his findings with any others who would listen. He was, in short, the prototypical little guy who had to stretch his limited physical abilities by using his head. He was a manager's dream. No wonder all of those instructors throughout the Braves' system loved him.

On that first road trip, to Prince William and Lynchburg, Marty had found a deal on a set of golf clubs and hauled them back in the cargo hold of the bus. Golf had always seemed to him a game of the wealthy, but when he found that it was the pastime favored by ballplayers, he was determined to join them. He played one round, not too badly for a neophyte, but that was about it; golf was expensive, tiring, and too slow, so he put the clubs away in his closet. The other players and West liked to kid him about his country background, the Huck Finn stuff, and he had no aversion to furthering that image. It was true that nobody on the Bulls had come from so far back in the sticks as he, so he often brought it up before they had a chance, holding forth on matters from tracking deer to making biscuits from scratch, regaling them with tales of the hard-charging stock car driver Dale Earnhardt and the country singer George Jones, arguing the merits of Chevys versus Fords, feeding the preconceived notions of the Californians and Yankees and other "foreigners" who were his teammates by overplaying his Florida Cracker drawl

and exaggerating his backwoods roots. He relished going out
into the parking lot of the Willowdale Apartments wearing his
cowboy boots and jeans and Florida Gators T-shirt, turning up
the volume on the local country-music radio station so he could
change the oil in his Chevy pickup to the strains of "A Country
Boy Can Survive."

You'll be okay as long as you remember where you come from. His
father's advice never left him. He still addressed his elders as
"sir" and "ma'am." He ate his vegetables. He didn't smoke,
thanks to a vision of his grandmother, who chain-smoked,
coughing and wheezing under the air conditioner on her visits
to Trenton. He shuffled over to the Spa in the strip shopping
center next to the apartments to get in his work with weights
whether he felt like it or not. He might go out and have a few
beers with the boys after a game, to yuk it up and ogle the ladies,
but he hadn't touched hard liquor since the night Randy Ingle
had plied him with tequilas in Macon to celebrate his twenty-
first birthday. He got his rest, called home at least twice a week,
remembered birthdays and anniversaries, pampered his truck,
made up his bed, obsessively went for a haircut every two weeks,
did his share of cooking and housekeeping at the apartment,
took to dressing neatly in Duck Head twill trousers and bright
polo shirts and Topsiders when he went out. He wasn't particularly religious—"Aw, I pray and stuff"—but he was always
among the dozen players who gathered in the runway beneath
the stands at the DAP for Sunday morning "chapel" services. He
was the product of a stable home in Trenton, Florida, a small-
town America that hardly exists anymore, and doing the right
thing came naturally to him in all matters, from obeying stop
signs in the middle of the night to backing up first base on
throws from the other infielders. Even when his life became
complicated for the first time, with the birth of a child out of
wedlock, he was trying to do what he thought was right: support

the kid, don't run, and hope that something could be worked out with the mother. The support money wasn't enough to break him, of course, but many accidental fathers his age would have walked away entirely from their obligation.

Curiously, given their different backgrounds, a mutual respect had evolved between him and Matt West. Marty missed the commonalities he had shared with Randy Ingle and Bobby Dews and Paul Runge, with their drawls and laid-back manners and Southernness, but he soon found that this can-do Californian was a baseball man to the core. "Matt's pretty intense about everything, even shouts orders while we're out there stretching, but he knows the game and he cares," Marty said. West had pulled Marty aside only three weeks into the season to say it wasn't necessary for him to show up an hour early for extra work in the batting cage every day: "You don't have to impress me with your work ethic, so save your energy for July." Marty hastened to say he wasn't a snitch, but often he served as a conduit between West and the players. (Once, when Bobby Smith had snarled at West after a round of batting practice, Matt asked Marty to find out what was up with Bobby. "It was lousy BP; he didn't give me anything to hit," Smith said. "Hey, look," Marty told him, "the man's out there throwing every day. Give him a break." The issue had been defused.) "If I had twenty-five Martys I could just sit back and enjoy the games," said West.

In spite of West's admonition to take it easy and save his energy for the dog days of the summer months, Marty couldn't help showing up early at the ballpark to hound Rick Albert or the instructors passing through to give him some extra work in the batting cage or around the bag. He saw those players who had vast natural talent wandering onto the field each day to do only what they were told to do, and he was truly puzzled: "Hollins won't work on playing fly balls off the fence, and Nunez won't spend any extra time around first base. It must be their upbringing. I don't know how Damon grew up in California, and I sure don't know how Raymond was raised in the Dominican. Maybe Grijak really did hurt his back that time, but I can't imagine anybody taking himself out in the middle of a streak like he had going." As he spoke, at a workingman's café called the Golden Corral, where the all-you-can-eat buffet cost $5, he still winced from the ingrown toenail, had strawberries on both knees from headfirst slides, and was going to the park early each day so Jay Williams could apply heat treatments for the pinched nerve in his back. "I'm not gonna sit anymore. You tell the trainer you're hurt, and bells go off in Atlanta: 'Make him sit; gotta protect our investment.' The hell with that. I've got all winter to sit."

"Somewhere in there," Willie Stargell had said during the '93 season at Macon, "your passion for the game becomes a way of life." Not being particularly articulate, few of these baseball men could find the words to describe how they felt about the game. "One day you wake up," said Randy Ingle, "and it's not a game anymore; it's your livelihood." Marty was no more articulate than the others, but after his shakedown period with the Bulls, playing before those rapt crowds at the DAP, he had begun to feel that baseball was, indeed, his life. All of the people he hung out with were ballplayers, even the two best pals back home, who hadn't quite had the stuff to turn pro. Everything he did now was related to his career: eating correctly, getting the proper sleep, learning how to dress more sharply, giving radio and newspaper interviews, even keeping his hair neatly trimmed. Nothing else mattered. He had no interest in books, movies, politics, or current affairs except as they related to baseball, and about the only time he watched television was when sports was involved. "What can I say? Baseball is it. Baseball is everything. I can't imagine my life without it now." He had joined the fraternity, the brotherhood of baseball, and even if he didn't ultimately make it to the major leagues he would live forever with the knowledge that he had been a ballplayer.

If report cards were to be issued after the first month of play—and they were certainly keeping track at the big house, in the minor-league offices in Atlanta–Fulton County Stadium—Marty's would read B plus. "If Marty hits two-eighty in the Carolina League," said West, "it will have been a hell of a year." His .281 led the club, now that Grijak had taken his act to Greenville, and he had clearly established himself as the best defensive second baseman in the league. Looking closer at his batting line for the month, his superiors were most heartened to see that he was becoming more disciplined at the plate. The key figure to look for in one being groomed for the two-hole was the ratio of strikeouts and bases on balls, and Marty's numbers had been disappointing in his first two seasons. At Idaho Falls, swinging at the first good pitch he saw in each at bat, he had struck out once every 5.8 at bats (forty-three strikeouts and only eleven walks in 251 at bats). At Macon, his strikeout ratio had risen to one every 5.1 at bats (seventy strikeouts, just thirty-nine walks). Now, after eighty-nine appearances, he was striking out once every 6.8 at bats, with thirteen strikeouts against seven bases on balls. This was still insufficient—Mark Lemke, the current Braves second baseman, had struck out only once per ten at bats and always had more walks than strikeouts during his long apprenticeship in the minors—but there was evidence that he was getting his primordial urges under control.

Those urges were double edged, could work for him and against him at the same time, and Matt West had understood that from the beginning. He had relegated Marty to the bottom of the order at the beginning of the season, he said now, as a form of punishment for his having "gotten away from his game" toward the end of spring training: swinging away more like a power hitter than a little guy in the two-hole whose job was to get on base or move runners along. West told of a night on the road, early in the season, when he was checking curfews in the motel and found that Tom and Marty had sneaked some beer into their room. "I told 'em I was going to have to take the beer, but I wound up staying there and drinking with them. I told Marty, 'You're scared to death you're going to strike out, aren't you?' He denied it at first, but I stayed on him. I know it's a stereotype about Latin players, but the reason they're such wild swingers is they're afraid to lose face by striking out. It's a part of their culture, a macho thing, and pitchers love to see somebody like that coming." West took the rest of the beer with him when he left—Marty later said it seemed like West had stayed for two hours—hoping he had left a message.

The fear of losing face by striking out was a part of Marty's culture, too, West said, and changing him wasn't going to happen overnight. "He's got to get it through his thick skull that if he's going to make it to the big leagues it's going to be as a great defensive second baseman and a smart little two-hole hitter," West was saying one day after he had faxed his daily report to Atlanta. "There's no doubt about his work habits and his instincts, but he's stubborn, thinks he can hustle his way out of any situation, and that works against him. Everybody says, 'Yeah, that Marty Malloy, he's a tough little guy; he'll battle you all the way.' We all agree on that. It's what we like about the kid. This hardworking-country-boy image is for real; that's Marty; but that alone won't get him to the big leagues. He's got to refine the tools he's got, find out what his game is and stick with it. This isn't high school. This isn't college. It's pro ball, the road to the major leagues. We don't care half as much about what kind of Durham Bull he is as we do about what kind of big-leaguer he can be, so when he's putting in all of this hard work he's got to keep that in mind. Frankly, I cringed when he hit that home run, because that's not his game."

Meanwhile, as warm weather came to Durham and the long hot summer loomed ahead of the Bulls, Marty couldn't keep from peeking at what was going on elsewhere in the organization. Several middle infielders ahead of him seemed to be faltering—most notably Ramon Caraballo, once deemed the Braves' second baseman of the future, who was barely hitting .100 at Richmond and might be playing himself out of the picture, leaving Tony Graffanino as Marty's main challenge. The hardened son of a retired New York cop and quite a different animal from Marty (rangy and powerful at six one, two hundred pounds, he had hit fifteen homers and been the Carolina League's best second baseman while with Durham in '93), Graffanino was batting .349, fifth in the Southern League, with the Greenville Braves. The kid immediately behind him in the Braves' order of things, a cocky Californian named Mike Eaglin, who had hit .326 in '93 with Idaho Falls, was now out for the season with a separated shoulder after batting only .237 in seventy-six at bats with Macon. Still, Marty knew that the only performance he could control was his own. "I've got enough on my mind without worrying about those guys," Marty said, convincingly, as he headed off to the DAP to work in the batting cage with Rick Albert.

CHAPTER 9

Once the summer came and the short-season leagues began play, the world of minor-league baseball would swell to 5,260 players on 213 teams in nineteen leagues. They ranged from triple-A to some rookie leagues, like the one in the Dominican Republic, that were structured more like extended spring-training camps than full-blown competitive leagues. Except at that lowest level, where games were scheduled throughout the day on back-to-back playing fields and few but scouts were in the rickety stands, a ballpark was the mother church for everyone involved. These parks ranged in size from 33,500-seat Cardinal Stadium, home of the Louisville Cardinals of the triple-A American Association, to fifteen-hundred-seat Joe O'Brien Field in Elizabethton, Tennessee, where the Minnesota Twins had a rookie team in the Appalachian League. Regardless

of the size of the ballpark and the average attendance—
Louisville could expect ten thousand fans every night, Elizabethton only five hundred—the ballpark was the center of
attention, the main stage, the center ring.

Durham Athletic Park never slept. A day in the life of the
DAP began, in fact, just when most fans thought it had ended—
after the last putout, around ten o'clock at night, as the players
finished showering and the stands emptied and all but a few security lights were shut down for the night. On his way to the
Bulls' offices in the trailers behind the ballpark, to fax his daily
report to Atlanta–Fulton County Stadium, Matt West was likely
to bump into the first of the people who kept the club and the
park running. Romeo McKeever was his name, laundry his
game, and all through the night he would sweat in the bowels of
the DAP washing and drying the uniforms, from shirts to jockstraps, that were tossed into giant hampers by the Bulls on their
way to the showers only half an hour after the game. At daybreak, just after McKeever had hung the last clean uniform in its
stall and was heading for home, he would say good morning to
the city crew arriving to begin their sweeping and hosing down
of the grandstand.

And so the cycle continued, whenever the Bulls were at home,
from the first week of April until Labor Day. By eight thirty, ad-
ministrative types, from the general manager, Peter Anlyan, to
Leisha Cowart, the director of community and media relations,
would have arrived at the cramped trailers that served as the
Bulls' offices. By nine o'clock, Bill Miller and his grounds crew
would be out on the field mowing or watering the grass. At ten
thirty, the first delivery trucks would come with kegs of soft
drinks and beer for the concessions stands, and by eleven, Jay
Williams, the trainer, would have unlocked the doors of the
clubhouse to make ready for the first of the wounded. By noon,
the last of the support people would have arrived: Matt West and

his coaches, to begin preparations for the afternoon's work and the night's game, and Steve Barnes, the play-by-play radio announcer, to start updating the statistics he would need for his pregame show and broadcast of the game.

Meanwhile, the other actors in that night's drama would be stirring: Bobby Dews on the phone in his room at the Hilton, checking his voice mail and getting reports from last night's games throughout the Braves system; Marty Malloy scrambling eggs at the Willowdale Apartments; the visiting Spirits trudging across the asphalt parking lot at the Red Roof Inn for breakfast at Honey's; the two umpires, stuck with each other until game time, awakening at a separate motel and wondering what to do with the long day spread out before them. Then someone became the first customer of the day at the Ballpark Corner, the concrete-block building across from the park: a fan from New Jersey who couldn't wait to buy an authentic fitted Bulls cap. Then someone else who knew the Bulls from the movie *Bull Durham*, a couple from Kansas, knocked on the door of the trailer and bought tickets for that night's game. And through all of this, about a mile from the DAP, across from what passed for a skyline in little Durham, there could be heard the whumping of pile drivers and the groaning of cement mixers as the construction crew continued laying the foundation for the new park that soon would render the DAP a piece of history.

The first players would show up around two-thirty in the afternoon, to be attended by Jay Williams or to work in the batting cage outside the park with one of the coaches or roving instructors, and for the next five hours all action would point toward the moment of the first pitch. While Jef, the actor who played Wool E. Bull, practiced clubbing rolled-up Bulls T-shirts into the bleachers with his five-foot plastic bat (a nightly giveaway promotion), the hilly gravel parking lot across the street would begin to fill up with the players' cars. By three-thirty, half a dozen of them would have drifted out from the clubhouse to get in some individual work on the field. At four, everybody in uniform now, the full team would begin its stretching exercises down the right-field line, overseen by West and his trainer. At five, while the Bulls took batting practice, the visiting club would arrive in uniform, having dressed at the Red Roof Inn. At six, as the visitors took their whacks, the gates would be opened. At seven, after both clubs had completed pregame infield, the grounds crew would begin laying fresh lime down the baselines and dragging and watering the infield. Finally, after he had played a taped tune called "Welcome to the Show," Bob Guy would formally convene the proceedings and announce the starting lineups. And then, to much fanfare, Wool E. Bull would gallop onto the field in full uniform to exhort the crowd; Leisha Cowart, like a mother hen, would shepherd the night's Field of Dreams Team so they could run onto the field with the Bulls as they were announced; and finally, Guy would say the magic words: "And now, we ask you to please stand and honor America . . ."

Show time.

At two-thirty on the day that the crowd would applaud the promotion of Grijak and May to Greenville, Jay Ward was working with Raymond Nunez in the special batting cage that sat in the gravel parking lot outside the DAP, beside the trailers and behind the first-base bleachers. Now that Grijak was gone, Nunez had first base all to himself, and he was having trouble; a stoical, powerfully built twenty-one-year-old from the Dominican Republic with great possibilities as a power hitter, he had hit only one homer so far and was batting just .257. Nunez's natural power was to right center, to the inviting short porch in the DAP, and in this park he should already have half a dozen homers. His problems traced to his inability to think along with the pitcher, to anticipate the next pitch, and Ward, the Braves' roving batting instructor, had been summoned to Durham especially to work with him. Ward had arrived in Durham unannounced the night before, having driven all day from his home in St. Petersburg, and sat quietly in the stands to observe Nunez at work. Like most instructors, he had never made it to the majors himself and hadn't been exceptional as a minor-league hitter, but he knew how to teach. The players loved these one-on-one sessions in the cage with Ward because he was so intense and had flair. Sometimes, Marty said, he would go out to the park early just to watch Ward put on his show.

And now, here was Ward, with a gray burr haircut, in white Braves uniform pants and a silver nylon shirt cut off at the elbows, kneeling on a neatly folded towel, plucking baseballs from a bucket and softly tossing them up to Nunez, who stood facing him not six feet away. "*We* come tearing through the strike zone, but *they* drag-ass through it, right, Raymond?" It was anybody's guess how much English Nunez was absorbing, but he nodded an assent and then snapped at a ball tossed up hard and belt high to simulate a fastball on the hands, the ball rippling the nylon net as it flew off his bat. "All right, what're we gonna do now, Raymond?" Ward said, reaching for another ball, juggling it in his hand. "He's thrown us a curve outside and now two straight fastballs on the hands. We've seen everything he's got, right?" A mumble from Nunez. "Now we've got the sonofabitch right where we want him, Raymond. What do you think, a change low and away?" Nunez said, "Change, mebbe?" With that, Ward tossed the ball so low and far from Nunez's reach that he had to golf it, one-handed, and Ward was ecstatic: "We did it, Raymond, we got the bastard, single to right on his change. *Comprende?*"

Marty had parked his pickup on the hill across the street and paused at the cage, still in his street clothes, to watch the Jay Ward show for a few moments, then checked in with Jay Williams in the training room for some more heat treatment on his back. At three o'clock, he sat on the stool in front of his locker and finished suiting up for the long day ahead of him. He had lots of room now, having taken over the adjoining cubbyhole that had been Keeline's, and he had been able to bring some order to his corner of the cramped clubhouse. Still, the two spaces were a mélange, like Fibber McGee's closet: four bats, three gloves, half a dozen pairs of baseball shoes, shower clogs, a pile of clean jockstraps and stirrups and sanitary hose and T-shirts, a Polaroid shot of Corbyn standing on his own power, uniforms hung by Romeo McKeever sometime during the night. Floating up from the tiny room shared by Matt West and his coaches were the sounds of a Braves afternoon game on television. The other players who had arrived early were welcoming a young outfielder who had just been brought up from Macon: Wonderful Terrific Monds III, a name tracing to his great-grandfather, who had shouted, "Wonderful, terrific!" upon the birth of a boy after eight straight girls. Someone told Marty that Jason Keeline had gone 5-for-9 in his first two games with the Greenville Braves, and he nodded with some pride and amazement.

Soon he was on the field, at work on his bunting with Rick Albert. The temperature was in the mid-seventies, jet contrails streaking the cloudless sky, as he and Albert pulled away the tarpaulin to reveal a lane of grass five feet wide down the third baseline. That would be the target area for the day's drill. Marty took his stance in the batting cage, already rolled into place for batting practice, and Albert stood on the front edge of the mound beside a shopping cart full of smudged dead practice balls. In a scene reminiscent of that day in January at the little ball field in Trenton when Tommy Malloy lobbed pitches and

Marty dropped bunts, Marty and the coach labored for half an hour. Albert did most of the talking. "Uh-huh, got a nice dead sound . . . Okay, good . . . How do you shoot a gun? You aim it first. That's right, angle the bat, aim for the spot where you want it . . . Nice, very nice . . . On our grass, there's a lot of base hits there . . . Head down, spread the hands . . ." Marty ended the session by dragging a bunt on the first-base side, breaking away from the plate for a base hit.

He would put that practice to work that night. Mike Warner was on the disabled list again, his arm aching so badly that he couldn't even swing a bat, so Marty was moved to leadoff for a six-game series against Salem and Frederick. In the opener that night against Salem, he dragged a lefty's inside fastball past the mound and slid headfirst into the bag to win a footrace with the first baseman and get his third bunt hit of the young season. Rick Albert, coaching first base, was there to slap him on the butt, and they grinned at each other as though they had pulled off a conspiracy. The Bulls would go on to lose that night, 4-2, on two late-inning homers by the Buccaneers, although Matt Murray wasn't guilty this time. The towering right-hander had his best outing of the year, striking out eight and walking none, but he could only watch in despair as his bull pen frittered away the lead and lost the game. John Simmons came on in relief to start the eighth, and when Salem's leadoff batter bombed his second pitch over the wall in right, West stormed out of the dugout to take the ball from him—Simmons, none too pleased with himself or his manager, stomped off for the clubhouse to rearrange the furniture—and Matt Byrd, after getting two outs, delivered another home run pitch. Byrd skulled the very next batter, no doubt bringing a smile to West's face, but it was too late.

There was more evidence in the next game that Marty was growing and learning from all of those hours in the cage and the four o'clock repetitions on the field. In the sixth inning, with runners at first and third, game tied at 2-all, Salem pulled a double steal. Marty was moving to take the throw at second, but when the batter struck out swinging and the runner broke from third, Marty cut in front of the bag and nailed the runner at the plate. It was a textbook execution of a play he had rehearsed hundreds of times. Then came the bottom of the ninth. Durham had pulled to within 5-4 on a two-run single by Wonderful Monds, and the game was in Marty's hands when he stepped up with two outs and runners at first and second. On the mound was a frightening sight, a fireballing six-five, 240-pound right-hander named Mark Pisciotta. Marty fouled off two straight devastating sliders from Pisciotta and stepped out of the box, with the crowd of 3,061 on its feet and the runners pleading, sure that Pisciotta now would try to jam him with a fastball. Marty got the smoke, all right, but it was out over the inside half of the plate, and he drilled the pitch to the gap in right center to score the tying and winning runs. It was the high point of the new season for him, and he was nearly buried by his teammates when they rushed out en masse to mob him at second base. Even Bill and Retta Law, veterans of many a thrilling finish at the DAP, were high-fiving each other in the box seats behind home.

He was in the midst of a hitting streak now, 17-for-47 over the past twelve games, running his batting average up to .286, but more important to West and Albert was how he was managing it. He was being more patient at the plate since being moved to the top of the order and was responding according to the situation. Baseball people call it (what else?) situational hitting—batting according to the count, the pitcher, the score, the outs, the runners, the needs at a given moment—and Marty was having smart at bats more often than not, even when the box score showed that he had failed. He would get only one hit in five at bats on the night following his game-winning hit, but it was a meaningful night's work against three different left-handers. Leading off the first, he lined out to short. They were throwing him curve-balls now, having learned better the night before, and on his sec-ond time up he walked on four straight curves that missed the mark. On his third trip to the plate, he badly missed a sweeping outside curve on an 0-2 pitch. But when they came back with the same pitch in the same situation his next time up, he drilled a single to center. Finally, with the score tied in the bottom of the ninth and a runner on second, he drove the first pitch to the wall, advancing the runner to third, leaving him only ninety feet away from scoring what could have been the winning run. The rally died there, and a two-run DAP Special that slinked over the 305-foot mark in right center won it for Salem in the eleventh, but Marty could walk away from the park confident that he had done his job.

Jay Ward had moved on, taking his act back down the inter-state to Greenville, and he missed the fruits of his labor on Fri-day night. With an overflow crowd of nearly six thousand in attendance for the opener of a three-game series against the Frederick Keys, a Baltimore farm club the Bulls were seeing for the first time this season, Raymond Nunez came up with two out and the score tied in the eleventh inning and blasted a homer over everything in right center, precisely where every-body knew his power lay. It marked another milestone in Marty's career—his two-hundredth game in pro ball—and he contributed with a walk and two runs batted in on five trips to the plate in a game where, once again, the Bulls had to claw back from a deficit created when their pitchers gave up a grand-slam homer in the early innings.

The largest crowd of the year (6,132) got its money's worth the next night. They had hardly settled into their seats when Bobby Smith steamrolled the pitcher, who was trying to tag him on the baseline near first, bringing both clubs out of their dugouts. It was the usual toothless baseball fight, with more taunting and posturing than fisticuffs, but the Bulls and Keys were out of luck. The president of the Carolina League happened to be in the box seats to witness the proceedings, and when it was over he announced fines of $100 and two-day suspensions for every player involved (excepting only the previous night's starting pitchers, who were charting pitches in their street clothes from the box seats, and Durham's Matt Murray, who had been using the toilet in the Bulls' clubhouse). Frederick was cruising along with a 2-0 lead until Durham tied it in the eighth, and then the Bulls pulled out another one when Mike Warner, back from the DL, bounced a single past the second baseman to score Monds, who had doubled and been moved along on a sacrifice, for the club's third win in the final at bat in their last four games.

They almost pulled off another last-second reprieve in Sunday's game. Wonderful Terrific Monds III was fitting in quite nicely, thank you very much, since his call-up from the woeful Macon club. He was "Mondsie" now to his new teammates—"Ain't no way I'm calling *anybody* 'Wonderful' or 'Terrific,' " said Marty—and in five games as a Bull he had already stolen two bases, driven in three runs, and twice scored the game-winning run. On this bright afternoon at the DAP he clubbed a homer onto the roof of one of the brick buildings beyond the tier of fences in right center, to give Durham a short-lived tie, and his chance for more heroics came in the bottom of the ninth, with Frederick clinging to a 4-3 lead. There were two outs and Nunez was on first with an infield single when Monds came to the plate. The strains of "I Need a Hero" rang through the park. The count went to two balls and one strike, bringing the crowd to its feet again, and they went berserk when he wound up and whammed the next pitch to the deepest corner of the park, at the 410-foot mark below the picnic area in center field; but the

Frederick center fielder made a running catch at the wall to end the game.

At daybreak on Monday the Bulls parked their vehicles in a well-lighted area at a shopping mall north of town and got on the bus for the mother of all road trips, to Wilmington and Frederick. Marty had stayed up as late as possible Sunday night, calling home, doing his laundry, and watching television well past midnight so he would be tired enough to sleep on the six-hour ride to Delaware. This visit to the northernmost points in the league not only would complete their swing around the cir-cuit but would be critical for a club beginning to slither toward the cellar. The Wilmington Blue Rocks and the Frederick Keys were clearly the strongest clubs in the league in the early going, and their proximity to large metropolitan areas (Wilmington forty miles from Philadelphia, Frederick less than an hour's drive from both Baltimore and Washington) had them battling it out for the league lead in attendance. The young Bulls were accustomed to large crowds, of course, but here they would not be among friends.

Wilmington turned out to be the most pleasant stop in the league once they got there. Visiting clubs stayed at the spacious downtown Holiday Inn, hard by a pedestrian mall filled with a good selection of franchise restaurants that stayed open late at night, and the Blue Rocks played in the best park in the league: fifty-six-hundred-seat Frawley Stadium, off an exit ramp from I-95 near downtown, built in the winter of 1992. With such an edi-fice as a dowry, the city of Wilmington had easily enticed the Carolina League to move the weakest franchise in the league—the Tidewater club in tired old Newport News, Virginia, where crowds of two hundred had not been unusual—to their Delaware metropolis. The Blue Rocks, stocked with some of the most promising prospects in the Kansas City Royals' organization, were threatening to run away with the pennant and were averaging nearly five thousand fans a game even now, before school let out and decent baseball weather set in.

The Bulls won the opener there 6-3 thanks to three runs batted in from the carefree teenager Damon Hollins and a six-hitter in eight innings from Blase Sparma. They lost the next two, though, Wilmington scoring five runs in the eighth inning of one and then winning the other in a tenth inning remembered mostly for a drive that hit pitcher Ken Giard in the head and caromed into the outfield for a crucial double. Forty games had been played now, which left them with an even hundred to go, but it was still the same old story for the Bulls—careless pitching with the game on the line—and the scheduled fourth game of the series was canceled, mercifully, by a biting all-day rain. Marty's performance in the series was mixed: he still hadn't committed an error after seventeen games in the month of May, but he went only 3-for-12 at the plate, with three strikeouts and a couple of bases on balls.

Durham came within one out of sweeping the three-game weekend set that followed at Frederick, witnessed by crowds estimated at an average of 8,876 in a new ballpark with only fifty-five hundred seats. (Steve Barnes, the Bulls' radio announcer, was astounded by figures he deemed more than dubious: "There's a lot of hedging on attendance in the minors, but this is ridiculous. They can fill that park without cheating.") In the first two games, won 7-3 and 6-4 by the Bulls, Marty was 3-for-9 with a two-run double. But he would most remember the Sunday afternoon game that ended the set. The Bulls lost that one when Jeff Bock gave up a single with two out and the bases loaded in the bottom of the ninth. Marty's angst was compounded when he struck out three times, the first time in his life he had done that in one game, and he dreaded the next phone call home. The game was televised by Home Team Sports, easily picked up by the dish in Tommy Malloy's backyard; sure enough, "half of Trenton" had been invited to watch the game in the Malloys' den, the first glimpse any of them had gotten of Marty in a Bulls uniform. Good friends and kind neighbors, they watched the game in respectful silence.

Now, with summer approaching, the inevitable movement of players up and down every minor-league system was under way in earnest. Managers were on the phone, pleading their case for one more starter or a left-handed stopper or "somebody who can catch the ball" at shortstop. Personnel directors were leaving their air-conditioned offices and hitting the road, to sit in the stands of their minor-league affiliates from triple-A to low-A, clicking their stopwatches and aiming their radar guns and making notations in their black books, reassessing the talent. The stocky power hitter Micah Franklin of Winston-Salem had been promoted to double-A Chattanooga after delivering twenty-one wind-assisted home runs and forty-four RBIs in only forty-two games in the Carolina League; many of the pitchers who had been overpowering in the first month and a half of the Carolina League season, like Prince William's lefty Mike Bertotti, were being measured for double-A. A lot can happen in forty games—a pitcher who didn't prepare himself in spring training shows signs of fatigue; an infielder is maimed on a double play; a player turns out to be either overmatched or playing better than the organization had predicted—and so the wires were humming in minor-league headquarters from Seattle to Miami.

There had been minimal movement on the Durham roster to date, mainly the promotions of Kevin Grijak, Darrell May, and Jason Keeline to Greenville and the addition of Wonderful Monds from Macon, and although Matt West's roster would undergo less tinkering than most of those in the league, some fine-tuning was necessary. It began when the Bulls were joined in Frederick, on that weekend of the Home Team Sports telecast, by center fielder Miguel Correa; he had been in over his head in the Southern League, it appeared, hitting only .202 in 124 at bats with Greenville, and the Braves didn't want to see his confidence jangled. Any addition meant a subtraction, one move begetting another, and at times West felt like a traffic cop. Over the next ten days, there would be this: Trapaga would go on the DL, forcing the Braves to reassign Keeline from Greenville back to Durham; Monds, batting .200 in spite of some promising moments, was sent back to Macon for more seasoning; Darrell May would come back from Greenville to help out the Bulls' pitching rotation; and West, for the first time as a manager, would have to go through the ugly business of releasing a player—lefty Jason Butler, whose forty-six base runners in twenty-seven innings had led to an ERA of 5.93. "The only way to look at it is, I did him a favor so he could get on with his life," said West, who then talked the big club into sending him a replacement, left-hander Aaron Turnier, whose ERA at Macon was 2.84.

The addition of the fleet-footed Correa, a willowy Puerto Rican who had shown speed and power at Macon in '93, gave West two natural leadoff men. Mike Warner could bat second, as the DH, until his throwing arm came around, but that still didn't assuage his feeling that he was an orphan. He was the only .300 hitter on the club and was the leader in on-base percentage, but he had played in only twenty-nine of the Bulls' first forty-three games, all as a DH. He wasn't even taking pregame fielding practice, so weak was his arm, in a season that should have found him leading off and playing center field at Greenville in only his third year of pro ball. His sense of disassociation even extended off the field: tired of sleeping on the sofa at Marty's apartment, he had moved in with Julio Trapaga; but he was driven to further distraction when he found that Trapaga, the homesick teenaged

Mexican, stumbled out of bed at daybreak to watch Spanish-language television until it was time to leave for the ballpark at midafternoon.

And then, as a result of events he felt were beyond his control, Jason Keeline went AWOL. It all began on the opening night of a three-game set at the DAP against Kinston, following the trip to Wilmington and Frederick, when Trapaga went back on the DL after pulling a groin muscle while turning a double play. This coincided with the demotion of the floundering former second baseman of the future in the Braves' organization, Ramon Caraballo, from Richmond to Greenville, where it was deemed he would play shortstop as a last hope of redeeming his career. Keeline was being boxed out, told to report to Durham, and he was furious. "As long as I'm wearing the shirt, I've got a chance," he had said one day late in the '93 season at Macon, when his batting average was hovering at .215. Now he had hit .290 in a week at Greenville, more than anyone could have hoped for, and if this demotion was his reward, then he was taking off the shirt himself. Randy Ingle and Bobby Dews tried to talk him out of it—there would be a dearth of defensive shortstops in the organization while the Braves waited for a sixteen-year-old million-dollar Australian, Glenn Williams, to develop—but Keeline wasn't satisfied. He couldn't see going back to A ball at age twenty-five, not when he felt he could play double-A or even triple-A shortstop, so he refused to report to Durham and was put on the suspended list.

Keeline's defection and Jason Butler's release rattled Marty. "I wish Keeline would change his mind, because he's the best shortstop I ever played with," he said, puzzled that anyone would voluntarily give up baseball. Even during the summer before, at Macon, he said, Keeline had shown some interest in a job offer from a restaurant chain out of Atlanta; the word now was that he had fled to Macon, where he had a girlfriend, and Marty guessed that he was pursuing the restaurant job. The release of Jason Butler, who had lived right across the landing from him at the Willowdale Apartments and become one of his best friends, completely floored him: "Jason and I had been to see a movie together, and when I got to the park that afternoon I saw him swinging a bat and wandering down toward the bull pen like he was lost or something. That was the first I knew about it." It never got easy for anyone, seeing the dream die.

There is a camaraderie among professional baseball players that can be likened to the fellowship of men who have seen war. "You've been in battle together, for better or for worse, so there's the bond," said Bobby Dews, looking back at his decade as a player in the minors. "But, just like in war, when a friend gets released he might as well be dead, so pretty soon you're careful about who you make friends with." Marty's first lesson on this had come when his and Tom Waldrop's roommate from the year at Macon, Jay Noel, was quietly released during the off-season after a decent year, and he never did call to commiserate ("What could I say?"). Now there was Butler, followed by Keeline, and one wondered what would happen to his morale if the cleaver were to fall on his very best friend, Tom Waldrop, whose wretched season to date bade ill for his future. "You go through a lot of stuff together," Marty said. "You sit around late at night, talking about your dreams and your fears, making the big leagues, *not* making the big leagues, and you really get to know what makes each other tick. Tom and I will always be good buddies, no matter what happens, but I don't want to think about him not making it. In the end, I guess it's every man for himself."

· · ·

With Paulino filling in at shortstop until Trapaga came off the DL, the Bulls won only two of their final eight games in the month of May and landed with a thud in the Southern Division cellar. Marty was dropped to fifth and sixth in the batting order while West tried to work both Correa and Warner into the lineup, and in those eight games he hit above .300, got his third home run and his fifth bunt base hit, and fielded superbly in spite of the shaky situation at shortstop. There was a note taped to his cubicle in the clubhouse, left by Jay Ward after his last visit—"Gator: Don't forget what we worked on"—and he was trying, always trying. He had batted .289 for the month, with the three homers and not a single error, and he had reason to feel good even if playing on a last-place ball club was something he would never get used to. The first half of the split season would end in three weeks, at which time everybody would restart with a clean slate, so there was that to look forward to: a time for renewal.

CHAPTER 10

The Bulls had plenty on their minds already, what with the afternoon workouts and the games nearly every night, and they tried not to concern themselves with how their peers elsewhere in the organization were faring as the season moved along. Still, they couldn't help themselves. Information flowed up and down the baseball grapevine as freely as gossip over a backyard fence. They read the same publications available to the fans, from the daily newspapers to the tabloids like *Baseball America*, but they had additional access to what was going on in the game: from comments dropped by the roving instructors and scouts as they passed through Durham, from late-night phone conversations with former teammates like Kevin Grijak at Greenville or John Knott at Macon, from players who had just joined the club and had the very latest skinny from the various outposts. (They had heard the story from Knott, for instance, about how the young Macon Braves had been treated to a trip to Atlanta–Fulton County Stadium on an off-day and how the Braves' Terry Pendleton, mindful that a $30 pair of batting gloves is hard to come by on Class A pay, pointed toward a crate of them in the Braves' spacious clubhouse and said, "Help yourselves, boys.") Bud Waldrop, Tom's father up in Illinois, was paying $90 for a season's subscription to the Howe News Bureau's weekly statistics covering every club in the Braves' organization, and much of the time he spent on calls to his son dealt with how Tom's competition was doing up and down the line.

No matter how hard Marty continued to insist that he couldn't be concerned with how the other infielders in the organization were doing, he wasn't very convincing. *Of course* he knew that Tony Graffanino, one step ahead of him in the parent Braves' scheme, was having a solid season at Greenville, batting .300 and having made only three errors after forty games. *Of course* he knew that the second baseman looking over his shoulder, Mike Eaglin at Macon, had played poorly and gone down for the season with a separated shoulder after less than a month in the Sally League. *Of course* he knew that the bevy of older middle infielders ahead of him at Greenville and Richmond, most pointedly Ramon Caraballo, seemed to be faltering in what might turn out to be their last season with the Braves' organization. Mark Lemke was having the best year of his career with the big club in Atlanta as the Braves and the Montreal Expos began battling neck and neck in the National League East, but it was becoming clearer now that Tony Graffanino and then Marty Malloy, in that order, had become the best bets to challenge him for his job in the next two or three years.

So Marty was in good spirits when his parents finally found the time to get away from Trenton and make the nine-hour drive to Durham to see their son in person, for the first time, in the uniform of the famous Durham Bulls. Tommy's Trenton High baseball team had wound up in the state play-offs, his young gaggle of freshmen and sophomores ultimately losing in the finals to a private academy made up mostly of seniors, and now, no longer coaching football, he was free for the summer except for having to oversee the American Legion baseball program in Gilchrist County. He and Beverly drove straight through, took a cheap motel a couple of miles from the Willowdale Apartments, and went directly to the DAP for the opener of a series against Prince William on the first weekend in June. Corbyn would turn one year old that Friday, but they felt he was too young for such a trip. It was "about to break Beverly's heart," Tommy said, that Nikki wasn't bringing the boy around more often than once or twice a week, and he was thinking about going to court over grandparental rights. As for Beverly, she was trying not to bother Marty with details of the situation: "He needs to concentrate on baseball. I'm older, and I can take it."

A three-run homer by Tom Waldrop in the seventh and a clutch 5-4-3 double play in the bottom of the ninth, with Marty scintillating in the pivot, had iced a 5-3 Durham win at Lynchburg the night before the Malloys' arrival. Tommy and Beverly rushed to the ballpark after their long drive up from Trenton, barely having time to hug Marty, and settled into their box seats behind the plate for what would turn out to be a vexing weekend. Trapaga was serving out his two-day suspension for his part in the brawl, so Marty was being thrown in at shortstop, where he hadn't found it necessary to take any ground balls all season. That, plus the fact that he would be facing Prince William's troublesome corps of left-handers, made for a long night. Marty went hitless in four trips to the plate and made an error at short in a game that Durham seemed to have under control—Sparma had a two-hit shutout after eight innings—until Carl Schutz and Matt Byrd came out of the bull pen and threw it away. Prince

William won it 3-1, scoring their runs on two walks, a wild pitch, a hit batsman, an outfield error, and a single.

There was time for Marty and his parents to do some catching up that night—they all went out to eat at a barbecue place Marty had discovered, and Beverly gathered his shirts so she could press them in the motel room with the iron she always hauled around—but on the next two nights Marty and the Bulls fell apart. Marty struck out twice and made two more errors in a 9-7 loss on Friday night, and he struck out twice again Saturday, when the Cannons scored twelve runs in the last three innings to win 14-5 for their ninth straight victory. Prince William had turned out to be Durham's worst nemesis, winning ten of the two clubs' thirteen games against each other, and to Tommy Malloy they looked like the beloved New York Yankees of his youth in the fifties. He and Beverly had to get back home to their jobs, so on Sunday, as they drove back to Trenton, they missed seeing Durham finally win one (Marty went hitless, again, in a 4-1 win remembered for Darrell May's twelve strikeouts against one walk in seven innings). It had been comforting to see his parents after nearly two months, but Marty felt a foreboding. Over the first five games of June he was 2-for-21, with four strikeouts and the three errors, and his time to sit out his two-day suspension came not a moment too soon.

Like most minor-league clubs, the Bulls were always pulling off some sort of public relations gimmickry in order to "bond with the community." This was the bailiwick of Leisha Cowart, the energetic young woman who handled media and community relations for the club. Barely older than the players themselves, she was kept busy arranging for them to participate in various public relations functions around the Triangle—benefit golf tournaments, baseball clinics, autographings at malls—even rousting the Latin players out of bed so kids at a public school in Durham could hear real Spanish being spoken. ("But I no spik Spanish," cracked Raymond Nunez when she was briefing him and the others.) Later in the summer, in a scheme that always netted more than $1,000 for a local charity, there would be the popular Bid on a Bull date auction, wherein the modern version of baseball groupies paid for a night on the town with a player. And for every home game, of course, it was Leisha who rounded up the Little Leaguers—the Field of Dreams Team—who would trot onto the field with the Bulls prior to the singing of the National Anthem.

Marty was a trouper. He had dusted off his golf clubs to play in a pro-am with a bunch of doctors and media types, had volunteered his body for the date auction, and was more than happy to help out with one of Matt West's clinics at the DAP for kids when he learned that West would pay him a welcome $50. "No harm done," he said. "You can meet people and maybe have a little fun." (Once, in fact, when he got hurt during a game and had to be rushed off for X rays, the attending physician was the one he had been paired with in a charity golf tournament.) He didn't have to think twice, then, when Leisha called the apartment on the first Monday in June, a rare off-day for the club, frantically asking if he and Tom Waldrop would pose for a poster to be given away a couple of weeks hence. They were sprawled in front of the television set, drinking beer and talking baseball, and they agreed. An hour later they and Wool E. Bull were all in uniform, posing with pitchforks and leaning against a split-rail fence on the grounds of a preserved Civil War homestead, for a poster: THE DURHAM BULLS, AMERICA'S FAVORITE FARM TEAM! The first one thousand fans through the gates on a night later in the month would receive free posters, but nobody wanted to get her hands on one more than Beverly Malloy, the keeper of the flame, who was already checking prices at a frame shop in Chiefland so she could have it laminated onto a plaque to be hung over the fireplace between the studio portraits of Marty and Amie.

Win or lose, public relations or not, it didn't seem to matter to Bulls fans. Durham was third in the league in attendance, even with the club in last place, and the DAP was filled over its five-thousand-seat capacity more often than not. (Leading the Carolina League in attendance for the second straight year were Wilmington and Frederick, but they were helped immensely by their proximity to major cities.) There was no way the Bulls would break the all-time Durham attendance record set the year before—305,692 in sixty-nine home dates, an average of 4,430— because the '93 season had been heavily promoted as the final season at the DAP and management knew better than to try that two years in a row. Besides, said Peter Anlyan, the Bulls' general manager, they were more concerned with holding their place as "the Triangle's team" over the Carolina Mudcats of the AA Southern League, forty miles away in Zebulon, who were claiming an average attendance of some five hundred per game more than the Bulls. (Most minor-league clubs, the Bulls included, arrived at their official-paid-attendance figures by looking in the stands and making an educated guess.) "We're competing with them [Carolina] for the same advertising dollars," said Anlyan, an intense man in his forties, whose background was in broadcasting rather than baseball, and he was steaming over what he perceived as cheating on the part of the Mudcats: "I hesitate to say this publicly, because then people will say, 'Well, they all cheat on their attendance figures in the minors,' but one night I sent somebody over to personally do a head count, and they were cheating big-time. They had about half the people in the stands that they claimed they did."

Minor-league baseball, once a foolish roll of the dice by civic patriots or millionaires who had the money to lose, had become big business in the nineties. Peter Anlyan's ultimate boss was

Capitol Broadcasting of Raleigh, which had just plunked down more than $3 million for rights to broadcast games of the National Football League's Charlotte-based Carolina Panthers, and they had known what they were doing when they paid Miles Wolff $4 million for the Bulls franchise in '90. The movie *Bull Durham* had given the Bulls a national following—their logo on caps and other souvenirs was the third most popular in the minors, behind the Hickory Crawdads' and the Carolina Mudcats'—but what made the investment worthwhile was the core of die-hard baseball fans in the Triangle. Management had the usual arrangement with the parent major-league organization, wherein the Braves paid all team costs (salaries, equipment, travel) and Durham Bulls Baseball Club Inc. took care of local costs, ranging from office salaries to upkeep of the DAP. What the Braves got out of it was a suitable environment to continue the development of their young players. What the Durham Bulls got out of it was every single dollar generated by staging seventy home games, from gate receipts to billboard and radio advertising to the sale of hot dogs and T-shirts. Was it making money? Basic arithmetic would show that gate receipts alone in '93 came to $1.5 million; twice that amount would be generated if each of those 305,000 fans dropped $10 for eats, a scorecard, and a souvenir of some sort. It was not only profitable in Durham, one of the hottest Class A tickets in the country, but even down the road at Kinston, one of the weaker draws in the Carolina League, with an average attendance of around fifteen hundred. "Oh, that's more than the break-even attendance we need here," said North Johnson, the young general manager who helped a local consortium buy the franchise from a group of baseball-loving lawyers from downtown Atlanta so the Kinston club could be more efficiently home owned and home operated.

One could couple those numbers with the growing possibility of a strike or lockout at the major-league level and see why minor-league baseball was enjoying unprecedented popularity in America. Several pages in every issue of *Baseball America* were devoted to advertisements for souvenirs of minor-league clubs with titillating names (Bulls, Mudcats, Greenjackets, Crawdads, Sea Dogs, Killer Bees), minor-league card sets, weekly league statistical services, advice on buying and operating a franchise. When major-league baseball saw that the minors were healthy and self-sustaining, it pressured its minor-league counterpart, the National Association of Professional Baseball Leagues, to upgrade its ballparks. If the major-league organizations were going to continue laying out millions of dollars every season to subsidize the product on the field, they had every right to insist on better playing conditions for their chattels. Thus, in the early nineties a whole new generation of ballparks like the one now sprouting in Durham was beginning to replace crumbling "quaint" venues all over the country. Now everybody was happy—the parent clubs, local investors, players, fans—and in 1993, for the ninth consecutive year, minor-league attendance grew. The all-time record for minor-league attendance had been set in 1949, when fifty-nine leagues drew nearly 40 million fans, but in '93 only nineteen leagues drew better than 30 million. Rarely, now, did one see the minor leagues referred to as "the bushes."

Following that off-day when Marty and Tom posed for the farm team poster, the Bulls began to improve ever so slowly. There was no dramatic turnaround, no sudden blossoming, and Matt West was having a hell of a time fielding the same lineup two games in a row because of niggling injuries and his having to dole out the two-game suspensions resulting from the brawl of mid-May. But the club was shedding its Jekyll-and-Hyde personality now, showing signs of jelling, becoming more consistent, avoiding the losing streaks that had numbed them in the early going. The major reason for it was the maturing of the starting pitchers—Matt Murray and Jamie Arnold had begun to avoid the home run ball now—and it seemed to put a spark in the others when the irrepressible Mike Warner, his arm pronounced fit, began playing left field for the first time in the season and took off on a hitting streak from the leadoff spot in the batting order. If not for trouble in the bull pen, where five of the relievers had earned-run averages above 5.00, they might have dug themselves out of last place in the Southern Division before the end of the first half.

They came home on the middle weekend of June, after sweeping three at Salem but then dropping two at Winston-Salem, for a set against Wilmington that would end the first half. Marty was in a genuine slump now, the only one he had ever experienced, having gone 8-for-42 in the first eleven games of June (a .190 batting average), and more often than not he was penciled in toward the end of the batting order as punishment while he worked it out. Maybe it was a sign that he was maturing as a pro when he shrugged and said, "These things happen," even though he had lost twenty points off his average in a blink. Jay Ward was coming back to town, he said, and "maybe we can work on some things while he's here."

A doubleheader was scheduled for that Friday night, the result of a rainout earlier in the season, and when the first game between the Bulls and the Blue Rocks got under way at six o'-clock, Ward was found sitting in the top row of seats beneath the grandstand roof behind home plate. He had driven nonstop from his home in St. Petersburg and now was wolfing down a couple of hot dogs and a Coke and calling it dinner. He would check on the Durham hitters from there, unannounced, on the first day of his visit—"Sometimes it inhibits them to know I'm watching"—before checking in with West and Rick Albert, and then going one-on-one in the batting cage for the next few days. His was a job without end, requiring him to put on about thirty thousand miles by car each season, and it had been compounded by business at home; no sooner had his parents retired to Tampa than his mother died, and then his father learned that he had cancer. Clearly, with that on his mind, Ward was glad to be here sitting in the stands, watching young men live and learn, talking about the science of hitting.

"I can't think of anything in sports that's harder to do than hit a baseball," he said after watching Bobby Smith hit a grounder to deep short that scored Mike Warner for a Bulls run in the bottom of the first inning. "They call baseball a game of inches, but it's more like microinches. Think about it. You've got a round ball, a round bat, and the pitch is coming at you, maybe ninety miles an hour. Could be a fastball, could be a curve or change, could be up or down, inside or outside, and you've got a split second to figure it out. *He* knows what's coming, but you don't. And look at all of the moving parts involved: feet, hips, hands, elbows, shoulders, head, eyes. If there's a breakdown anywhere along the line, with the feet or the hands or whatever, then the whole machine falls apart. There's nothing as complicated as that in any sport."

For no discernible reason, except perhaps that Wilmington's starter was a right-hander, Marty was batting leadoff that night. He went down swinging in the first inning and bounced to short in the third, then reached base in the sixth when the Blue Rocks' first baseman kicked his ground ball. But when he ran to second on Smith's long fly to center and had to quickly reverse his field when it was caught, he fell to the ground with a twisted ankle and was doubled off. He was helped off the field by Tom Waldrop and Jay Williams, and the doctor who was summoned to the clubhouse pronounced a severe sprain that would keep him out for a couple of days. Darrell May was on the mound, pitching as cleverly as any Durham pitcher had all season long, and the game was tied at 2-all going into the last inning. In the top half, with Wilmington's leadoff man on second and no outs, Ward shook his head when the Blue Rocks' leading RBI man came to the plate and fouled off a bunt attempt. "Now he's got one pitch to do it," Ward said. "The third strike is the pitcher's, not his." The batter, a free-swinging left-hander named Larry Sutton, tried to pull an outside fastball from May but, sure enough, got it with the end of the bat and grounded meekly to short.

As the Bulls came to bat in the bottom of the seventh and final inning (doubleheaders in the minors consist of two seven-inning games), Ward became the first instructor to say flat out, publicly, that Marty "is going to play in the big leagues." Not even Bobby Dews had gone that far. "It might not be with the Braves, given the situation with Graffanino ahead of him, but he doesn't have any control over that. He's in a little bit of a slump right now, I see, but his numbers are very good, given what's he's had to do this year. His fielding is fine and he's working on his things with the bat." Not so, he said, with Raymond Nunez, who now had six home runs and twenty-five RBIs with a .281 batting average. "With that fence out there in this park, Raymond should be fifteen [homers] and fifty [RBIs] by now. His power is to right, to the porch, but he keeps swinging at bad pitches and taking the good ones. He and I work on it all the time, but sometimes they just have to figure it out for themselves in games." Ward was the first on his feet when Nunez came to the plate, with Bobby Smith on second with a double, and ripped a single past the shortstop to win the game for Durham.

The Bulls lost the second game of the doubleheader 3-1 on a two-run DAP Special off Carl Schutz with two outs in the top of the seventh, and Marty went home to ice his ankle. He drove to the park early Saturday afternoon, suiting up and testing the ankle by running in the outfield, but Matt West and Jay Williams overruled his contention that it was okay, forcing him to sit through a sloppy slugfest ultimately won by Wilmington 9-5 before an overflow crowd of 5,429. Waiting for him outside the clubhouse door after the game were a couple of pals who had driven up from Trenton, one of them Scott Guthrie, who had been something of a three-sport star at Trenton High and just might become his brother-in-law. The boys went out to howl that night in what was, to them, the big city, and on Sunday morning Marty showed them the basketball palaces at Duke, North Carolina, and North Carolina State. When he reached the ballpark that afternoon—from now on, with the coming of hot weather, Sunday games would be played at night—he found that he was back in the lineup for the last game of the first half.

It was Father's Day, so hot and muggy even in the late afternoon that the half dozen scouts who had shown up behind home plate with their radar guns and notebooks were playing one-upmanship: "Christ, I remember one day at Golden Park in Columbus, back in the seventies; it was so hot the flags were sweating . . ." The Bulls got behind early when Blase Sparma, quickly pitching himself out of the rotation and into the bull pen, gave up three homers in the first two innings. But they kept chipping away and finally won it with three runs in the bottom of the ninth, the winning run coming when Damon Hollins, who had hit two homers the night before, rattled a double off the billboard in center field, one that advertised DAMON'S CLUBHOUSE, THE PLACE FOR RIBS. Marty, back to seventh in the order, went oh-for-two officially but walked and scored a run and drove in another with a sacrifice fly deep to left center with the bases loaded; he also turned a sensational pivot on a crucial double play late in the game.

So, the Bulls finished the first half mired in last place with a record of 28-40, seven games behind Winston-Salem in the

Southern Division and a whopping twenty games off the pace of the runaway Wilmington club (48-20) in the North. It was the first Durham club to fail to win at least thirty games in the first half since 1960, and West blamed it on inexperience. Because the parent Braves were concentrating these days on signing high school graduates rather than college players, he said, ten of the twenty-five Bulls had yet to celebrate a twenty-second birthday. Some had reached the Carolina League ahead of their time, he pointed out, which made the first half of the season a shakedown period for them. "I don't think there's a better combination up the middle than Hollins in center and Trapaga at short and Malloy at second," he told the *Herald-Sun*, then addressing the club's real problem: the pitching. The Bulls had given up an astonishing one hundred home runs in those sixty-eight games, and it could only get better.

Most of the young pitchers on his Durham staff had been high draft choices right out of high school, and there was never any doubt that they could *throw*. They were big and strong and had gotten substantial bonuses to sign because they could bring it at ninety miles an hour. But now they were learning the hard way that what had worked for them in rookie ball and at low-A Macon wouldn't necessarily cut it in the Carolina League. "There's a big difference between throwing and *pitching*," said Slack, and that is what had him out at the DAP every afternoon, down in the right-field bull pen, quietly counseling (and consoling) the twelve pitchers placed in his care. Slack had been a marginal pitcher himself through eleven years in the minors, a little guy (five nine) without blazing speed, one who relied on a curveball and control and smarts, and it was those qualities that informed him as a coach. "Not much teaching went on in the minors in my day," he said. "A lot of the veterans in the fifties wouldn't help rookies unless they were asked, so you learned by the seat of your pants." As expected, Slack would counter Jay

Ward's contention that nothing is harder than hitting a baseball by saying that nothing is harder than pitching one, that there are just as many moving parts involved in a pitcher's delivery as in a hitter's swing. "Almost all pitching is situational, too, just like hitting. While Rick [Albert] has his hitters up in the cage, trying to teach 'em how to adjust to the pitch count and the situation in the game, I'm down here in the pen doing the same thing with my pitchers. First you've got to get the mechanics right, and then you've got the old guessing game between the pitcher and the batter."

There is an obscure poem about all of that, "Pitcher," by Robert Francis—"He throws to be a moment misunderstood . . . making the batter understand too late"—and Slack's daily lectures dealt with the mental part of pitching as much as with the mechanical. Matt West had also been a pitcher, of course, and the propensity of the Bulls' pitchers to carelessly offer up a fat pitch just when they had the hitter on the ropes was driving him and Slack to distraction. At the halfway point in the season, the Bulls as a team were batting .241, but their pitchers were being hammered at a .260 clip. Durham pitching was last in the league in earned-run average, complete games, and shutouts (only one of each) and led the league by a mile in homers allowed. They had certainly seen adversity, and Slack kept telling them that there was something to be learned from it. "I was managing at Winston-Salem in the sixties," he said, "and one of my guys finished with twenty wins and two losses. The [parent] Red Sox had a place on their evaluation form that asked how a player handles himself in adversity. What could I say? A guy that goes twenty-and-two doesn't *know* adversity."

Because of their high draft status (and thus the Braves' investment in them), Murray and Arnold were being monitored more closely than any of the other Bulls starters, and scouts from Atlanta and other organizations seemed to show up at the DAP in greater numbers whenever those two were scheduled to pitch. The scouts sat together in the box seats directly behind the plate, a convivial group, raising their radar guns in unison to record the velocity of each pitch and then writing the number down in their notebooks, seemingly more interested in *how* a pitch was thrown than what became of it. At the midpoint in the season, their numbers were lacking—Murray was 5-7 with a 4.08 ERA, Arnold 5-4 and 4.52—but that wasn't what the scouts were looking for. There was such a thing, to them, as a good wild pitch: Did the fastball hum and slam against the backstop when it sailed over the catcher's head? Did the curveball snap wickedly and leave a rooster tail when it broke into the dirt? The wild pitches may have been maddening to the manager, Matt West, but they could be music to the ears of men who still chose raw power over clever pitching at this point in a pitcher's career. There were those in the game who sneered and called it "the cult of the radar gun," wherein a smart pitcher like the reliever Matt Byrd (the league was batting only .162 against his softer offerings) was overlooked in favor of the hard throwers with busy fastballs, but it was a sad truth that Byrd and Darrell May (whose 3.86 ERA led the club) had to live with every day. The scouts looked at the flamethrowing Murray out on the mound, a six-six, 235-pound hunk, and salivated even when they saw him serve up a 420-foot home run ball on an 0-2 count that lost the game for the Bulls.

Likewise, the scouts were looking at the Bulls' position players from a standpoint not so much of whether they were helping Durham win but of how they were projecting as future major-leaguers. Mike Warner, happily, was scoring high on both counts since recovering strength in his throwing arm and returning to the outfield. More and more, the little guy with the lopsided country grin was looking like a possible leadoff man for the big club: leading the club in average (.300), walks, stolen bases, triples, slugging percentage, and on-base percentage after a twenty-seven-game stretch in which he hit .330 and scored twenty-six runs. Damon Hollins, who had turned twenty in June, was leading the Bulls in doubles, homers, and RBIs, and turning out to be a scintillating center fielder whose raw speed overcame his inexperience. And soft-spoken Bobby Smith, the "man among boys," although leading the club only in errors, was showing glimmers of being the Braves' third baseman of the future: solid numbers in every hitting category across the board, getting his glove on balls that most Carolina League third basemen waved at, in the lineup every night, still learning the game. Those three, plus Marty and Raymond Nunez, were driving the club offensively. The three catchers were batting an aggregate .200, the shortstops Trapaga and Paulino .180. Of the other outfielders, Miguel Correa still hadn't gotten comfortable after the demotion from Greenville, playing part-time and batting just .233; Juan Williams had hit some moon shots between strikeouts but was at .237; and with Tom Waldrop it was feast or famine: seven homers, four of them grand slams, gave him thirty RBIs on thirty hits, but he was striking out once every 3.3 at bats and batting just .210.

The boys at 707 Willowdale were sleeping later these days. They were tired, waiting for a second wind, and all three of them were mired in the worst slumps of their careers. Marty had gone 8-for-47 in the eleven games he had played during June, to lose twenty-one points on his season's average, now down to .260, and there were signs that he was beginning to press. But his problems were slight compared to those of his roommates. Waldrop had only eight hits in his last seventy-one at bats, an average of .113, and he was spending more time than any of the Bulls petitioning Matt West about playing time: "I hit three-run homers on back-to-back nights back in April, then I sat for four games. That's the way Matt's been using me." John Simmons, much more placid and stoical than Marty and Tom, had pitched the second-fewest innings of anyone on the staff, and his line was not a pretty sight: fifty-two base runners allowed in thirty-three innings, an opponents' batting average of .281, five homers allowed, ERA of 5.67. When he wasn't reading business manuals and giving more thought to his father's dream of their going in together on a scheme to sell gourmet foods by mail (the sort of business one sees advertised in the back of *The New Yorker*), he was out for a silent morning jog on the apartment grounds. Often they were bypassing breakfast now, driving over to the Golden Corral to load up on the buffet special and talk about anything but baseball, biding their time until they were due to check in at the DAP for another day of what was becoming more and more like work.

CHAPTER 11

The practice of breaking a season into halves, almost as old as the game itself, was a device of owners to rescue clubs that had gotten off to poor starts and, as a result, lost favor with their fans. Wilmington in the Northern Division and Winston-Salem in the Southern had won the first-half championships and would qualify for best-of-three play-offs against the second-half winners at the end of the regular season, and then the two survivors would play a best-of-five series to determine the league's overall champions. The off-day separating the end of the first half and the beginning of the second represented a wiping of the slate, then, a fresh start for everybody, and in the minor leagues it was meaningful. The "break," as it was called, was the time when the parent organizations sometimes made roster adjustments on a wholesale scale—listening to their managers' cries for help, reassessing talent, moving players up or down the system according to their first-half performances, fine-tuning rosters—and often it worked just as it was intended. The clubs that had been hot in the first half were stripped of their key players by promotion, while the stragglers were improved with promotions from below, which created instant parity. As a result, not many clubs in the minor leagues won both halves of the season.

Although there would be no wholesale personnel changes at the break this season in the Carolina League—two of the big ones had come earlier, when Winston-Salem lost Micah Franklin and Durham lost Kevin Grijak by way of promotion to AA—the emotional young players on some of the weaker clubs during the first half, especially the Bulls in the South and the Frederick Keys in the North, took to heart the idea of getting a fresh start. Two weeks into the second half, Frederick (32-35 and sixteen games behind Wilmington in the first half) was 8-3, the only club in the Northern Division over .500, and the Bulls were 9-3. In the case of the Bulls, as Matt West had projected at the break, it was a matter of his young players' jelling after a shakedown period that had gone on quite long enough.

The Bulls came roaring out for the second half, sweeping three from Winston-Salem at the DAP and then splitting four at Kinston. It didn't seem to dampen their spirits when Matt Murray was called up to Greenville in the midst of all that—he had finally put it together, eschewing the home run ball, beginning to overpower hitters with his fastball, losing only one of his last five starts as a Bull—because Darrell May and Mike D'Andrea were nearly untouchable and nobody could get Mike Warner out with any consistency. This was an entirely different ball club from the one Durham fans had seen earlier, one with consistent starting pitching, explosive power, and a bull pen that meant business. During that stretch there was one embarrassing moment, a 12-2 drubbing of Sparma at Kinston, but the rest was dotted with heroics: a string of sixteen scoreless innings by D'Andrea; a fifteen-inning stretch over two games by May, during which he struck out nineteen and walked only two, giving up just three runs on six hits; a night when Correa had a homer, a triple, and two doubles and scored three runs and drove in three others; even an electrifying steal of home by Hector Roa, a veteran shortstop who had been brought down from Greenville when Trapaga again went on the DL with a pulled groin. The new Bulls of the second half could do little wrong.

That didn't apply to Marty. While the club was winning fifteen of its twenty-seven games in June, he was sinking deeper into a slump the likes of which he had never experienced. He had been batting .286 overall on the last day of May, a month that had seen him doing all of the right things—bunting, taking left-handers to the opposite field, working for a base on balls, moving the runners along—but on the last day of June he was down to .248. In the twenty-two games he played in June, he had batted .169. The key number to be found on his line for the month was his nineteen strikeouts in seventy-eight at bats, a ratio of one strikeout every 4.1 appearances, compared with one every 6.1 prior to June. Overnight, it seemed, he had abandonded everything he had worked so hard to learn, returning to his old habits, answering the primordial call to rear back and take his hacks, becoming easy pickings for pitchers who could sense a wounded animal when they saw one. A pattern of pitching to him had developed, all of it based on the perception that he was panicking and losing his patience: smoke a quick strike past him, follow with the curve or change away for strike two, and finish him off with a tantalizing fastball up but out of the zone. "He's an aggressive hitter," said Rick Albert, "and when one like that starts going bad the pitchers take advantage of it. You've got three chances [strikes]. Only one of 'em is going to be your pitch. The higher you go [in classification], the less often you'll get that pitch. It's his aggression that's causing the strikeouts."

Bobby Dews, the coordinator of field instruction, had been forced to watch most of Marty's season from afar. He had caught the Bulls in person for two games in late April at Winston-Salem and had been at the DAP that first weekend of June when Marty went 1-for-13 and made three errors at shortstop with his parents looking on. Other business had kept him away for too long—spending ten days helping assemble the rookie club at Idaho Falls, joining the young Macon Braves at home and on the road during their early-season travails, then rushing home to Albany when massive floods inundated southwest Georgia—but he had kept up over the Braves' electronic bulletin board and on phone conversations with Matt West and he didn't like what he heard. "He was a tough little out earlier, but now I don't know," Dews said by phone from Albany, where he was helping out with flood relief operations. "Part of it's that ballpark [the DAP]. I hate these little parks for young players. They look at that short porch and all of a sudden they think they're home run hitters. What's he got, forty-two strikeouts already? Marty shouldn't have forty strikeouts in a whole *season*, and it's barely halfway over. I'd hoped he would learn some things from Mike Warner about being patient, but that hasn't happened."

The kid himself was defensive. "Hell, I've hit a lot of balls on the nose that just got caught, that's all," he said. "I've been in the game long enough now not to panic. The home runs [four now] just happened, you know, when I got something in the wheelhouse." He had been maintaining his weight at 160, keeping up his strength with regular trips to the Spa, and continuing to take early BP in the cage with Albert, pointedly trying not to change his daily routine. There had been no panic in his voice when he called home during June, said Tommy Malloy, although Marty had expressed the idea that he "might be getting too much conflicting advice" from Ward, Albert, Dews, and even some team-mates. "I decided I was going to concentrate on my defense this year, anyway," Marty said on the eve of another visit from his parents. That part was working, because only the night before, in the last game of June, he had helped save a shutout for D'Andrea against Salem at the DAP with two brilliant plays—a shovel toss from his glove on a slow roller to get a batter at first, and a backhanded stop deep behind second base for a force play—and nobody doubted that he was the classiest second baseman in the league. Still, as further punishment from West, he was back to the bottom third of the batting order while he fought through the slump. "I still say I can hit three hundred in this league," he said, not altogether convincingly. "In the meantime, I've got my glove. And we're winning."

In spite of his protest to the contrary, one got the sense that Marty had been humbled by the Carolina League. Here was a kid who heretofore had been "undefeated," as Dews said of young prospects, had always been able to hitch up his pants and work his way out of trouble through sheer grit; and now, as West had predicted, that old work ethic wasn't enough. It was working against him, in fact, because the harder he pressed, the worse it got. This slump was likely to cost him a spot on the league's mid-season all-star team, which was being voted on even as he spoke, and it might have a more serious implication if he didn't pull out of it soon. There was the very real possibility now that the men at minor-league headquarters in Atlanta–Fulton County Stadium were looking ahead to the '95 season, measuring and juggling the talent, perhaps thinking that Marty ought to be returned to Durham for a second year, at least long enough for him to complete his remake at the plate. The heat was off him from below with Mike Eaglin out for the season, and maybe they would hold Marty back while that gaggle of middle infielders currently playing second fiddle to Tony Graffanino got their last chances at Greenville and Richmond. It all depended on whether he could turn it around in the second half of this season.

A batting slump is like an earthquake. It comes without warning, leaves its victims helpless and demoralized, departs when it is good and ready, and the only thing to do is hunker down and ride it out. Willie Stargell, with his looping home run swing full of moving parts, certainly went through slumps during his days with Pittsburgh, but even as a batting savant he was puzzled and defensive on the subject. "It's like catching a cold," he said. "It's in the air and anybody can get it. It just happens, and there's not much you can do about it. But look here, everybody has slumps. How about the accountant who has a bad day? His pencils keep breaking; he keeps using an eraser all day; but nobody's looking over *his* shoulder. That's a slump, isn't it? But then he goes out to the ballpark that night and sees a ballplayer who suddenly isn't hitting, and he's all over him. 'Come on, hit the ball. What the hell's wrong with this guy?' Too much is made out of it, if you ask me."

Even Stargell had no magical cure for a slump, except to say that it "depends on the individual, what's inside his shirt," a variation on his theme that the great hitter is the one "with a great set of nuts." Marty Malloy had determination above all else, but that wasn't enough to protect him. Like a golfer who suddenly can't drop a putt—the "yips," they call it—he was spooked and didn't know what had hit him. He began taking extra batting practice. He began asking for advice from others. He began going into Matt West's office to watch tapes made of him during BP, comparing May film with June film. He may have begun to think about it too much, to become overly conscious of every one of the moving parts involved in swinging a bat at a ball. It was like trying to swim in quicksand; the harder he tried, the deeper he sank.

"The drunks never had slumps because they never thought about hitting; they just did it," said Bobby Dews. "There's a story about how Paul Waner [the Pirate Hall of Famer] was hitting about three-seventy-five in May one year and somebody said, 'Hey, wait a minute, if he was sober, hell, he'd hit four hundred.' They offered him a big bonus if he'd quit drinking, and the minute he stopped he started hitting one-sixty." Dews, too, had been surprised when Marty went into a slump because "the bunters and contact hitters, guys like Luke Appling [the White Sox Hall of Fame shortstop], don't have 'em. What you need when you get into one is a base hit, any kind of base hit, and the bunter or the contact hitter is going to have a better chance to pick one up." Had Marty been pressing? "I was a fielder, not a hitter—I averaged two-seventy-three, lifetime—but when I got into a slump I'd start thinking, 'Let's see, now, if I go oh-for-fifty I'll still be hitting two-twenty-five, and that ain't so bad.' If you're going good, all you see out there is green pastures, but when you're slumping it looks like there's eighteen pairs of gloves and hands, bodies all over the place. You start showing up at three for BP, then two, and soon you're in the cage right after breakfast. You're tired, you're pressing, so it gets worse."

For Bob Montag, the Atlanta Crackers slugger of the fifties in what is now the Class AA Southern League, where Marty hoped to play the coming year, a slump is "fatigue, then it becomes mental. Early in fifty-four I was hitting four-something. Hell, I was worn out just from being on the bases all the time. Then we went on the road, to Chattanooga and Nashville. The first night I went oh-for-four on four line drives, and I got to thinking that if I'd been off the plate maybe just a few inches I'd have hit all four of 'em out. Now pitches that looked outside were called strikes on the black. I went oh-for-twenty-seven on that trip. I was tired from running, and my hands were dragging, and hitting's all in the hands. I needed a hit real bad, so I shortened up and moved up on the plate, and when I hit a bullet past the second baseman it was all over. That's the year I hit thirty-nine homers."

Looking from afar, where he now served as a coach with the Greenville Braves, Randy Ingle, perhaps Marty's greatest believer in the organization, was watching with great interest: "I knew when I had him at Macon that Marty would cope with whatever came up. He learns his lessons the first time and never forgets. This slump's probably going to be the best thing that happened to him. It's going to teach him a lot of things. One, it's impossible to get three hits in one at bat. Two, you play this game one day at a time, one at bat at a time, one *pitch* at a time. Three, he's a contact hitter, not a power guy, and if he's making contact he won't have any more slumps like this. That's going to be the most important thing he'll learn, I think. Who is Marty Malloy, as a hitter?"

On the first weekend of July, with the Bulls in the midst of an eight-game home stand against Salem and Frederick, Marty's parents, with his sister Amie in tow this time, made their second visit of the season. His twenty-second birthday was coming up, on Wednesday the sixth, when the club would be en route to Wilmington, and the Malloys came bearing gifts: a graphite rod and some fishing tackle so Marty could fish the nearby Noe River, some shirts, some cash; Beverly, of course, had her iron with her so she could press her son's shirts. Also converging on Durham were Tom Waldrop's parents and his girlfriend, who had driven the 850 miles straight through the night from Illinois. The Malloys and the Waldrops had become good friends in support of their sons and would sit together behind home plate for the weekend set.

They were not disappointed. Both Marty and Tom homered

in the Friday game, won by the Bulls 9-3, but the night would best be remembered for some hotdogging by Hector Roa, the newest Bull. Roa was a muscular little guy (five eleven, 170 pounds), a switch-hitting shortstop and second baseman from San Pedro de Macoris. He was twenty-five, in his fifth year of pro ball, another of those middle infielders living on the edge in the Braves' organization. He had experienced so-so years at Macon, Durham, and Greenville during the past three seasons, just good enough to earn advancement each year, and now he had come down from Greenville to fill in at shortstop until Julio Trapaga recovered from the latest of his injuries.

The trouble flared up in the seventh inning when Roa came up and drilled a cannon shot over the left-field wall. It appeared to be some icing on the cake, another run to fatten the Bulls' lead to 6-2, but Roa wasn't content with that. At the moment he connected, he flung his bat to the ground and stood in the batter's box to admire his handiwork, departing for his slow trot around the bases only when the ball had disappeared over the wall. The Buccaneers were not amused, least of all the Salem pitcher Chris Peters, a left-hander who had just joined the club from low-A Augusta. Roa had violated one of the cardinal rules—don't show up the opposition—and he was met at the dugout steps by the veteran Bulls catcher Brad Rippelmeyer, who reamed him out for the benefit of the infuriated Salem players. Somebody was going to pay for this, Rippelmeyer shouted at Roa, and the somebody, for whatever reason, turned out to be Marty. When he came up in the next inning he was promptly plunked by Peters, an event that Marty accepted stoically ("That's baseball"), and a moment later he trotted home when Tom Waldrop slammed a three-run homer to ice the game for the Bulls.

Marty had gone 2-for-3 in that game, with the homer, two runs scored, and a stolen base, but on Saturday night, with the Frederick Keys in town for a four-game set, he went hitless in three trips and kicked a double-play grounder for only his tenth error of the season. That error and two by Rippelmeyer, filling in at first base for the slumping Nunez, proved problematic for Durham, but three home runs in the late innings, including yet another by Tom Waldrop, brought the Bulls from behind to win 8-7.

That night the Malloys and the Waldrops and their sons, plus Amie and Tom's girlfriend from back home, gathered around Formica tables pulled together at Honey's restaurant. Much of the talk was about how every time Bud Waldrop showed up at the DAP, Tom put on a show.

"Looks to me like the Bulls ought to spring for an apartment for Dad, fly him in when we're at home," Tom said as he hunkered over a hamburger and fries.

"How many of 'em have you seen, Bud?" said Tommy.

"Well, let's see. That was his ninth tonight, right?" Bud began to count them off on his fingers. "There's that one, the one last night, and—what?—two in three games back in the spring. I've seen four of his nine so far."

"Kind of makes up for the long drive, then."

"Tell me about it!"

"We decided to break up our drive this time into two stops, with Amie along," Tommy said. "I don't see how you do it, eight hundred and fifty miles in one whack."

Bud shook his head. "Fifteen and a half hours. I counted eleven deer just in West Virginia. Maybe he'll hit another one for me tomorrow night. It makes the driving a lot easier."

The conversation was aimless, light, and jocular, all about baseball. The women seemed content to stay out of it. Hector Roa couldn't be recalled to Greenville soon enough for the other Bulls, said Marty: "We've only got a five-hole shower at the park, and he jumps right in ahead of people when he's ready. I mean, that's just not *done*, you know?" Tom said that six of his nine homers had come off left-handers, so that certainly wasn't the reason he wasn't getting more at bats; he kept complaining to West, to no avail, winding up on the bench every time he got hot. Kevin Grijak kept calling in the middle of the night, the boys said, still on a tear with Greenville. There had been no further word from Jason Keeline, who apparently had retired for good. Warner was thinking about smashing the TV set so Trapaga couldn't watch the Spanish-language station anymore. Correa was homesick, too, like Trapaga, and was ready to go back home to his wife in Puerto Rico. "The Latin players live in some other apartments, not Willowdale," said Marty. "It's a cultural thing. We don't have much in common off the field."

"You boys are starting to turn it around a little," Tommy said as he and Bud wrestled for the check.

"Couldn't be any worse than it was," said Tom.

Marty, who had never been on a championship team in his life, said it for both of them. "I want me a ring."

Early the next day, Sunday, Marty checked in with Rick Albert for some work in the batting cage. They had reached the dreaded month of July, when the suffocating heat and the tedium traditionally begin to take their toll, and West was cutting back on pregame work as a means of conserving his players' energy. This was one of those days when the position players would only take a round of "hacks"—no pressure, no teaching, just some freelance swings to loosen up—after the pitchers took a spirited round of BP. Down on the field, the pitchers were whooping and placing bets as they got one of their rare chances to take over the batting cage, and their gaiety echoed through the DAP as Marty, wearing shorts and a gray Bulls T-shirt, whacked away at pitches from Albert in the auxiliary cage in the parking lot. Around six o'clock, as fans began to drift through the turnstiles, Marty was among the Bulls, who were in full uniform now, sprawled on folding chairs or squatting on the concrete floor in the runway beneath the stands, amid the rakes and hoses and other groundskeeping paraphernalia, bowing their heads during the regular "chapel" service being led by a member of the Fellowship of Christian Athletes.

The biggest crowd of the season (6,215) showed up that night to see the Famous Chicken, a touring mascot dressed in a hairy red-and-yellow costume with floppy feet and a beak, and between his slapstick gyrations and a lusty hitting show by both clubs, the fans got their money's worth. The Bulls scored eight runs in the first inning—the big blow being a three-run homer by Tom Waldrop (he had now generated twenty-eight RBIs on his ten home runs alone)—setting the tone for the game. It was tied 12-all after six innings, and the old ballpark was rocking. Fans never tired of the Chicken's routine, it seemed (one gambit found him in the first-base coaching box trying to distract the rival pitcher by waggling an enlarged *Playboy* centerfold), and they were still laughing at him when Bobby Smith capped a 5-for-5 performance by driving in the winning run on a single in the seventh. The Keys and the Bulls combined for twenty-nine hits that night—Marty singled and scored a run in five at bats—and Bud Waldrop had another big smile on his face as he cranked his car for the all-night ride back home to central Illinois.

Marty's parents were on the road home, too, when he dropped in for lunch on Monday, the Fourth of July, at the Golden Corral. He had already been advised by West that he would be sitting that night against Frederick in order to give him a needed rest and allow Nelson Paulino some playing time. Except for the two backup catchers, Adrian Garcia and David Toth, Paulino had the fewest at bats on the club of those who had been with Durham from the beginning: 140, against Marty's 256, for a

.179 batting average. Only three of the Bulls' next sixteen games would be at home, with pauses in the middle of that stretch for both the major-league and Carolina League all-star games, and for the first time in the season he was agreeable to a rest.

"I've got scabs on top of scabs from sliding," he said, "and my arm's sore just from throwing so much in infield and in games. It feels like a piece of dead meat hanging from my shoulder."

"Winning makes it easier, though," he was told.

"Tell me about it. Matt's more relaxed now that we're—what?—nine and three. There won't be BP or anything today. Just show up and play the game."

"The push begins."

"Right. Not as hot here as Macon, either."

"June was one to forget, huh?"

"I hope so." He dabbled with his spaghetti, shaking his head as though still trying to comprehend what had happened. "One thing I do know is, it's important how you finish a season. 'What about Malloy? How does he do late when it's on the line?' If I can get it going again, they'll forget June."

It seemed like more of his feigned confidence, the I-can-cope defense, but for the first time there was some evidence that Marty was readjusting his dream. He was understandably proud of his work at second base, but now he had begun taking some ground balls every day at shortstop and third base and was again giving thought to turning himself into a switch-hitter. He seemed to be lowering his sights a bit, beginning to feel that his future in the major leagues might be as a utility infielder rather than as a full-fledged second baseman. The Carolina League had taken its measure.

"What do you dream these days?" he was asked.

"Realistically?"

"Well, a dream is a dream."

"Five years in the big leagues," he said flatly. "That wouldn't be a bad career. Not many guys make it at all."

"And then?"

"It would depend on the money situation. I thought for a while that I'd like to be a coach in the minors after I retired as a player, like Dews and Hubbie and them, but now I don't know. I've been watching guys like Jay [Ward] come through. They don't make much money and they live out of the trunk of their car. I mean, I've got this son and I don't even know him. I figure I'd quit if I didn't make it to the big leagues by the time I'm twenty-five or twenty-six, and either take a job in the organization or get a degree so I could coach high school like my dad."

"That's quite a comedown from spring training."

"It's reality," he said.

The Fourth of July game against Frederick had been scheduled for six o'clock, Bob Guy announced on the public address system, so fans could "attend the fireworks of your choice" afterward. In truth, there was such a plethora of golf courses and lakes and parks and other entertainments in the Triangle that Sundays and holidays observed on Monday were not the Bulls' best days at the gate. With the flags rippling in the breeze, the sun shining brightly, and Guy running through John Philip Sousa's entire repertoire on the PA system, the loyalists trickled into the DAP for what once had been an American standard: baseball on the Fourth of July. At twilight, with the park barely half filled, the fans were momentarily stunned when a guest singer strolled to a microphone at home plate to sing the National Anthem—the only time all season when anyone but the crowd would handle the chore. She was a local blues singer, an ample black woman, and when she laid a startling a capella rendition on them, the crowd gave her a clamorous ovation.

The players had congregated only in time for their light stretching exercises in the outfield, and when the game got underway Marty was found rooted to the aluminum bench in the bull pen down the right-field line, head bared to the sun, arms folded, legs stretched out and crossed at the ankles. On the mound where his grandfather's ashes had been strewn was Jeff Bock, the hometown boy signed out of a tryout camp, making his first start at the DAP. The season had not gone well for him so far—his ERA was 5.72, he had given up thirteen home runs in only forty-six innings, and opponents were hitting .281 against him—but on this day he would pitch well enough to pick up a win, giving up five hits and three runs in five innings. When he had showered and dressed after finishing his stint, he wandered through the grandstand toward the box seats behind the plate and sheepishly acknowledged the scattered shouts from the crowd: "Nice job, Jeff" and "Attaway, homeboy!" The bull pen held it for him, and the Bulls won their fifth straight, 5-4.

Marty was back in the lineup the next night, pitching in with a single and a walk in three official trips to the plate, as the Bulls romped, 8-3, behind a six-hit effort from Mike D'Andrea, only the second nine-inning complete game of the season for the Durham staff. They had swept the Northern Division leaders in four straight and now led their own division by a mile, with a record of 11-3, and as they hit the road again for six games in the lions' dens at Wilmington and Frederick, they appeared rested and confident. The championship ring Marty hankered for wasn't an idle dream anymore, and there was something else for him to look forward to: the announcement of the Carolina League all-star rosters for the game to be played later in July.

CHAPTER 12

They would always remember the ensuing six-game foray into the North country as the road trip to hell. The bus had barely lumbered onto the interstate leading out of Durham when the air-conditioning broke down, which forced the players to open windows and caused the driver to nurse the engine along at fifty-five miles an hour rather than his usual sixty-five, and it took them eight hours rather than the normal six to make it to Wilmington. For the first time, they were envious of those minor-league clubs whose buses were equipped, like giant airliners, to show movies on board. They barely had time to check into their motel and get to the ballpark for some batting practice, and when the game got under way against the Blue Rocks they were tired, and it showed: they were shut out for five innings (by a pitcher who would be promoted to AA immediately after the game), committed five errors, and went meekly, 5-0, to end their six-game winning streak.

For Marty, it wasn't much of a way to celebrate a twenty-second birthday. Although he went 2-for-3 at the plate, he made one of the errors leading to a four-run fourth by Wilmington. There would be no hoorahing at a sports bar after the game, as there had been for his twenty-first, not even a birthday cake from superfan Martie Byron, since they were on the road; but he had some consolation when the Bulls received a nice surprise. Awaiting them at the motel in Wilmington was a pitcher who might make a difference during the rest of the season: Roger Etheridge, a towering left-hander (six six, 215 pounds) who had been the "player to be named later" in a trade wherein the Braves swapped Deion Sanders for Roberto Kelly of the Cincinnati Reds. Etheridge was as country as grits—from Linden, Alabama, deep in the forests on the Mississippi line, a fanatical Auburn football fan, a connoisseur of country music who wore wrinkled jeans and scruffy gray boots best suited for oystering and had a drawl as thick as molasses—so there was instant rapport between him and Marty. At noon the very next day, to catcalls from the players, the two walked off together to pig out for lunch at the Black-Eyed Pea, a Southern-style meat-and-three restaurant in the nearby pedestrian mall.

That night, the Bulls righted themselves behind Darrell May. The quiet and poised young left-hander seemed to be collecting himself after being delayed with tendinitis in spring training and his brief fill-in stint at Greenville and was settling in as the most consistent starting pitcher on Matt West's staff; he was not long for Durham, it appeared, if he kept this up. On this night he slammed the door on Wilmington, striking out seven and allowing only five scattered hits in seven innings, and the Bulls won 4-0, Marty getting a single in five at bats. The Bulls took a 6-5 win the next night, to run their second-half record to 13-4, and they looked forward to motoring over to Frederick for a three-game set, their memories still fresh of having swept the Keys in four a week earlier at the DAP.

It seemed like an omen when the air-conditioning still failed to work on their bus and a backup had to be chartered for the two-hour run from Wilmington to Frederick. They lost all three games, scoring only seven runs in twenty-seven innings, and Marty was relieved to know that the club was scheduled to return to Frederick only one more time during the season, for their last four road games, in late August. It was there that he had his three-strikeout game in May, and in these three games he struck out six times in eleven trips to the plate and saw the end of a promising seven-game hitting streak during which he had gone 8-for-27. The only salvation, as far as he was concerned, came in the finale of the series when his new friend, Roger Etheridge, allowed only four hits over six innings in his debut for the Bulls, although he lost a 2-1 decision. The Bulls limped home on the crippled bus, crawling beneath their bedcovers in the wee hours.

That day, July 12, was an off-day throughout the minor leagues so the stage would be cleared for the major-league all-star game at Three Rivers Stadium in Pittsburgh. Marty's only chore was to show up that night at the downtown Hilton for the annual Bid on a Bull date auction, where he was won for $100 by a pretty young secretary named Robin—they had met before, as it turned out, one night at a hangout called the Long Branch Saloon, and although she would be seen later waiting for him outside the clubhouse door, not much came of it—and he hurried back to the apartment to watch the major-league all-star game on television. The Bulls players, like fans all over the country, felt uneasy as they watched the proceedings from Pittsburgh.

More and more, every day now, the sports pages were filled with news of the standoff between the major-league owners and the players' union, and there was a helpless feeling, bordering on disbelief, that this season might come to an abrupt halt.

Throughout the minor leagues, from rookie ball to AAA, crowds were at a peak now. One reason, no doubt, was the fans' growing disgust over the shenanigans at the major-league level, but they had reached the precise time of the year, any year, when baseball was truly the national pastime: kids out of school, pennant races engaged, no other sports occupying the mind, no better place to be on a hot summer night than out at the old ballpark, with the flags flying and the hot dogs sizzling and the players in their best form. The announced crowds at Wilmington and Frederick on the Bulls' six-game swing had averaged more than six thousand; while they were gone, an exhibition game at the DAP between the touring all-women's Colorado Silver Bullets and the over-thirty Roy Hobbs All-Stars had attracted nearly five thousand. The summer game was in its full glory now, in the middle of July, a time when it was okay for grown men, whether they shuffled papers in air-conditioned offices or slumped over production lines, to gaily hum the strains of "Take Me Out to the Ball Game" while anticipating a night at the park with the wife and kids. For the remainder of the season, in spite of a stretch of rainy weather, crowds at the DAP would average slightly more than the park's capacity of five thousand.

So it didn't seem to matter to Durham fans that the Bulls had lost those three in a row at Frederick. On the night following the major-league all-star game, an overflow crowd of 5,448 squeezed into the DAP for the opener of a three-game set against the Kinston Indians. (Awaiting Marty in the clubhouse was a belated birthday cake, courtesy of Martie Byron.) It was baseball they wanted, any kind of baseball, and the Bulls would oblige them by sweeping the series. Matt West's club was pumping at full bore now. Little Mike Warner was on a tear, slashing hits to all corners of the park, seriously contending for the league lead in batting average and runs scored, starting every game in left field now that his throwing arm had healed. Raymond Nunez was in the midst of a hitting streak that had begun, not coincidentally, when the Braves dispatched their Latin American supervisor, the Spanish-speaking Carlos Rios, to work one-on-one for a full week with the confused and often sullen young Dominican. (Nunez would hit .346, with seven homers and fourteen RBIs, in the twenty-two-game stretch beginning with Rios's visit.) Most important, the pitchers were finally coming into their own: Mike D'Andrea's heavy fastball now had him among the league leaders in strikeouts; Jamie Arnold seemed to have broken his tendency to serve up home run pitches; and Darrell May and Roger Etheridge gave the club a pair of wise left-handers who knew how to throw, as the poem says, "to be a moment misunderstood." There were only two negatives to speak of: the careless play at shortstop by Hector Roa, who was committing an error every third game; and the loss of the veteran catcher Brad Rippelmeyer, out for the season after surgery on a ruptured disc he had failed to reveal on account of some desperation (a Carolina League all-star two years earlier, he was twenty-four now and his career might be in jeopardy).

The story of the first game of that series was May, who went 7-2 and dropped his ERA to 2.71 by allowing Kinston only six singles in seven and two-thirds innings; Hollins and Nunez each homered and combined for five of the RBIs in a 6-1 win, the Bulls' seventh straight victory at home. The next night (Bulls, 7-5) belonged to Nunez, who stroked two homers, although he was almost overshadowed when the free-swinging Juan Williams, third on the club in homers despite a .220 average and one strikeout every third at bat, launched a shot that might have traveled five hundred feet had the ball not struck the lights above and beyond the scoreboard in left. Marty's turn at heroics came on Friday night before the biggest home crowd of the season (6,326) when he stroked a two-run double to the gap in left for the tying and winning runs in a 7-6 victory, the Bulls' thirteenth win in their last fourteen games at the DAP. It was the second time during the season that Marty had driven in the game-winning run, and West happily noted on his faxed report to the big house in Atlanta that both times it had been accomplished against a left-hander.

When the rosters, drawn up by the managers, were announced that week for the Carolina League's midseason all-star game, Marty's name wasn't there. The second baseman picked ahead of him for the Southern Division squad was the Salem Buccaneers' Chance Sanford, a slope-shouldered, bandy-legged kid from Houston, Texas, who wore his trousers in the old style, hitched just below the knees, revealing knotty calves. Like Marty, he was twenty-two and in his third year of pro ball. It was a close vote, for at the time of the balloting both were batting slightly over .250; what it came down to, much to Marty's chagrin, was Sanford's power versus Malloy's defense: Sanford had eight homers to Malloy's five and double the number of RBIs, but Sanford, on the other hand, had an ugly twenty-five errors to Marty's ten. It galled Marty, especially when he later watched the all-star game by way of cable from Wilmington and saw Sanford play all nine innings, but he was somewhat mollified when, a week later, *Baseball America* named Marty Malloy as the best defensive second baseman in the league.

In spite of their rueful performance as a team during the first half, the Bulls placed six players on the midseason all-star team. Mike Warner was the only one picked as a starter by the managers, and five others were selected by the all-star team manager,

Mark Berry of Winston-Salem: Damon Hollins and Bobby Smith as reserves and the pitchers Jamie Arnold, Darrell May, and Carl Schutz. Hollins was leading Durham in both home runs and runs batted in and was now being considered the best prospect in the entire Braves' system. Smith was hitting a strong .280 and was among the club's leaders across the board, from runs scored to stolen bases; and although he was making errors by the bushel, it was understood by everyone in the league that they were errors of commission (he, like Marty, was named the best defensive player at his position in the Carolina League by *Baseball America*). The numbers of May and Arnold spoke for themselves. Schutz made the all-stars not so much for his numbers (1-3, 5.29 ERA, seven saves) as for his role as a left-handed spot reliever with a devastating strikeout pitch; he had fanned fifty-six in only thirty-six innings. (Alas, boys will be boys. Schutz, feeling perky about his selection, was horsing around in the outfield during batting practice when he tried a flashy Barry Bonds snatch catch of a fly ball wending his way. He pulled his glove too soon, which resulted in a broken nose and his being replaced by D'Andrea in the all-star game.)

Elsewhere in the Braves' organization in the first half, both Richmond in the AAA International League and Greenville in the AA Southern League were playing above .500 and on the upswing. (Of the Bulls promoted earlier to Greenville, Kevin Grijak was playing full-time at first base and leading the club in homers and RBIs; and Matt Murray had been clubbed for twenty-five hits in his baptismal first fourteen innings with the G-Braves, as they were clumsily known.) The most heartening story in the farm system was found at Macon, where the overmatched Braves not only had suffered through the worst start in all of professional baseball but had been orphaned by the severe floods that had struck south Georgia and buried little Luther Williams Field under four feet of silt and water, forcing them to play twenty-four straight games on the road. Playing some of their home games at Columbus, Georgia, and some others at Greenville (where they would play at noon and then, furthering their education, watch Greenville play at night on the same field), they had recovered from their 1-19 start to go 27-22 the rest of the way in the first half. The most productive player on the club was the only veteran, the third baseman John Knott, Marty's roommate during spring training, who was leading the club in homers, RBIs, and stolen bases. And what of the fancifully named Wonderful Terrific Monds III? Had he played there full-time instead of losing those two weeks filling in at Durham, he likely would have been leading Macon in every offensive category.

For the remainder of July, the Bulls would see only the Prince William Cannons and the Lynchburg Red Sox, in home-and-home series, interrupted by a three-day layoff for the league all-star game. They were 16-7 so far in the second half, the hottest team in the league, maintaining a four-game lead over the Winston-Salem Spirits in the Southern Division, and as they boarded the bus for the four-hour run to Woodbridge, Virginia, only twenty miles south of the White House, they sensed an opportunity to make a serious run for the second-half pennant and a spot in the play-offs. Lynchburg had collapsed after going only 30-40 in the first half; Prince William, in spite of the bevy of wonderful pitching prospects dispatched there by the parent White Sox, was riding along slightly above .500 because of a lack of offensive punch.

They were shut down in the opener at Prince William, losing 6-0 before a boisterous crowd of more than seven thousand on a Saturday night at the Cannons' little Erector-set park hard by I-95, but they came back with a crisp performance in a rain-shortened game on Sunday. Marty singled in a run in the third inning; Tom Waldrop did the same in the fifth; and they hung on for a 2-0 win as Roger Etheridge allowed only four hits and a walk before the rain clouds fell open. The Bulls won again on Monday in a 10-7 donnybrook, returning home immediately afterward for the all-star break. For Marty, it had been a profitable little business trip: 4-for-10, another game-winning hit, one double, a walk against only one strikeout. He now had another modest hitting streak going, this time 8-for-21 over six games, and the appalling slump of June was becoming a memory.

In the gloom of their apartment in Durham, with midsummer rains pounding on the roof, Marty and his roommates cracked open beers and scrunched down to watch the Carolina League all-star game on cable television. It wouldn't do for Marty to smirk (cluck his tongue, perhaps), but the North was still leading by a score of 1-0 after eight innings because Chance Sanford had bungled his first chance of the game, fielding a ground ball with a man on third in the first inning but losing it in the transfer from glove to hand to allow the runner to score. In the top of the ninth, they cheered as Bobby Smith drilled a two-out single to tie the game at 1-1. The game had a storybook finish, though, when Blue Rocks catcher Lance Jennings thrilled the home crowd—at 6,983, it was the largest of the year at the glitzy new ballpark in Wilmington—by launching a dramatic game-winning solo homer over the left-field wall in the bottom of the ninth. Of the other Bulls who made the trip, Mike Warner had two singles, Jamie Arnold was a bit shaky in two innings of relief (two hits, a wild pitch, a hit batsman), and Mike D'Andrea pitched a harmless inning. Damon Hollins didn't bat and Darrell May didn't pitch. What the boys at 707 Willowdale didn't know was that the papers were being cut for May to rejoin Matt Murray and Kevin Grijak at Greenville of the AA Southern League.

Following the break for the all-star game, the Bulls had an appointment for four games at Lynchburg. Attendance might be soaring elsewhere in the league and, indeed, throughout the minor leagues, but that wasn't the case in Lynchburg. An old textile town on the Dan River, now home to Jerry Falwell's Moral Majority and his Liberty University, Lynchburg had soured on its floundering Red Sox' farm club. They had never quite put their act together during this season, and now they had lost their premier gate attraction: Trot Nixon, the teenaged big-bucks prospect from Durham, only a year out of high school and aluminum bats, had mashed an impressive twelve home runs with forty-three RBIs and stolen ten bases in the first half of the season but now was out for the year with a bad back. (Ah, the gulf between the hot prospects and the wannabes! A low-round draft choice might have been told to take two aspirin and go home for the winter, but Nixon was flown to Boston for observation by the Red Sox' own specialists.) With Nixon gone, it seemed doubtful that Lynchburg would attract a total of a hundred thousand for its seventy games at the tired old downtown ballpark where Carolina League games had been played since 1966.

Thus, the zealous Durham fans who followed the Bulls' bus 113 miles up the road to Lynchburg for the weekend series felt they were in the majority when, on the first night, only 884 were in the stands. Marty went 1-for-4 with a stolen base in the opener, stretching his hitting streak to seven games, as the Bulls took a 4-2 win. But he went hitless in eight trips as Durham lost 4-3 and 7-1 decisions on the next two nights. He sat in the final game of the set, won by the Bulls 3-2, when Etheridge again came on strong by striking out five, walking none, and allowing only six hits in eight innings. The laconic left-hander from Alabama's piney woods was turning out to be a more than adequate replacement for the departed Darrell May. He already had a 2-1 record and an ERA of 0.90 in his three starts, presenting Matt

West with the same old double-edged quandary faced by all minor-league managers: the big club giveth, and the big club taketh away.

Now, in the dead of the summer, rains of monsoon proportion were a daily occurrence. Epic black thunderclouds, remindful of Noah and the ark, began rolling in from the west around noon every day, flooding the bottoms where the DAP lay downtown, keeping all plans on hold: no individual work, no batting practice, no pregame infield; just show up at four and see what develops. It was like that on the last Tuesday of July, the Bulls' one-hundredth game of the season, with Prince William in town to open a six-game home stand. The game finally got under way at nine o'clock after many false starts, and the low point of the Bulls' 9-5 loss was a three-run homer by Pete Rose, Jr., a third baseman and designated hitter for the Cannons. The novelty of seeing the son of the troubled former star of Cincinnati's Big Red Machine—big Pete had been banished from the game for gambling and assorted other offenses—had worn off now, for Pete Jr. was twenty-four, still in Class A after six years in the minors, a slow, thick-bodied kid who was often hurt (he was batting .277 in only 130 at bats) and appeared to have little future left since being drafted high by the Orioles in 1989. About fifty fans remained, huddling beneath the grandstand roof, when the digital clock on the right-field foul pole flashed 12:00 ("Good *morning*," said the announcer, Bob Guy, his voice startling them from their vigil), and soon the soggy remnants of the crowd of nearly three thousand awakened the children who had been asleep in their laps and drifted off to their cars.

Marty was able to pick up some more pocket change by working Matt West's baseball clinics each of the next two mornings—his $100 would cover child support for a month—before the rains descended and canceled the games scheduled for those nights. Prince William had come all of that distance to play one game, biding the rest of their time by rattling around the Red Roof Inn and snacking across the parking lot at Honey's restaurant, and no sooner had they checked out of their rooms than they were replaced by the Lynchburg Red Sox. About the only notable occurrence during the long and miserable days was the news that yet another shortstop was on his way to Durham: Manny Jimenez, a Dominican who had played the entire '93 season at Durham (batting .225) and was coming down after seeing little playing time at Greenville. Jimenez's demotion meant that Hector Roa was going back to the Southern League, and Marty had mixed feelings. "I say good riddance, as far as Roa is concerned," he said, noting Roa's eleven errors in only twenty-eight games and the general discord he had wrought. "But Jimenez will make five shortstops I've worked with this year. You can't get much rhythm going when that happens." He still missed the long-gone Jason Keeline as a double-play partner.

When Friday rolled around, the weather situation was much the same. Bill Miller and his grounds crew were out at daybreak siphoning water from the field, thinking they had it licked, but then another gale of rain swept through at three o'clock in the afternoon. By six, when the gates opened, the early arrivals for the opener of a weekend set with Lynchburg came upon an odd sight: dozens of men—grounds crew, ball boys, Matt West and his coaches, some of the players, even general manager Peter Anlyan and the office staff—were crawling over the playing field sopping up puddled water with towels taken from the training room and clubhouse, tossing them into hampers, demanding more towels. They would, by God, get this one in, come hell or high water.

For Wayne Williams and his wife, Sharon, who had followed Beverly and Tommy Malloy all the way up from Florida to take their first look at Marty as a professional baseball player, this was a hell of a note. Wayne was thirty-one now, paunchy and balding, manager of the Winn-Dixie on the main highway in Chiefland. He had played football for Tommy Malloy at Chiefland High as a teenager and then, immediately after graduation, gone to work at the grocery store. He knew that this was about as good as life was going to get for him, although his wife had just been accepted by a community college for further study toward a license as a registered nurse, and he was somewhat agog over what he was seeing in what was, to him, the big city of Durham.

"This is great," Wayne was saying as the frantic work continued to dry off the field for that night's game. He had taken a seat under the grandstand roof, behind the Bulls' dugout on the first-base side, and he had spotted Marty lolling against the chain-link fence, chatting with fans, in front of the bleachers. "I've got to talk with Marty about this."

"The field's wet, is all," he was told.

"No, I mean getting paid to play ball."

"If you call it *pay*. He only gets about forty dollars a game, you know."

Wayne Williams tried to compute that, convert it into Levy County, Florida, dollars, but it came out the same. Interminable bus rides? Uneven playing fields? Endless sessions of batting practice in a cage on a gravel parking lot in the broiling sun? The search for something besides pizza to eat after a game in Salem? Left-handed pitchers snapping curveballs on the black? *Poor Marty*. Wayne Williams knew that a twenty-two-year-old stock boy at the Winn-Dixie in Chiefland, earning little more than minumum wage, could make that kind of money only by spending a full eight-hour day on his feet, affixing sticker prices on cans, trundling fresh meat from the freezer, and dealing with persnickety customers counting out their coupons. There were no autograph shows for grocery-store clerks, as far as he knew.

"You think he might make it to the Braves someday?"

"He's got a chance."

"That'd be something, wouldn't it?"

"Well, the odds are long. But, yeah, that'd be something."

"I'll sure be there if he does, but I don't know," Wayne Williams said. "I've never been to Atlanta, but I've heard the stories. Friend of mine told me he was up there once and he was driving eighty-five miles an hour on the expressway and somebody *passed* him. You reckon that's true?"

"Your friend exaggerated," he was told. "I'd be more worried about some logging truck coming up out of the woods around Trenton like a turtle, doing a mile an hour."

He thought about that for a minute. "Well, anyway, even if this is as far as Marty gets, this is really something." Now, he saw, Marty was autographing a scorecard for a kid. "About the only time I ever sign anything, it's to okay somebody's check."

The field was a quagmire, but they finally got back to playing baseball again that night, following a half-hour delay, and the two days of inactivity showed. Mike D'Andrea got raked for nine hits in five innings, and the Bulls let in three unearned runs with sloppy play in the field to lose the game 9-7. They weren't much more pleasant to behold the next night, when Jamie Arnold experienced a nightmare—in five and one-third innings, he gave up ten hits, three of them homers, to account for eight earned runs, and was flustered into committing two balks—and West was in a snit after the 8-2 loss. "When Mr. Arnold made a mistake, they hit it on the roof," he snapped, noting that Durham had won only seven of nineteen games against the worst club in the league. "There needs to come a point in time when he has to get beyond having learning experiences and become his own kind of pitcher."

This would likely be the last chance for Tommy and Beverly

Malloy to see their son play for the Durham Bulls—unless, of course, the Braves decided to return him there for another season—and they had sat in the box seats rather glumly through the proceedings of Friday and Saturday nights. On Sunday, having pointed Wayne and Sharon Williams back in the direction of home, they took Marty to lunch at the Golden Corral. He had doubled in six at bats during the two games and was charged with a tough error on a twisting ground ball that came up on him in the wet grass in short right field, and he wasn't in the best mood himself. "We're going to hear it from Matt if we lose again tonight," he said, playing with his food, only nodding when his father said he had learned that the concrete-pouring job was available during the off-season if he wanted it. After lunch, Beverly tried to lift her son's spirits by driving him to a cut-rate drugstore and buying him a pair of thonged clogs to wear in the showers at the DAP.

That night's game was the most exciting of the year at the old ballpark. Roger Etheridge was on the mound for the Bulls and was in complete control of a game that had something for everybody. The fun began in the top of the second when Hector Roa, playing his last game at Durham before going back to Greenville, got ejected for continuing to bitch about a called third strike. In the sixth inning of a game that was still scoreless, two Bulls were called out at home on close plays, one of them Mike Warner on an attempted steal of home, arguably the most exciting play in baseball. Then, in the seventh, both Marty and Matt West got tossed in the rhubarb following a blown call by the umpires—Marty's one-hop shot to the third baseman with runners at first and third was ruled a catch, and when the shouting died the Bulls had nothing to show for it—and the two of them had to leave the field with the game still scoreless.

The first thing West did when they reached the clubhouse was to fling a trash barrel across the training room (Marty cleaned up after him, not wanting to invoke Jay Williams's anger), and then he promised to pay the kid's $100 fine ("I got you into it"). Then they sat to hear the rest of the game on the radio. Bobby Smith botched a play at third base to give Lynchburg a 1-0 lead in the top of the tenth, but he came right back in the bottom half to hammer a two-run single with the bases loaded to win it for the Bulls 2-1. Etheridge, who was relieved by Bill Slack only one out away from going the full ten innings, had given up only six singles and had now allowed just two earned runs in thirty innings with Durham. The Bulls' lead in the division was back up to four and a half games, Winston-Salem having lost that night, but somebody besides Etheridge was going to have to become a stopper if Marty was to have a chance at a championship ring.

CHAPTER 13

There is a *Peanuts* cartoon in which Linus calls time during a sandlot baseball game and shuffles out to the mound, his shin guards and chest protector dragging in the dust, for a conference with Charlie Brown about the pitching signs. "One's a fastball, two's a curve, three's a change, four's a knuckler, five's a down-shoot," he begins, continuing through a fanciful repertoire of pitches that ultimately totals sixteen. "Got it?" says Linus. "Got it," says Charlie Brown, whapping the ball into his glove. Linus is halfway back to his position behind the plate when he stops, turns, and says, "On second thought, throw anything you want."

For much of the season, Marty had felt like Charlie Brown, with all of the complicated signals he had been getting: *do this, try that, maybe this is it, I don't know.* Matt West had been just as puzzled as anybody over Marty's slump in June, and at first he had joined Rick Albert and Jay Ward and the others in offering advice. Although there had been some improvement in the early games of July, when Marty put together a seven-game hitting streak, it became obvious to West that the constant tinkering with Marty's mechanics had left him in an unnatural crouch, forcing him to overstride and leaving him vulnerable to both the fastball on the hands and the change on the outside corner. Only when he got the pitch he was looking for did he make solid contact—the rest of the time he was badly fooled—and that was no way for a little man with neither power nor blazing speed to get out of the Carolina League.

It was in the middle of July when West, playing Linus to Charlie Brown, pulled Marty aside and told him, on second thought, to simplify: straighten up, spread out, shorten the stride and the swing, hit the ball where it's pitched. This was essentially the way he had hit during the successful seasons at Idaho Falls and Macon, and after all of that conflicting advice, this came as a great relief. Almost immediately, Marty began to cut down on his strikeouts and spray line drives all over the field, and his numbers for the month were a marked improvement over June: .272 average, eight walks against eleven strikeouts (an average of only one strikeout every 7.1 at bats, the best of his career). Pleased with the results, West went a step further: beginning on the first of August, no matter what, Marty would bat leadoff or in the two-hole for the rest of the season.

That decision was made easier when Mike Warner finally got the call to Greenville. It had been a long season for the spunky little outfielder, who had batted .319 with twenty-nine stolen bases for Durham in a '93 season shortened by injury, but when his throwing arm recovered and he was able to play full-time he became a terror for West's Bulls from the leadoff position. One wouldn't have suspected this from looking at the official team photograph, made early in the season, in which Warner, flanked by the husky Grijak and D'Andrea, looked like a batboy. The kid was a gamer, a pesky contact hitter with an insatiable greed to get on base at any cost, a ghost of Pete Rose and every other overachieving little man who'd had to fight for every inch. When he departed, he was leading the Carolina League with a .321 batting average and headed the Bulls in several important offensive categories, in spite of limited playing time: runs scored, doubles, triples, bases on balls, stolen bases, on-base percentage, even slugging average (he also had thirteen home runs). He had been the dream leadoff man, a driving force on the club, and now Marty was expected to take up the slack.

West had not passed the baton to Marty whimsically or because of a lack of options, but rather because he knew his man. It had been liberating for Marty to be unshackled at the plate, to be told it was all right for him to go ahead and follow his instincts, and now he was being made to feel that the fate of the club was in his hands. By now the manager knew what a competitor he had in Marty Malloy, how brightly his flame burned. To tell Marty Malloy to go get 'em was like throwing Br'er Rabbit into the brier patch. Handed this mandate as the Bulls headed into the final month of the season, Marty would respond with the most productive stretch of his young career.

His transformation came immediately, on the first day of August, when the Bulls got off the bus at Salem for the start of a seven-game road trip. Batting in the two-hole, with the speedy Miguel Correa leading off and starting to find himself, Marty replaced Warner as the pest in the Durham batting order. The Bulls won only one of the four games at Salem because of some inconsistent pitching, but Marty had three two-hit games and added five bases on balls. When they moved on to Winston-Salem, to win two of three against the first-half division champions, it was the same story: ripping line drives, showing bunt to bring in the infielders, going with the pitch, even working for walks, he seemed to be in the middle of everything offensively. It was a remarkable seven games for him: 10-for-25 with four doubles, a triple, two stolen bases, seven runs, seven walks, only four strikeouts.

This was the Marty Malloy the Braves had been waiting for. Somebody should have spent the time and effort to film his every move during this stretch of his third season in pro ball and file it away for future reference, for they would have recorded a kid at the precise time in his career when he put everything together. He was perfection on the double play, on the pivot and the feed, no matter how many shortstops they put alongside him, and not once all season long had he been seriously endangered by an oncoming base runner. Through trial and error, good times and bad times—the surest way to learn, in the long run—he had finally found himself at the plate. Surviving the June slump had sobered him, calmed him down, shown him that the only way to play a long season in professional baseball is one game at a time. In place of the skittish kid whose heart pounded as he raced onto the DAP on opening day, anxious to please and afraid to make a mistake, there was now a mature young man who might be on his way to the major leagues. He would say it later for himself: "I think I'll always be able to look back and say this was the year it finally came together for me. Durham is where I learned professional baseball."

The Bulls themselves weren't exactly sailing along through calm seas, and the reason was obvious: when they got good pitching from their starters, they won; when they didn't, they lost. The trip to Salem and Winston-Salem was a perfect case in point. Their only win in the four games at Salem came when Mike D'Andrea scattered seven hits over eight innings, all but one of them harmless singles, for a 5-1 victory. They were outscored in the three losses, 21-9. Then, at Winston-Salem, they had won two of the three games when Etheridge threw a four-hitter and when a newcomer up from the Macon Braves, a tall right-hander named Carey Paige, also gave up just four hits in his Carolina League debut (Durham won a 15-0 blowout, thanks to six homers). Even after going only 3-4 on the road trip, though, they had actually managed to stretch their Southern Division lead over second-place Winston-Salem to seven games, with twenty-six to play. The Spirits were playing badly, and it appeared that the Bulls might back into the play-offs in spite of themselves.

When they arrived at the DAP on the second Monday in August for a weeklong homestand against Wilmington and Winston-Salem, it was under a troublesome black cloud that was not of their making: the imminent probability that the major-league baseball season would come to a premature end. All season long—indeed, for a couple of years now—the major-league owners and the players' union had been dug in and were refusing to give an inch. The owners wanted to impose a salary cap in order to stem the runaway salaries that they themselves had brought about; and the players, in spite of an average salary of $1.2 million, had the audacity to say that they were tired of being jerked around by management. It was a sorry state of affairs, mind-boggling to minor-league players who earned about $1,100 a month and to Durham fans, who might not earn $1.2 million in a lifetime of labor, and as the deadline neared for reaching an agreement—midnight, Thursday, August 11—the Bulls and their fans seemed to draw even closer to one another.

Minor-league baseball fans have always understood the fleeting nature of their relationship with the young players dispatched to their town each year by the major-league organization. The kids have been loaned to them for their enjoyment during the hot summer months, in small towns not exactly pulsating with entertainment, and the fans tend to pamper them as though they were exchange students, making them feel at home, applauding their successes while overlooking their failures, delighting when they are rewarded with a promotion, sometimes maintaining correspondence with the good ones over the years as they become stars in the major leagues. One of the great joys of being a minor-league baseball fan is being able to say, "*Hell, I remember when he was just a kid, getting the hang of things,*" and Durham fans had enjoyed plenty of that in recent years. Ten of the twenty-five Atlanta Braves who were about to join their brethren in a strike had matriculated at the DAP, the best known of those being pitcher Steve Avery of the '89 Bulls and outfielder David Justice of the '86 club, and everyone seemed to know that shortstop Jeff Blauser still corresponded with the woman who had been his landlady in Durham nearly ten years ago, when he was Marty Malloy's age. But now, with the knowledge that Avery and Justice and Blauser and Mark Lemke and all of those other former Bulls now with the Braves were about to go on strike, the Bulls faithful found themselves clucking like parents whose kids had gone astray. They would rather remember them as innocent children, full of spit and promise, than as hardened adults who had fallen in with the wrong crowd when they left home.

The issues surrounding the impending strike seemed beyond comprehension for fans at this grassroots level, in the low minor leagues, and the Bulls themselves had little more understanding of it all. They didn't spend a lot of time talking about it. Marty had been saying all along, when asked, that he guessed what the players' union was doing might help him in some way down the line if he made it to the big leagues. When Tom Waldrop was asked if he would cross the picket line to play for the Braves, if it came to that, he first yelped, "Sure, in a New York minute," before rolling his eyes and trudging off to the batting cage for another confrontation with the fastball on the hands. The only strike the young Bulls were concerned with at this point was the one that sonofabitch called in the third inning last night with runners in scoring position. To them, the brouhaha between the owners and the players was grown-up stuff, hardly their concern. They felt like kids caught in the crossfire of an ugly marriage, cowering beneath the bedcovers while their parents raged at each other in another room, hoping it soon would end so they could go out and play.

If the big boys didn't want to play baseball, by God, the young ones did. A heightened sense of joy seemed to permeate the DAP when the Bulls bounded onto the field to open their home stand on that second week of August. Less than a month remained for the summer game to run its course—a sobering thought that had suddenly occurred to the townspeople and the players alike—and a glorious magenta sunset settled over the little ballpark like a halo, as though a spectral blessing had been bestowed on the occasion. Few of the five thousand seats at the DAP were empty for that night's game, which would be true for the remainder of the season, and there seemed to be a pronounced spring in the steps of everyone from the peanut vendors to the ragamuffin Field of Dreams youngsters who raced onto the field for the full-throated singing of the National Anthem. It was time to play some ball.

Minor-league games are usually brisk affairs consuming little more than two hours, primarily because most hitters swing at the first good pitch available, and this would be no exception. The Wilmington Blue Rocks scored in the first inning, on a two-out double off the boards in right center, but Miguel Correa gunned down the trailing runner in a thrilling play at home plate. Correa evened the score in the third by singling to right but then was thrown out trying to steal second. The two clubs continued to chip away at two fireballing starting pitchers who were in prime form at this point in the summer, the Bulls' D'Andrea and the Blue Rocks' Mike Bovee, and it was tied at 3-all in the bottom of the ninth when Tom Waldrop came to bat with Damon Hollins standing on second, courtesy of a crucial two-base error by the Wilmington third baseman. "When Damon got on, my mentality changed a little bit," Waldrop would say afterward, saying reams about a season which found him with forty-four runs batted in on only fifty hits. He rifled the first pitch he saw down the right-field line, raising chalk, to score Hollins with the winning run. The game ended at nine thirty-eight, which gave fans time to rush home and watch the last innings of the Atlanta Braves game from Cincinnati if they cared to, but nobody seemed in a hurry to leave the DAP on a night like this.

Marty had singled and walked in three official trips to the plate in that game, but when he reported for duty the next afternoon he found that his legs were cramped and, ruefully, he would have to go down to the bull pen and sit this one out. Filling in for him at second base and in the two-hole was Nelson Paulino, who had been the Bulls' odd man out all season long, now showing only 170 at bats compared to Marty's 360. Paulino was hitless in four trips, as were most of the other Bulls (Juan Williams had two of their three hits, one of them another monstrous home run over everything in center field), and Wilmington coasted to a 6-1 win behind a right-hander named Bart Evans, now leading the league's pitchers with a 10-1 record and an ERA slightly above 2.00. In spite of Durham's loss, the overflow crowd of 5,482 respectfully applauded the play of the Blue Rocks, whose overall season record was 76-37. Their parent Kansas City Royals had stacked the deck at Wilmington this year, vowing to leave the roster intact, and the Blue Rocks were leading everybody by a mile in team batting and team pitching.

In fact, the only club Wilmington had been unable to dominate during the season was Durham, which had won half of their fourteen meetings until this night's loss.

Roger Etheridge was at it again the next night, even when he didn't have his best stuff. The left-hander from the Alabama outback had been with the club for only a month, but it was clear that he had the unwavering respect of his teammates. He had uncommon presence for a twenty-two-year-old—tall, all business, his body language indicating *Gimme the ball, I'll take care of this myself*—and it seemed to rub off on the others the moment he had finished his warm-up tosses and hitched up his trousers and scowled at the first man he would face. His fastball didn't pop the mitt, and scouts behind the plate rarely bothered to raise their radar guns when he threw, but somewhere he had learned how to pitch. Against Wilmington, in this third game of the series, he walked an uncharacteristic five and struck out just one, but when he departed after eight innings, having reached the pitch count of one hundred ordained by the Braves, the Blue Rocks had only five scattered hits and no runs to show for it. His fastball hadn't worked from the beginning, so he had adjusted by keeping the hitters off balance with a popping slider and a change-up that died on the corners like a duck winged in flight. The Bulls won 4-1, Damon Hollins's homer and double for two runs batted in being all they needed, and Etheridge's ERA plummeted to 0.79, with opponents batting exactly .181 against him.

The pattern was becoming too familiar for the Bulls—they were winning with D'Andrea and Etheridge on the mound, in dire trouble otherwise—and on the next night they were out of it before another sellout crowd could settle in for the evening. Jeff Bock, the local boy now being used as a spot starter, got shelled for twelve hits and six runs in the first five innings, and lanky John Simmons was brought in to take one for the team (six hits, three walks, and five more runs in two and one-third innings), giving Wilmington an 11-1 lead. There were some fireworks in the bottom of the seventh, when thirteen Bulls came to the plate and produced eight runs, but it was too late to avert a sloppy 11-10 loss. A game like that gave minor-league baseball a bad name: five errors, eight walks, thirty-three hits (eleven for extra bases), and twenty-one runs in a donnybrook that consumed nearly three hours. It "looked as if the Durham Bulls might have been better off joining the major-league strike," wrote Mike Potter in the next day's Durham *Herald-Sun*.

When that strike finally became a reality that night, on Friday, the twelfth of August, it was business as usual at the DAP. The Winston-Salem Spirits were in town for a weekend series that might presage a postseason play-off, provided that the Bulls quit fooling around in their lumbering pursuit of the second-half championship in the Southern Division, and that seemed to be the focus as another sellout crowd began gathering. Those who expected a huffy monologue over the public-address system from the loquacious Bob Guy were disappointed. "What else is new?" he said in an aside from his ground-level burrow beneath the home plate box seats, then proceeding to routinely announce the starting lineups.

It was another splendid night for baseball, but the Bulls' starting pitching failed them against the power-hitting Spirits, who were on their way to setting an all-time record for Carolina League home runs. The second start by right-hander Carey Paige, the newcomer up from Macon who had scattered four hits in five innings against the same club in his debut on the previous Sunday, blew up in his hands when Winston-Salem exploded for five runs in the third inning. He gave up three more runs in the fifth, failing to record an out before West came with the hook, and a late rally wasn't enough to overcome the early deficit. Marty had one of his more productive games of the year—a homer, two singles, two runs scored, two RBIs—but it was wasted, forgotten in the 9-6 loss.

Ichabod Crane took the mound for Winston-Salem the next night, with 6,120 crammed into every corner of the park, and he was a joy to behold for those fans who liked to disparage the radar-gun mentality. Will Brunson was his name, and he was a bespectacled stringbean from small-town Texas, six six and not likely to survive a windstorm. As it was with all of the Winston-Salem pitchers forced to work in a power hitter's haven, the home run ball had gotten him into some trouble during the season (one every seven innings), ballooning his ERA to 4.04, but he, like the Bulls' Roger Etheridge, was a control pitcher who knew how to change speeds and work the corners. Marty and the catcher Adrian Garcia would reach him for doubles on this night, Marty's shot to the gap in right being his one-hundredth hit of the year, but that was the extent of the damage; Brunson struck out ten and walked nobody in his eight innings of work, and four errors and some uninspired pitching by Mike D'Andrea and three relievers doomed the Bulls to an 8-1 defeat, their third straight loss. With twenty games left on the schedule, the Bulls were still six games ahead of Winston-Salem. Their magic number for clinching the second-half pennant was now fourteen (the total of Durham wins and Winston-Salem losses needed to sew it up), but that brought little solace to Matt West. He called them together afterward in the cramped clubhouse to remind them, not gently, that it ain't over 'til it's over.

It had been nearly a month since the Bulls had won an "ugly" game, one in which the opposition scored seven runs or more. That had occurred in mid-July at Prince William, in the last game before the break for the league all-star festivities, and since then they had won only when the pitching held up. In Sunday's game to end this set against Winston-Salem, they were about to lock up a 7-6 victory when Marty again had trouble with the same twisting ground ball near the bag that had handcuffed him during the opening home stand of the season. There were two outs and runners were at first and third when it came at him, hopping like a rabbit, ball and runner arriving at the bag simultaneously, and when he failed to smother it and make the force at second, the tying run crossed the plate. It was scored as a hit, benevolently, but it was soon forgotten. Raymond Nunez, who had been on a sustained binge ever since the Spanish-speaking Carlos Rios had been rushed in for special tutoring back in early July, and now led the club with a .281 average, looped a two-out, three-run homer over the billboards in right to win it 10-7. To hell with the big-league strike. The three games at Durham Athletic Park, held on the first weekend without major-league baseball, had attracted 16,081 fans.

In the thirteen games he had played since West's decision to bat him at the top of the order for the rest of the way, for better or for worse, Marty had hit better than at any point during the season. He had averaged .404, and the nine walks plus one hit by pitch, added to his nineteen hits in forty-seven official trips to the plate, put his on-base percentage at .508 during that stretch. His batting average for the season was now back up to .270, third on the club behind Nunez and Bobby Smith, and if this kept up there was every reason to believe he could finish at an impressive .280 in a league that had only six players averaging .300 or better. This was more like it, he was saying as the Bulls took a day off (he intended to dust off his golf clubs for a round at a public course) before gearing up for the last three weeks of the regular season.

CHAPTER 14

There would be only one more road trip of consequence during the regular season, the long haul to Wilmington and Frederick on the next-to-last week, so this little run down the road to Kinston for a three-game set in the middle of August was looked upon by the Bulls almost as a respite to break the monotony of a season that was about to run its course. The Kinston Indians had just broken a nine-game losing streak with a win over Wilmington at home on Sunday night, but they remained buried in the cellar of the Southern Division, eager to get this thing over with and go home for the winter. In the late-season shufflings within the Cleveland organization, they had lost some of their key players by way of promotion to Canton-Akron of the Class AA Eastern League (most notably, right-hander Daron Kirkreit, whose ERA of 2.68 had been second best in

the league). About the only force left on the club was Jon Nunnally, the outfielder who had beaten out Marty as Florida's ju-
nior-college player of the year back in '92 and now led Kinston
with seventeen homers and sixty-two RBIs. The Kinston fans,
not surprising, had all but lost interest by now.

Fifteen times the Bulls had gone through the routine of em-
barking on a road trip, so it was no big deal anymore. They ran
by the DAP at ten-thirty on this Tuesday morning to collect the
$45 per man for the three-day allotment of meal money and to
load their personal equipment bags in the cargo hold of the bus,
then raced back across town to leave their cars in the relative security of a parking lot at the Northgate Mall, which was well
lighted at night. The bus was right behind them, and they
slumped aboard at eleven o'clock for the ninety-eight-mile run
through flat fields of alfalfa and tobacco to the easternmost
point in the Carolina League; the nappers, like Marty, sprawled
out in the front seats with their pillows and Walkmans and paperback thrillers, the poker players gambling their fresh meal
money in the center of the bus, the Latins talking among themselves in the rear. Riding shotgun were Matt West and his
trainer, Jay Williams, the two of them conspiring over a laptop
computer for a report to be faxed back to Atlanta when they
reached the motel.

Groaning in low gear, the bus reached the motel at one o'-
clock. "Okay, listen up," said West, straddling the aisle up front.
"The bus leaves at four-thirty, and we'll dress at the park." WEL-
COME DURHAM BULLS, read the marquee in front of a Sheraton
on the edge of downtown Kinston, a sleepy little town on North
Carolina's sandy coastal plain, not fifty miles from the Atlantic
seaboard. "This place is literally the end of the line in the Carolina League," said Bill Slack, who had spent nearly half of his
adult life playing or managing or coaching in the league. When
the bus shuddered to a halt, he and Albert and West debarked,

followed by their young charges, and they all made a beeline to the front desk for room keys. By two o'clock, while the coaches sampled lunch in the motel dining room, the players walked across the asphalt parking lot shimmering in the midday heat to pig out at a Hardee's and then . . . to wait. Another numbing afternoon on the road lay ahead of them: napping, playing cards, revisiting Hardee's, aimlessly perusing free tabloid shoppers in the motel lobby. And to think: this Sheraton, with its well-appointed rooms and spacious lobby, was regarded as the poshest stop in the league.

"Yo, somebody hold Marty down," a voice rang through the bus as it rolled into the parking lot at the Kinston ballpark late in the afternoon. It was East Carolina Speedway Night at Grainger Stadium, with three gaudy stock cars parked in the concourse, their rear ends jacked up like cats in heat, and Marty and Roger Etheridge peered through the windows of the bus for a glimpse before the bus stopped and everybody piled off to enter the clubhouse and begin another day's work. Although they would miss the excitement of the big crowds at the DAP (only 1,598 would show up that night), they did appreciate the amenities awaiting them: a spacious carpeted clubhouse with stalls around the walls, plenty of showers, a large table in the center that was laden with slices of watermelon and oranges and cartons of fruit drinks. Kinston had been a member of the Carolina League off and on for nearly forty years, and the new local owners had recently spent upwards of $1 million to build the clubhouse and offices and generally refurbish the park. It was a neat little ballpark, better lighted than most; its only drawback was, as far as the players were concerned, unforgiving outfield walls built of concrete building blocks brightly decorated with advertising. When the Bulls took the field for their brief round of batting practice, Marty spent much of the time observing how batted balls ricocheted off the concrete fences like rockets.

He wouldn't need that information on this night, because his buddy Etheridge was on the mound. The lefty gave up a run in the first inning on a sacrifice fly by Jon Nunnally, but when he found he couldn't get his fastball over he simply went to his change-up and breaking stuff and was virtually untouchable, giving up two singles over six innings to win his fifth decision in six starts and lower his ERA to 0.88. The Bulls won it 5-4, with Tom Waldrop driving in two of the runs on a two-out single, but the signature moment in the game came in the eighth when Juan Williams launched an orbital homer over the triple tier of signs in center field. In the game before, the 10-7 win over Winston-Salem on Sunday, he had sailed one clear out of the DAP—possibly the longest shot ever hit there—but this one was downright awesome. "As Eastern North Carolina braces for a possible visit from the remnants of Tropical Storm Beryl later this week, fans at Grainger Stadium got a look last night at another devastating force of nature arriving from the Piedmont," the local baseball writer gushed in the next day's Kinston *Free Press*.

If Williams was becoming known for his moon shots, Marty was playing his game, too. He had batted in the leadoff spot that night, going hitless in four trips, but he left his mark in the fifth inning. Having worked his way around to third after drawing a walk, he chanced an ill-advised dash to the plate on a bouncer to the mound. The catcher—two inches taller and twenty pounds heavier—was braced for him, ball in hand, when Marty lowered his shoulder and drove his helmet into the catcher's breastbone. It was a vicious hit, delivered like a lead blocker laying out a linebacker on a toss sweep, and the crowd was hushed when the catcher, Mitch Meluskey, went flying through the air and landed on his back with a deathly thud. There were cheers when

Meluskey staggered to his feet and triumphantly held the ball above his head, bringing the out sign from the umpire, and as the dazed catcher was being led off to the hospital for observation, the crowd began raining boos on Marty. *That's baseball.* He didn't hang around, choosing instead to wait until he got to the dugout to dust himself off.

In the bar off the lobby at the Sheraton, with his ballplayers probably playing poker in their rooms on the second floor by now, Matt West, dressed in a polo shirt and black nylon wind pants and sneakers, was having a couple of beers before calling it a night. He had already faxed the obligatory game report back to the big house in Atlanta, a sort of detailed box score with commentary from him on the club's play in general and from Bill Slack on the pitching of Etheridge and the two Bulls relievers, and he was grinning, in spite of himself, about Marty's leveling the catcher at the plate. Flanking him were Jay Williams and Steve Barnes, the radio play-by-play man.

"He probably shouldn't have gone," he said, "but that's Marty."

"The catcher had twenty pounds on him," said Williams.

"And don't forget the equipment. That's another five, at least," Barnes said.

"Yeah, well, that doesn't much matter to the kid. He okay?"

Williams said, "He might have a headache. But, hey, he probably feels great."

West frowned. "That's just another example of Marty thinking he can fight his way out of any situation," he said. "A hopper to the mound, and he thinks he can score. Didn't have a prayer. Ah, well"—he gobbled a palmful of peanuts and washed them down with a swallow of beer—"better that than the other. Some of these kids with big bonuses wouldn't have *thought* about going. Why can't they go hard all the time, like Marty? Cal Ripken could take it easy, but he doesn't. Lou Gehrig could have taken it easy, but he didn't. I can't understand it when a kid doesn't run the ball out, just walks back to the dugout. These big bonuses can ruin some of 'em. They've got a great opportunity to go to the major leagues and make all of that money, but they won't even run out a ground ball. Can you believe it? They don't understand that their chances won't be there forever."

Not an hour after the Bulls' arrival at the motel that afternoon, the marquee had been changed to welcome a convention of realtors. Some of them had been in the lounge when West entered: middle-aged men, ties loosened and coats off, huddled at tables where they knocked down drinks and talked earnestly about real estate deals. Now, as the lights were being blinked to announce closing time, West dismounted from the bar stool and paid his tab and strolled toward the lobby. He shook his head when he saw Roger Etheridge shambling across the lobby toward the elevators, unkempt in his oyster boots and wrinkled jeans and an Auburn baseball cap, looking more like a shade-tree mechanic than the hottest pitcher in the Carolina League.

"There's so much for these kids to learn," he said, "and some of it doesn't have anything to do with baseball. I was telling some of 'em earlier in the year that when they get to double-A they'll have to wear a shirt with a collar. 'A *collar?*' one of 'em said. 'That's right,' I said, 'and when you get to Richmond you'll have to wear a jacket on the plane.' 'A *jacket?* Hell, Skip . . .' Well, Marty doesn't miss much. He'd been wearing jeans and those macho cowboy boots, you know, keeping up his image, but then one day he shows up to get on the bus, and there he is in a sharp polo shirt and some Duck Head shorts and a pair of Topsiders, like something out of a Land's End catalogue. He had that cock-eyed grin on his face and said, 'What do you think?' Marty picks up on stuff. We'll make a pro out of him yet."

• • •

Late the next morning, most of the players would board the bus and ride the mile to a mall for an hour's work on weights at a fitness center, under the eye of Jay Williams, followed by a lunch at the fast-food joint of their choosing, and as it turned out, that was about as productive as the day would get. There were fewer than twenty games remaining on the schedule, and the long season was beginning to wear on them, even if it did appear to be only a matter of time before they backed into the postseason play-offs. The tone seemed to be set for a long afternoon and evening of grumbling and minor insubordinations when the bus was idling, ready to leave for the ballpark at four-thirty, and a head count revealed that Jamie Arnold wasn't on board. West was about to give the word to leave without him when Arnold raced across the parking lot and boarded without a word, stuffing his shirttail in his jeans, ducking his head to avert the malevolent glare from his manager. The bonus baby had napped overlong, and on that note they rolled away.

Marty did his bit that night, getting two singles and a walk and a stolen base, but the Bulls got clobbered 9-1, with boiling thunderclouds holding the crowd to only 826 of the faithful scattered in the metal folding chairs that served as box seats. The hapless Indians teed off on Jeff Bock, who gave up seven runs on five hits and four walks in an eight-run fourth inning, taking his sixth straight loss. The Bulls came up with only six hits and struck out eleven times against four pitchers, but what was more disconcerting to West was their surly attitude. Several of those strikeouts came on called third strikes, most of them loudly protested by the Durham batters, which led to an ongoing dialogue between the Bulls and the home plate umpire.

The last straw came on the last at bat of the game, in the top of the ninth, when Raymond Nunez took a pitch on the outside corner. Hearing the umpire bellow, "Strike *twooo*," he looked back in pained disbelief, flashed a dark scowl at the umpire, and threw up his right hand in disgust as he walked away from the batter's box. Everybody in the box seats behind the plate could see the umpire's mask working up and down as he chewed out Nunez, who peered down at West in the third-base coach's box as though looking for a second opinion but found no comfort there. With his manager glowering at him and the umpire letting him have it, Nunez petulantly stepped back into the box, dug a new hole in the dirt, and promptly took a called third strike to end the game. West came charging to the plate, not to argue with the umpire but to roughly lead his player away, and then he followed the umpire all the way to the umpires' clubhouse door up under the stands behind the visitors' dugout—holding his temper, doing more listening than talking, conciliatory. Umpires will allow a little bitching on plays in the field, but arguing balls and strikes is not only against the rules but also the surest way to ask for trouble on the next at bat.

They had been bad boys, and they knew it. They dressed in silence and quickly boarded the bus, ignoring the half dozen young women who had been waiting in the shadows cast by the faint lights of the parking lot. West had spent so much time talking with the umpire that he didn't have time to shower and change, and he was still in uniform when he got on the bus. He broke the glum silence by standing beside the driver and giving out the routine instructions for the final day of the trip—checkout time was eleven A.M.; three rooms would be held open until the bus left the motel at four-thirty; they would dress at the park—then taking his seat with a thud. The bus was as quiet as a tomb when the driver closed the door and found low gear and began the slow drive through the eerie streets of Kinston, boarded up like a ghost town. Not a peep came from the players shrouded in darkness in the bowels of the bus.

Suddenly, when they reached the motel, West jumped to his

feet and exploded. "I'm getting sick and fucking tired of hearing you pussies whine," he said, the veins on his neck and forehead about to burst. "How about if every time you fucking kick the ball or hit a fucking pop-up we just call it a fucking ball to get you off the fucking hook? These fat bastards [umpires] are fucking gonna remember this." Dead silence. He dropped his voice only to say, almost fatherly, "You're better than this," but then resumed his harangue. "I'm fucking tired of looking at you pussies. It's time you fucking grew up or get out of the fucking game . . ." The door flew open and West made his exit, stage right, trotting across the grass in full uniform and taking the outside stairs three at a time to his room on the third floor. The players, wishing to give West a wide berth, took their time about following him into the motel.

It didn't end there. Both Hardee's and the motel coffee shop had been closed when the club returned, the game having run a bit late, so there was an order for pizza to be delivered to the motel. Then, shortly after midnight, there was an irate call to the front desk from a woman who had unfortunately drawn a room on the second floor. If "those boys" in Room 201 didn't "shut up," she was going to call the cops. The desk called Jay Williams, who called Matt West, who threw on some clothes and flew down the stairs and found that the catcher Adrian Garcia and the pitcher Mike D'Andrea were hosting a poker game that had blossomed into a boisterous rumble spreading up and down the hallway. Marty and Tom Waldrop, fast asleep directly across the hall, cracked open their door and just as quickly closed it. "It's always the pitchers who aren't working," Marty would say the next morning. "They've got too much time on their hands." The matter would be addressed at the next caucus of the players' Kangaroo Court, trainer Jay Williams presiding, with proceeds from the resulting fines earmarked for the season-ending team party, which was fast approaching.

• • •

Raymond Nunez paid for his sins by being scratched from the lineup for Thursday night's getaway game, replaced at first base by the little switch-hitting utility infielder Nelson Paulino. Whether the game would be played had seemed doubtful even as they loaded their belongings into the hold of the bus at the motel, and when they arrived at the ballpark they found that the field was covered with a tarpaulin. Menacing low black clouds were scudding over the park, headed eastward toward the Atlantic coast, almost certain to return. "We see it all the time around here," said North Johnson, Kinston's young general manager, loosening a hand-painted tie dizzy with baseballs as he monitored the weather on a computer screen in his office. "The clouds run to the coast, fill up with moisture, then turn around and come back to do some serious business." Sure enough, the rains came and the game was officially canceled at eight o'clock. The Bulls quickly changed out of their uniforms and boarded the bus, assured of a late dinner on their own turf that night.

How many times had Bill Slack found himself hunkering down like this into a bus seat for a nighttime ride with a bunch of rambunctious kids? He was a sixty-one-year-old with snow white hair now, in his forty-fourth year of professional baseball, and his own four children were all older than any of these Durham Bulls. His record as the winningest manager in the history of the Carolina League (913 wins in twelve years, covering five separate stints with Winston-Salem) wasn't likely to be broken, since major-league organizations moved managers around nearly every year in the new scheme of things. This gig as pitching coach at Durham would continue for at least two more years, he hoped, before he finally retired. A native of Ontario, Canada (and still a Canadian citizen), he had been calling Winston-Salem home for more than thirty years. Whenever the Bulls played at the older towns in the league, such as Kinston, there was invariably a hardy group of old-timers waiting for him at the

park, to sit in the stands and talk of seasons past. Indeed, a fifti-
eth-anniversary Carolina League baseball card set had just gone
on sale, and Bill Slack's card was one of the thirty-five in it, right
along with the five CL players who had gone on to the Baseball
Hall of Fame.

His career as a manager and coach had followed twelve undistinguished years as a utility infielder and pitcher in the Boston
Red Sox' farm system, from High Point–Thomasville of the
Class D North Carolina State League in 1952 to the Seattle
Rainiers of the AAA Pacific Coast League in '63. "I was just a little guy, five-foot-nine, but I could do double duty in a time when
there were sixteen-man rosters," he was saying over the drone of
the bus and the slapping of windshield wipers. "I wasn't but
eighteen when I signed and they sent me to the Birmingham
Barons in double-A. I was way over my head there, but I hung
around long enough to see Jimmy Piersall get sent down and go
nuts. It was in the book and the movie [*Fear Strikes Out*] about
him shooting an umpire with a water pistol, getting kicked out
of half a dozen games in about a month, all of that stuff. One
night he'd been kicked out of the game and these kids in the
bleachers started yelling, 'Gimme a P, gimme an I, gimme an
E . . . Whaddya got? PIER-sall,' and we looked out there and
saw Jimmy right in the middle of 'em, leading the cheers." One
night at Sulphur Dell in Nashville, with its right-field fence only
250 feet from home plate, he was called on to protect a big Birmingham lead but lost it without getting anybody out in the ninth
inning. "The next day, the guy who'd hit about a five-hundred-
foot homer off of me to end the game came around asking,
'Where's Slack?' I raised my hand and he said, 'Slack, you still
owe us three outs,' and laughed and kept on walking."

"Sulphur Dell was some ballpark," he was told.

"This short porch at the DAP is nothing."

"The Nashville Vols were built around it."

He smiled at the memory. "All lefties. Big guys who could up-percut and lift the ball over the fence and the chicken-wire screen they had on top of that. The Dell was in a hole—used to be a sulphur mine there—and they'd bomb that ice plant behind the screen with home runs. Their batting averages were four hundred at home and two hundred on the road, because in Atlanta and Birmingham and everywhere else, they were just hitting pop flies to short right. Bob Lennon hit sixty-four homers one year for the Vols, poking 'em over that fence."

He had seen more home run balls than he cared to remember, in this year with the Bulls, who were still leading the league in homers allowed, even though Matt Murray was gone and Jamie Arnold seemed to have it under control. "At least these kids have got somebody to help 'em," he said. Every day at noon when the club was at home, even at his age, Bill Slack was in uniform at the DAP, meandering down to the bull pen to get in some early work with one of his pitchers. "There wasn't much teaching when I played. There were a lot of veterans in the minors then, and they wouldn't help a rookie unless they were asked. You learned the hard way, like I did that night in Nashville."

"Maybe that's the best way."

"Could be," he said. "About all you can do is tell 'em what's going to happen if they throw the wrong pitch to the wrong guy at the wrong time. Trouble is, they don't believe it until they see it. Some things never change."

There had been no poker game on the bus that night. The Bulls knew they had pushed Matt West's patience to the limit on this little jaunt. They sat up straight in their seats as the bus rolled onto the brightly lit streets of downtown Durham, closed for the night, and they craned their necks for a peek at the ominous dark silhouette of the new ballpark now rising on the edge of town. Soon the DAP and this season would be history.

CHAPTER 15

W hen they checked in at the DAP on Friday afternoon to open a weekend series against the Salem Buccaneers, the penultimate home stand in the fifty-year history of the ballpark, the Bulls found a celebrity of sorts waiting for them: Jimy Williams, third-base coach for the parent Braves, a familiar figure to the Durham players and fans because of his nightly exposure on TBS. Like all big-league managers and coaches, Williams was caught in the middle of the strike, neither union nor management, and in order to keep them occupied, the Braves had ordered their coaches and even manager Bobby Cox onto the road to visit the various clubs in the farm system. So Williams suited up in his white Braves uniform and pitched a round of batting practice, then submitted to interviews with Mike Potter of the Durham *Herald-Sun* and

Bulls broadcaster Steve Barnes before settling into a box seat behind the plate. "I've heard about some of these guys," he said, "but that's about it. I've been a little busy, you know?" He seemed a mite surprised when fans came over to get him to autograph their scorecards, chief among them being the indefatigable Martie Byron, and he had leaned back to finish a hot dog and watch some baseball when the rains came and forced a suspension of the game with the Bulls leading 1-0 after two innings.

Over lunch Saturday at the Golden Corral, with a double-header scheduled for that night, Marty talked about everything but the strike, something he still found to be incomprehensible. He had done some laundry after the trip to Kinston, called home, diligently lifted weights at the Spa, and checked his mail. (A letter had arrived from the league office, advising that he was being fined only $25 for his recent ejection, and since it was manageable he would pay it himself rather than accept West's offer, made in the heat of battle, to cover it.) He was as tired as he had been all summer, especially his throwing arm, "but I don't want to sit, because I don't want to hit two-sixty." He had heard that Tony Graffanino had a sore arm and a bad back and was in a late-season slide at Greenville, and he was very much aware that the big club wants to know how a guy responds down the home stretch. "Like they say, I've got all winter to rest."

"You'll pour concrete again, I guess."

"Looks like it," he said.

"That's not exactly a rest."

"It's a rest from baseball. They asked me if I wanted to play winter ball, but I said no. The Arizona League runs from October twenty-seventh to February eleventh. It's for guys who haven't played much anyway. I want to be fresh for spring training. Bobby [Smith] played winter ball last year, and when he showed up at West Palm he was dragging. Besides, I've always looked at Trenton as a kind of haven. Like a bear going into hibernation."

"Anything new there with Nikki?"

"Same old same-old. She'd like to see me give up this 'foolishness.' "

All signs pointed toward the end of the season now. He and his roommates, John Simmons and Tom Waldrop, had already arranged for their phone service to be cut off on the last day of August, when they would be playing at Frederick; since they couldn't be sure when the last game would be played, because of the probability of making the play-offs, they would be paying rent day-to-day at the Willowdale Apartments come September.

"Hey," he said, brightening, "the Gators have been picked number one in the preseason."

"Football already."

"Can you believe it? Duke opens here two weeks from today."

"I saw where Florida fired its baseball coach."

"It's gotten like pro ball, with the pressure to win. In fact, the guy who would've been my hitting coach at Florida is gonna be here tomorrow, interviewing for the job at North Carolina."

"No second-guessing about turning pro instead of being a Gator?"

"Nah. I'd just be finishing my rookie year if I'd done that. I would've gotten a bigger bonus, that's for sure, but I'd be headed for Macon or Durham in ninety-five instead of Greenville."

"You feel confident about Greenville for next year?"

"I think so. Bill [Slack] told me the other day, 'You'll never see Durham again.' It's a great town, and I wouldn't mind playing in the new ballpark here, but, hey . . ."

The largest crowd in the history of the DAP (6,534) was on hand that night to watch the completion of the suspended game

and the playing of another between the Bulls and Salem. The
Bulls won the first 3-1, when the smooth young left-hander recently called up from Macon, Aaron Turnier, allowed only a
homer to Chance Sanford, the Salem second baseman who had
won out over Marty on the all-star team. Salem took the seven-
inning nightcap 2-0, with Marty slicing doubles to the gap in
right and down the left-field line for two of the Bulls' three hits.
But the most gratifying moment for Marty came in the first inning of the second game when he ranged far to his left and five
feet back on the outfield grass to spear a ground ball, pivot, and
gun down his nemesis, Sanford, at first base. He and Sanford
were both hitting around .270, but Sanford had thirty errors to
Marty's sixteen, and to say that robbing Sanford of a hit did his
heart good would be an understatement. Marty still smarted
from being left off the all-star team.

The Braves' Jimy Williams wasn't there for Sunday night's finale of the season against Salem, nor was the tail of the mechanical bull atop the fences in right (stolen for the third time that
season by, it was presumed, fraternity boys from the local colleges), nor were most of the fans. In spite of another appearance
by the Famous Chicken, only 2,335 showed up on a rainy night
to see Jamie Arnold and John Simmons shut down the Buccaneers on seven hits and nine strikeouts, for a 6-2 victory that put
the Bulls' magic number at six to win the Southern Division's
second half. It had been a productive weekend for Marty—three
doubles to go along with two bases on balls, against only one
strikeout, plus a couple of RBIs from the leadoff position—and
he now led the club in walks, stolen bases, and, most important
of all for a top-of-the-order guy, on-base percentage.

The traditional season's-end team party was held at a seafood
restaurant in Durham on Monday night, an off-day, financed for
the most part by fines collected during the raucous meetings of
the Kangaroo Court. At least once a month the players had

gathered in the runway beneath the grandstand, amid the rakes and hoses and other groundskeeping paraphernalia, to assess penalties for a wide variety of sins. It was stupid kid's stuff, naturally, and all in good sport. Marty was docked for the time, on the opening home stand, when he made the wide turn around first and was motoring toward second, thinking double, only to find that the third baseman had made a backhanded stab and thrown him out at first. The now-departed Matt Murray was fined six dollars for fouling the air of the crapper on the bus during the club's first road trip. Nunez had to pay for bitching to the umpire that night at Kinston and causing West to go ballistic. Anything deemed unprofessional was dealt with—forgetting the number of outs during a game, failing to advance a runner, giving up an unpardonable home run (yo, Arnold and Murray!), missing a sign, taking the field on a Sunday wearing other than the white Sunday cap—and the coffers had filled to the point that the beer and the food were guaranteed not to run out during a party that howled far into the night. There were no arrests.

The Frederick Keys then came to town for a three-game set in the middle of the week. They had been the hottest club in the league during the second half and held a slim lead over Wilmington, which meant that if they kept it up they would force a play-off with the Blue Rocks to determine who would represent the Northern Division in the postseason play-offs; but once more they were swept by the Bulls at the DAP, which made it seven straight losses for them in Durham, and would never see first place again. The weather had cleared and the crowds were back—15,551 saw the three games, splendid for a midweek series in late August with no special promotional nights—and they saw superb minor-league baseball, the three games being decided by a total of four runs. Marty again was in the middle of everything from the leadoff spot, getting four hits and two walks, scoring three times, and anchoring an infield defense that had never looked surer.

Tuesday night's game was won 6-5 when the squat reserve catcher Adrian Garcia, batting .230 in just 150 at bats, looped a DAP Special over the right-field wall in the bottom of the eighth inning. It was Roger Etheridge's turn to star on Wednesday, a 4-2 Bulls victory, when he had a perfect game going through five innings and turned it over to the bull pen after walking the lead-off man in the eighth. On Thursday night it was time for heroics from the Bulls' other catcher, David Toth, who had been sharing duties with Garcia since Brad Rippelmeyer went down with back surgery in early July. The Bulls were down 3-2 in the bottom of the ninth, but Garcia evened the score with a pinch-hit homer, and then Toth came up with Raymond Nunez on first with a walk and doubled him home for the winning run. The Bulls' magic number for clinching the second-half championship of their division now stood at two, with eleven games left to play. Only an unimaginable disaster would keep them out of the play-offs.

Marty was hitting .375 for the twenty-one games he had played in August, and committed only two errors in that stretch. Since being installed at the top of the order on the first day of the month, he had seen his batting average climb twenty points, to .276, and if he continued at this pace he would easily reach the magical .280 that West had said would constitute "a hell of a season" for him. His body might have been aching early the next morning when they parked at the Northgate Mall lot and got on the bus for their last road trip of the regular season—seven games at Wilmington and Frederick—but the heart was more than willing. Stowed into the hold of the bus, along with their equipment bags, was a case of champagne. Maybe he would get the championship ring he coveted after all.

• • •

While the Bulls took batting practice, Jay Williams lugged the bubbly into the clubhouse at Wilmington's sleek new ballpark, where overflow crowds had been the rule ever since the big-league strike had shut down baseball thirty miles away at Philadelphia, and though the Blue Rocks were the most formidable opposition in the league—the pitchers who would be going up against Durham over the weekend, Mike Bovee and Bart Evans and Jim Pittsley, were one-two-three in strikeouts, with a composite ERA hovering at 3.00—the Bulls had in their grasp the first Durham championship since the 1989 club of Steve Avery. They took the field that Friday night at Wilmington with 6,237 fans filling the grandstand and the bleachers and even the glassed-in sky boxes, fully expecting a celebration afterward. It would be Jamie Arnold against Mike Bovee.

Oh, lads, please. With the score tied at 2-all and two outs in the bottom of the eleventh of a game that looked like it might go on forever, Adrian Garcia let a swinging third strike elude him, allowing the batter to reach first. The runner was off on the next pitch, and Garcia's throw to nail him at second wound up in center field. Backing up the play was Damon Hollins, and when he retrieved the ball and tried to head off the runner at third, his throw sailed into the dugout, enabling the Blue Rocks runner to trot across the plate with the winning run. Close, but no champagne. Matt West needed no reminder that these were, after all, kids still learning to play a very difficult game. The Little Rascals came to mind.

It was only a matter of time, though, and they finally clinched the division and popped open the champagne the next night, when Julio Trapaga, of all people—back from the DL, batting .180, sharing shortstop with Manny Jimenez—cracked two doubles to highlight a seven-run third inning, and a committee of pitchers held on for a 7-6 victory before an even larger crowd. They would go down meekly on Sunday night, losing 7-0 on a complete game five-hitter by Jim Pittsley, but now the waiting was over. As they motored over to Frederick to end the road season with four games against the Orioles' farm club, the Keys, Matt West and Bill Slack sat in the front of the bus and began juggling their pitching rotation to ensure that their best arms, Etheridge and Arnold, would be ready for the play-offs.

Suddenly, Marty couldn't buy a hit. He had gone 2-for-15 in the three games at Wilmington, four times hitting ropes that got no higher than four feet off the ground and were caught before he could leave the batter's box, and it got no better at Frederick. He was rested during the first game but then picked up only one single in twelve official appearances at the plate (he added two walks but made two errors). He couldn't believe it: 3-for-27 in his six games up North, after the great August he had been having, and now it was but a dream that he might finish the season at .280. The Bulls lost three of the four games at Frederick, making it a 2-5 road trip, and they quickly dressed in silence after losing the last to the Keys on a single with the bases loaded in the bottom of the ninth. None too perkily, they slumped onto the bus for the long ride through the night. The last Bulls team ever to play at the DAP was on its way home to close the books on the season and the historic little ballpark. Now, finally, the end was at hand.

CHAPTER 16

Nearly six months had passed since Marty trotted onto the auxiliary fields constituting the Braves' minor-league complex at West Palm Beach to open spring training—pale skinned, rusty from the winter's layoff, anxious about how he might fare at Durham—and those who knew him best recognized the subtle changes that had taken place. "Marty learned a lot about the game," said his father, "but he learned about himself, too, and that was probably the biggest thing." He had played in nearly three hundred professional games now, with slightly more than a thousand official at bats, and he had seen enough ups and downs to have developed the stoicism of one who had seen war. No one could describe a twenty-two-year-old Class A second baseman as grizzled, but he was on his way. He had long since passed the point where baseball had become, in the words of Willie Stargell, "a way of life," and to that he had added a layer of armor. There was no doubt now that the best thing that had ever happened to him was what had appeared, at the time, to be the worst: the month of June, when the kid who had never seen a pitcher he couldn't hit had batted only .169. He had, as they say, seen the elephant and heard the owl, and nothing could harm him now.

The schedule called for Durham and Kinston to play four games on the Labor Day weekend, ending the regular season, before the Bulls hosted Winston-Salem in the first game of the Southern Division play-offs on Monday. Sunday's doubleheader would end it for Kinston, already a cinch for last place in the division, and the Indians players who owned cars had driven them to Durham so they could begin the long drive to their homes (three of them were Californians) immediately after the last out. With the play-offs his primary consideration, Matt West would use only Mike D'Andrea of his top pitchers in the Kinston series, giving starting assignments to those not likely to figure in the play-offs unless the Bulls took it to the full eight games.

Torrential rains forced an early cancellation of the doubleheader scheduled for Friday, the second day of September, setting the stage for an orgiastic ending to professional baseball at the DAP: doubleheaders beginning at twilight Saturday and at two o'clock Sunday afternoon. The fans of Durham had set an all-time season-attendance record the year before, with 305,692 in sixty-five home dates, when the "final season at the DAP" was heavily promoted. Now, in this *final* final season, the Bulls' front office felt it unnecessary to say anything further about the last go-around at the DAP. *Open the gates and they will come* was the thinking of general manager Peter Anlyan. How right he was.

Even though rain clouds had been roiling in the skies over Durham for much of Saturday and Duke was opening its football season less than five miles away, a crowd that would swell to nearly thirty-five hundred had queued up early for the last week-end of baseball at the DAP. West had picked D'Andrea to start the first of the two seven-inning games, which would give the stocky fireballing right-hander sufficient rest to pitch a third and deciding game in the division play-offs if it came to that. D'Andrea was looking good when he took to the mound, pop-ping the mitt of catcher David Toth, but the one mistake he made would eventually cost him the game. With two runners on base and nobody out in the top of the second inning, Kinston's Mitch Meluskey, the catcher whom Marty had sent to the hospi-tal two weeks earlier in the home plate collision, sailed a homer out of the park.

Kinston's lead remained at 3-0 and the Bulls were getting nowhere after five innings against a six-four, 240-pound left-hander named Charles York. Then, in the sixth, the Indians were threatening to put the game away. They had runners at first and third, with two outs and a dangerous RBI man at the plate. Bearing down, D'Andrea induced a high pop foul into no-man's-land, a ball that at first appeared to be headed for the bleacher seats behind first base. Neither Juan Williams in right nor Ray-mond Nunez at first made a serious move for the ball. The fans in the bleachers were craning their necks and squinting into the lights, trying to locate the ball, and kids with baseball gloves were rushing to the fence with visions of snagging a souvenir. The home plate umpire was already fumbling for a new ball in the pouch cinched around his waist, and the runners were idly watching the flight of the ball as they walked back to their bases.

But here came Marty. A ball like that *always* sails back toward the playing field, often causing severe embarrassment to inexpe-rienced first and third basemen who misjudge the drift. The mo-ment it went up, Marty ducked his head and began a mad dash toward the bull pen about one hundred feet from his position deep behind second base. As he crossed the foul line at full speed, now only twenty feet from the long aluminum bench, he looked into the lights and saw that the ball was, indeed, curving back toward the field. On and on he came, his feet pedaling furiously, his glove going up. The half dozen Bulls pitchers suddenly scattered like frightened quail when it became obvious that Marty was soon to enter their midst. With his glove outstretched, he went airborne. "I got it!" were his last words. There was a faint *smack* as he gloved the ball, a sickening *thunk* as he slammed into one of the metal posts anchoring the bench to the ground, a shout of "Out!" from the base umpire, trailing the play and throwing up his right fist . . . and deathly silence from the crowd.

Marty lay there on his belly, motionless, still holding onto the ball, for nearly a minute. The fans were on their feet, expecting the worst, as Jay Williams rushed out to the bull pen, his fanny pack jiggling. "Don't move!" he said to Marty, going to his knees and crouching over him like a battlefield corpsman, checking for broken bones. The pitchers who had scattered now surged back and formed a knot around Marty and the trainer, hearts in their throats, and the other Bulls came trotting up to join them. The Kinston players had already gone to the dugout for their gloves and were taking up their positions in the field when Marty finally staggered to his feet, groggy and disoriented, hatless, the front of his uniform stained green. "I get him?" Marty slurred to Matt West. "You got him, kid," said West. The longest sustained applause of the season rolled through the DAP as Marty shook his head to clear it, brushed himself off, and then, with Jay Williams at one elbow and his buddy Tom Waldrop at the other, began to walk gingerly toward the clubhouse.

It was an ignominious but altogether fitting end to Marty's regular season. With two runners on and two outs, in a game that had absolutely no meaning, he had come perilously close to breaking his neck in pursuit of a foul ball. It was the moment that Marty's champions throughout the Braves' organization, especially Bobby Dews, had always feared; that the kid's aggressiveness was going to get him maimed or killed. He was loaded into a car and rushed to a hospital for X rays. The Bulls scored a couple of runs in the bottom of the seventh but came up short, 3-2, and they were taking the field for the second game when Marty returned to the ballpark. The X rays had found nothing wrong. Jay Williams wrapped his left shoulder in an ice pack and Marty watched from the dugout as the Bulls got a two-run DAP Special from Damon Hollins in the first inning and held on to win 3-1. He spent a long and sleepless night at the Willowdale, icing his shoulder and popping aspirin.

Sunday morning broke cool but sunny, with scant clouds over Durham, a perfect day for baseball. When Marty crawled out of bed on that last day of the regular season, he felt as though he had been hit by a truck; the aching in his left shoulder reminded him of those mornings after being sacked once too often as quarterback for the Trenton High Fighting Tigers. But, hey, this was the day of the grand finale at the DAP, in many minds the mother church of minor-league baseball, and he wanted to be in on it. He filled a bowl with cereal, swallowed some more aspirin, drove away to the park, and checked in with Jay Williams in the training room well before noon. He was told there was no way he would play that day; he should save it for the play-offs; but he was in denial. Williams and West could only cluck and shake their heads, not without a smidgen of awe, as Marty suited up and went onto the field. He stretched, he ran sprints, he took ground balls, he swung a bat, he presented his case. No go, said West. You sit.

Without any special promotion and to no one's surprise, the largest crowd in the fifty-six-year history of the DAP showed up that day to say farewell to the park. The attendance was announced as 6,636, but nearly ten thousand eventually came through the gates, those extra fans drifting in off the surrounding streets when the gates were thrown open during the second game, just checking in to say they had been there. In the final season at the DAP, the Bulls drew 259,758, third in the league behind Frederick (344,563) and Wilmington (335,024), an average of nearly four thousand per date. Also in attendance were four players who had been with the Bulls earlier in the season before being promoted to Greenville—Kevin Grijak, Mike Warner, Darrell May, Hector Roa—and, having finished their regular season on Saturday night in Jacksonville, they were biding their time until the G-Braves opened the Southern League play-offs on Monday night against the Carolina Mudcats in nearby Zebulon.

Some little touches were added to the pregame ceremonies to mark the occasion. As a souvenir, the paying fans received five-by-seven-inch ticket stubs. Bob Guy didn't get maudlin in his pregame announcements but did work in a few words about "this fine ballpark, with its idiosyncracies," and applauded the faithful for "making the Durham Bulls one of the greatest minor-league franchises of all time." As he spoke, a former member of the grounds crew who had driven many miles for this moment was raking the area around the plate while his infant daughter rode in a carriage strapped to his back. Both clubs were introduced and lined up down the baselines, play-off style; the Durham mayor, Sylvia Kerchoff, was given the ball after throwing out the first pitch and was told to safeguard it until she threw out the first pitch the next April to christen the new ballpark.

Finally, Matt West bounded out of the dugout and stepped to a microphone to present some special awards to the players. The most valuable player, to no one's surprise, was the young center fielder Damon Hollins. Best pitcher, in spite of his 9-10 record and 4.22 ERA, was Mike D'Andrea. Something called the Community Service Award went to Jamie Arnold, the pitcher, for always being available for public relations chores ranging from the Bid on a Bull date auction to a fashion show. The players had come out of the dugout as they were announced, to accept a plaque and a handshake from West and mild applause from the fans. Then West said, "Finally, we have the Team Spirit Award." He paused and cleared his throat. "This kid almost killed himself last night to catch a foul ball in a game some might say didn't mean anything, and now he's mad at me because he thinks he ought to be playing today. The thing about Marty Malloy is, there's no such thing as a game that doesn't mean anything . . ." Leaving the dugout in his little pigeon-toed trot, gingerly holding his left arm at his side, Marty got almost as big a hand as he had gotten the night before when he staggered off the field.

West's disclaimer on Marty's behalf aside, these two games meant nothing in the overall scheme of things. The Bulls had their minds on the play-offs, and the Kinston Indians were merely fulfilling their obligations, their minds already on the roads to home. "Now, Kevin, I don't want to see you smoking that thing," Retta Law chided to Kevin Grijak, who sat behind home plate wearing Ray-Bans and his old "Texas tan" Bulls cap, smiling cockily, clenching in his flashing teeth a Hav-a-Tampa cigar still in its cellophane wrap. As the Bulls took the field to a standing ovation, Marty slumped toward the bull pen to take up residence on the same bench he had nearly dislodged from its moorings the night before.

Partly because he was saving his best pitchers for the play-offs and partly out of a sense of drama, West had chosen as his starter in the first of the two seven-inning games the kid with the deepest personal connections to the DAP: Jeff Bock, the former Bulls batboy whose grandfather's ashes had been scattered on the mound and whose father had been the club's general manager when the Bulls returned to baseball in 1980. It had been a long year for Bock, a rangy kid (six five, two hundred pounds) who had been signed out of a Braves tryout camp right there at the DAP slightly more than a year earlier. His numbers were the worst on the Durham staff: 3-8, an ERA of 6.27, an opponents' batting average of .305. But what the hell; he was a likeable kid, like a favored nephew to such regular patrons as Tinker Parnell, and shouts of encouragement greeted him as the first Kinston batter stepped in.

A part of Bock's problem was that he had too many pitches and was a master of none—fastball, curve, sinker, slider, change-up—but the Braves' instructors could wait until spring training to work on that. (Larry Jaster, the pitching coach at Macon, once told of going to the bull pen to check out a young pitcher who had just joined the club. "I've got nine pitches," the kid said. "Not anymore, you don't," Jaster told him.) Bock admitted to having butterflies before the game, quite understandably, but he also had all of the intangibles going for him.

The kid was brilliant against a club that had gotten seven earned runs off him in three innings just two weeks earlier at Kinston. This time around, getting three early runs from his teammates (Miguel Correa, batting leadoff in place of Marty, scored two of them on two doubles and a triple), he allowed only three singles, struck out four, and walked only one. Seven innings or no, it was only the second complete-game shutout pitched by the Bulls staff all season long. When the Bulls went quietly in the second game, getting only four hits in a 2-0 shutout, it was thus recorded for posterity that the last Bulls regular-season victory at the DAP was rung up by a local boy.

And so the long season was over. The fans lingered for a while after the last out in the second game, some rushing down to the

Bulls' clubhouse to gather autographs, but most of them simply standing pensively for a last long gaze at the brightly painted outfield fences and the fading green grass of early September. There was a plan to transfer home plate and the mechanical bull to the new park (the bull to be enclosed in glass as protection from the frat boys), but for the nonce both the plate and the bull would be needed for the play-offs. The players on both clubs gathered up their equipment, some of them meeting on the field for a handshake and good wishes for the winter, then drifted toward the showers. Marty went out for dinner that night with Grijak and May and the others who had been promoted to Greenville during the season, to pick their brains about conditions in the Southern League. Tony Graffanino had batted an even .300 and led the G-Braves in stolen bases and was right on schedule, as the Braves' second baseman of the future, to move up to triple-A Richmond and clear the way for Marty to remain a step behind him on the organizational chart.

Even though his remake at the plate had not been complete, Marty had probably earned a promotion to Class AA for the '95 season. His slide in the last seven games had cost him dearly— he had gone 3-for-29 and made three errors in that span—but his final batting average of .264 held some promising figures. He wound up leading the club in on-base percentage, was tied with Bobby Smith for the lead in stolen bases, with eighteen (although he had been caught stealing twelve times), and was second in bases on balls (behind the free-swinging Juan Williams, of all people), with fifty-two. His ratio of one strikeout every 6.2 at bats was the best of the regular players and the best of his pro career. With every game he had proven himself to be the classiest defensive second baseman in the league; and, most important to everybody in the organization from Matt West to Bobby Dews, he had been the catalyst on the club—its driving force, its heart, its character. The kid had come to play some ball, and he had accomplished that and much more.

The postseason Carolina League all-star team had been announced in the papers on that Sunday morning of the last regular-season game, and not a single Durham player was on it. At the time of the balloting, Marty was outhitting his main competition, Prince William's Essex "Gas" Burton and Salem's Chance Sanford (Marty was at .276, Sanford at .274, Burton at .270), but his defensive work wasn't enough to make the voters forget Sanford's nineteen home runs and Burton's sixty-six stolen bases. The only mention of Durham in the postseason honors was Jay Williams's being named trainer of the year. The all-star team was dominated by players from Wilmington and Frederick, who had been the strongest clubs in the league throughout the season, and if any conclusion could be drawn from this it was that Matt West had done a hell of a job in his first year as a manager. The Bulls had finished the first half with the worst record in the league, 28-40, and turned around to go 38-30 after the break, finishing six and a half games ahead of Winston-Salem to win the second-half championship and force a play-off.

The position players almost certain to move up to AA Greenville the next year, along with Marty, were Damon Hollins, Bobby Smith, and Raymond Nunez. Hollins, who had turned twenty in the middle of the summer, had played a sensational center field and led the Bulls in most of the power categories at the plate (.270, twenty-three homers, eighty-eight RBI) and was now being regarded as the Braves' organization's best young prospect. Smith had become a spider at third base, in spite of his numerous errors, and his offensive numbers across the board were making him a long shot as the Braves' third baseman of the future; he finished at .266 with a dozen homers, seventy-one RBIs, and eighteen stolen bases in twenty-five attempts. The dark horse was Nunez, the moody Dominican first baseman, who had gone from only seven homers in '93 at

Macon to seventeen this year; he led the Bulls with a .276 batting average and was second to Hollins in slugging percentage. Among the pitchers who were with the Bulls at the end, those with the brightest future seemed to be the starters Jamie Arnold, Mike D'Andrea, and Roger Etheridge, along with the stumpy left-handed reliever Carl Schutz, who had rung up eighty-one strikeouts in fifty-three innings and tied an all-time Durham record with twenty saves.

Marty's roommates, Tom Waldrop and John Simmons, were left in limbo. Waldrop, particularly, was in a cold sweat. He would be twenty-five when spring camp opened the following season, with a trio of promising young outfielders coming up from Macon and breathing down his neck (Andre King, Jermaine Dye, and the redoubtable Wonderful Terrific Monds III), and he had batted only .215. It had been a feast-or-famine year for him: platooning with Juan Williams in right field and in the DH role, striking out nearly once every three at bats, producing runs in droves when he was on a hot streak, then returning to the bench to smoulder. Simmons's ERA had ballooned from 2.66 at Macon to 4.39 in the Carolina League, and he would be twenty-four when he reported to West Palm Beach for spring training in '95, but he had some things going for him: he was big and strong, he was intelligent, and he was a left-handed reliever.

There was one other, larger matter to be considered during this summer when the major-league players decided to go on strike. The Bulls had been averaging around thirty-eight hundred fans per game at the DAP, but that average jumped to 5,061 during the ten dates played poststrike, from August 12 to the end. There was a great anger across the land about this strike, one that ultimately would cause the first cancellation of a World Series in ninety years, and what it had done was to throw the

spotlight on the minor leagues. The minors had already been
swept up in another resurgence, closing in on an all-time attendance figure that had stood for more than four decades, and
when the strike came there were many minor-league general
managers who couldn't make enough room for people in their
meager little ballparks. Overall, attendance jumped by 11 percent in the last three weeks of the minor-league season, and it
was most pronounced in those cities and towns within an easy
drive of major-league parks now locked up and silent because of
the strike. Poststrike attendance was up by 51 percent in the
Class AA Eastern League, whose members included Bingham-
ton and Albany in New York, Reading in Pennsylvania, and
Canton-Akron in Ohio. It was up by 44 percent in the Class A
Midwest League, normally the domain of the St. Louis Cardinals and Milwaukee Brewers and Chicago's Cubs and White Sox.
The big-league strike had been a sobering experience for baseball fans everywhere, and on the radio call-in shows the senti-
ment was running nine-to-one against the players' union. *If these
guys don't want to play, screw 'em.* In the minors, at least, baseball
was forever.

CHAPTER 17

Marty awoke with a start on the morning of Labor Day. The left shoulder was okay, so there was no question that he would be ready for that night's game against Winston-Salem to open the best-of-three divisional play-off. He liked his chances of getting a championship ring this time. The Bulls had won six of their last nine games against Winston-Salem, and although they had finished a whopping twenty-seven games behind Northern Division champion Wilmington in the overall standings, their nine wins in twenty games was the best any club had fared against the mighty Blue Rocks, who had finished at 94-44. But then he became fully awake and realized that if the worst happened—losing two straight to Winston-Salem—this season would suddenly be over. He spent the morning packing his clothes and stuff in

boxes, and by noon he was out in the parking lot at the Willowdale Apartments, changing the oil in his pickup truck and then
giving it a good scrubbing.

Although it was too late now to work on fine points with Rick
Albert in the auxiliary batting cage or to fiddle with pitching
mechanics in the bull pen under Bill Slack's eye, most of the
players got to the ballpark early that afternoon. For postseason
play, they would be earning the usual prorated pay of about $40
per game, such a piddling amount that it was the last thing on
their minds. Even before the pregame calisthenics and batting
practice began, they were suited up and ranging over the ballpark, brandishing cheap cameras like so many tourists, taking
snapshots of one another and the DAP for their scrapbooks.
Some of them would not pass this way again. For others, it might
be the last evidence that they had once been professional baseball players.

It would be another splendid night for baseball, chilly and in
the upper sixties, but a certain edge seemed to be missing among
the players and in the stands. It was as though Labor Day was a
demarcation point between the end of the baseball season and
the beginning of football. The crowd that night would fall off
drastically from the record-breaking highs of the two previous
weeks—down to 3,479, the faithful—and there was none of the
constant humming in the stands that was a part of the DAP's
charm. The scouts were gone. The work had been done. The results were in. These play-off games were mere icing on the cake
for those who couldn't get enough baseball.

Both managers had juggled their pitching rotations to assure
that they would lead with their best, and the matchup promised
to be an interesting one, involving a pair of tall left-handers who
got by on control, guile, and off-speed stuff. The Bulls' Roger
Etheridge was looking like the sleeper in the swap of leadoff-hit-
ting center fielders at the major-league level earlier in the sum-

mer, which saw the Braves send Deion Sanders to Cincinnati for Roberto Kelly. Etheridge, the PTBNL in the trade, had moved over from the Reds' Sally League club at Charleston, West Virginia, to the Macon Braves, and after a so-so performance there he had been promoted to Durham and become virtually untouchable. The only time anybody had gotten to him was a week before this opening play-off game, when Frederick scored three runs on six hits in six innings, and he had finished the regular season with a 6-2 record and a 1.40 ERA. Will Brunson, Winston-Salem's bespectacled Ichabod Crane, was 12-7 with a 3.98 ERA but had been devastating in his two starts against the Bulls; pitching two complete games, he had allowed Durham only two earned runs on fourteen hits and three walks, against eighteen strikeouts, in eighteen innings.

There were two more season-ending presentations to be made—a plaque for Jay Williams as the league's trainer of the year and an oil painting of the DAP for the faithful groundskeeper, Bill Miller—and once both clubs had been introduced and lined up down the baselines and the National Anthem had been sung for the last time, the game was on. Alas, it was over soon after it started. The Winston-Salem Spirits had set a Carolina League record for home runs during the season, hitting 202 in 137 games, a disproportionate number coming in their windy little ballpark, and on this night they reached Etheridge for a solo homer in the first and a two-run job in the third. Brunson, in the meantime, was scattering nine hits and striking out seven in his seven-inning stint (Marty got a single and struck out twice in five trips to the plate). For the record books, the final outs ever to be made at the DAP came when Marty Malloy bounced into a 6-4-3 double play in the ninth inning at exactly 10:11 P.M. on Monday, September 5, 1994. Winston-Salem won 6-2, and now the Bulls had their backs to the wall, faced with a must-win situation the following night at Winston-Salem. "We'll have to do it the hard way, but this club's been down before," West said in the clubhouse after the game.

They were down more than West thought, if one could draw inferences from Marty's mood at noon the next day. The Bulls would suit up at the DAP and get onto the bus around three o'-clock for the hour-and-a-half ride west to Winston-Salem for a game they had to win to stay in the play-offs. If they won that one, and then again at Winston-Salem on Wednesday night, they would advance to a best-of-five championship round against the Wilmington Blue Rocks. But losing the opener at home, and with Etheridge on the mound, had been devastating to the kid. He piddled over lunch at Honey's, possibly the last meal he would ever eat in Durham, North Carolina, and his mind was on home rather than Winston-Salem. Championship ring be damned; wait 'til next year.

"This fucking shit's gotten old," he began, then caught himself. "I've got to clean up my language before I go home. Too much time on the bus and in the clubhouse."

"You packed?"

"Everything's inside the door. The truck's ready, the phone's been cut off, the rent's paid. Me and Jamie [Arnold, of Kissimmee, Florida] are going to follow each other to Florida. That means we'll probably win tonight, of course."

"Mr. Team Spirit doesn't sound too pleased about the prospect."

"Don't get me wrong," he said. "The game starts, I'll be into it. But the truth is, I don't want to go to Wilmington."

About fifty die-hard fans in Bulls caps and jackets followed the team bus to Winston-Salem in three chartered vans, and they would whoop it up by needling the smattering of Spirits fans. ("You call that a *crowd?*" one bellowed when attendance was announced as 1,156.) In spite of its neat refurbished downtown ballpark and its first-half pennant, Winston-Salem had finished fifth in league attendance with an average of 2,516. A chilly rain shortened batting practice and delayed the start of the game by half an hour. Pitching for Durham was Jamie Arnold, who had evened his record at 7-7, with a 4.66 ERA, but was the league leader in home runs allowed (twenty-six in 145 innings). He was going against the Spirits' Chad Fox, 12-5 and 3.86, a right-handed twenty-four-year-old Texan against whom the league had batted only .216.

Arnold didn't have his best stuff, and Fox did. The Spirits scored three runs in the second inning on four hits and a stolen base and Marty's inability to turn a double play that would have ended the inning with only one run scored. The Bulls evened it at 3-all after five, one of the runs scoring when Marty slashed a single to left and came home on Tom Waldrop's single, but three more runs off Arnold in the home half of the fifth made it 6-3. With two outs in the top of the ninth, still 6-3, Marty worked a reliever for a base on balls and was edging away from first, exhorting Bobby Smith to keep it alive, but Bobby went down swinging at a high fastball. It was over.

The bus sat in the gravel beyond the center-field wall, rumbling in a low idle, as the last of the Bulls swung aboard in silence. The main field lights were being flicked off now, as if to pronounce the end of the season for the Durham Bulls of 1994, and when the players had taken off their spikes and settled in for the last ride, Matt West stood at the front of the bus. "I only want to say a couple of things," he told them. "There's not a fucking loser on this bus. You went from worst to first, and I'm proud of every one of you. In these play-offs, somebody's got to win and somebody's got to lose. You're going to see these guys again along the way in your career, and the next time—maybe it'll be the World Series—you're gonna knock their dicks off." There was utter silence. "So I don't want to hear any bitching and moaning on the bus tonight. You can hold your heads high. Have fun. Talk to your teammates. You won't see 'em again until spring training. I'm proud of every one of you for the work you've done this year . . ." The overhead lights went off and the bus groaned away, headed home for the last time.

There was one final round of poker in the middle of the bus, but it was muted. The five Latin players huddled together in the rear, slumping down in their seats and trying to rest up for what would be a long day of changing planes at airports. "Have fun, talk to your teammates," West had told them, but most were lost in their own thoughts. Marty and Bobby Smith sat together toward the front, right behind Matt West and his trainer, Jay Williams, who were punching their last postgame report of the season into the laptop computer, and the two young players chatted softly about what lay ahead. Bobby and Damon Hollins, each only twenty years old, would spend a couple of weeks at the Fall Instructional League in West Palm Beach, but first Bobby was faced with a cross-country drive to Oakland that would take nearly a week. For Marty, whose scant bonus money had run out, it would be back to pouring concrete throughout the winter with Cotton, Spiderman, and Curly.

It was eleven forty-five when they rolled into the gravel parking lot at the DAP. "Okay, listen up," said West. "Turn in your stirrups, belts, and jackets. Pick up your travel money from Jay. For those of you who're flying out tomorrow, your tickets will be ready at ten o'clock, and Bill Miller has volunteered to drive you to the airport. And, hey, I want to speak to each one of you in my office before you leave." The door cranked open and they filed off the bus, casting eerie shadows beneath the bluish security lights, gathering their canvas equipment bags and trudging down the long concrete ramp leading to the clubhouse beneath the stands.

Marty showered, changed into some shorts and a T-shirt, gathered up the Polaroid snapshot of his son, Corbyn, and the other personal things in his cubicle, and shortly after midnight poked his head into the cramped little coaches' room, not much more than a closet, for the last words with his manager. West made it succinct: "You were the heart and soul of the club, kid. You were the burning light. You set the tone. You were there day in and day out, and I appreciate it." Marty didn't know what to say, except to mumble, "It was fun." He shook hands with West and Rick Albert, slung a bag over his shoulder, and shuffled across the deserted street to his pickup. Durham slept. He tossed his equipment bag onto the floor on the shotgun side, nestled down into his seat, took a deep breath, and cranked the engine. Patting the accelerator, making sure all systems were go, he slapped the cassette containing Hank Jr.'s "A Country Boy Can Survive" into the tape deck and roared off into the Carolina night. With any luck, he would make it to his grandmother's house in Waldo at daybreak, in time for the first real home-cooked meal he had seen in five months.

AFTERWORD

The winter of 1994-95 saw baseball in its deepest funk since the Black Sox scandal in 1919. The players' strike had killed the playoffs and World Series, and when no settlement was reached during the off-season the owners called for replacement players—scabs—to cross the picket lines during spring training. Marty was of a mind to do just that until he was tracked down at West Palm Beach by Brett Butler, the most militant of the striking major-leaguers, who advised him in no uncertain terms to forget about it. The point was rendered moot when Marty took the issue to Chuck LaMar, the Braves' director of player personnel, who said he was one of those choice prospects that they would never ask to play replacement ball.

So the kid moved on up to the Greenville Braves of the Class AA Southern League for the '95 season, and again he was right on schedule. Batting leadoff and in the two-hole, he hit .278, with 10 home runs, 15 bunt base hits, 73 runs scored, and 58 RBI (extremely high for the top of the order). His strikeout percentage of one per 7.9 at bats was the best of his career, his walks nearly equalled his strikeouts, and he batted a respectable .247 against lefties. With his range and only 16 errors in 124 games (he missed 10 due to minor injuries), he was arguably the best second baseman in the league. "The Braves know he's for real now," said Randy Ingle, reunited with Marty as a coach at Greenville. "There's no doubt any more that Marty's going to play in the big leagues."

But for whom? Now his path was being blocked by Tony Graffanino. The Braves' "second baseman of the future" had gone down with chronic back problems, holding him to a .190 batting average in only 179 at-bats with Richmond, and he would almost surely be back there for a full Triple-A season in '96. Marty had "hated" playing at sleepy Greenville, where crowds averaged 3,000 ("After Durham, it was like a demotion"), and he didn't look forward to returning.

His roommates from the season at Durham appeared to be on their way out of baseball after poor performances in '95. Tom Waldrop never recovered from injuries in spring training and went back down to Macon, a twenty-five-year-old among teenaged prospects, where he batted .237 with three homers and struck out 52 times in only 194 at-bats as a DH. John Simmons was the forgotten man on the Greenville staff, with a 4.62 ERA in only 60 innings out of the bullpen. Shortstop Julio Trapaga was shipped back to the Mexican League, and the recovering alcoholic Ken Giard was sent all the way down to a rookie league to find himself (which he did, with a 2.38 ERA and 44 strikeouts against five walks). Five other '94 Bulls were released—utility infielder Nelson Paulino, catcher Adrian Garcia, and the pitchers Blase Sparma, Tony Stoecklin, and Aaron Turnier—and the twenty-five-year-old catcher Brad Rippelmeyer might be joining them after batting only .182 as a backup catcher for Greenville in his fifth year of pro ball.

The sluggers Kevin Grijak and Juan Williams were too hot for the Southern League to handle, and early on were promoted to AAA Richmond; and the pitchers Matt Murray and Darrell May were late-season callups to Atlanta. (Eight Greenville players were promoted during the season, leaving manager Bruce Benedict with a next-to-last-place club). Murray's career had taken a curious turn. He was 4-0 with a 1.53 ERA at Greenville, 10-3 and 2.78 at Richmond, but after a baptism with Atlanta (10 hits in 10.2 innings) he was abruptly traded to the Boston Red Sox for two young Class A prospects. After all of that—the big bonus, the two seasons lost to injury, the nursemaiding, the fruiting at long last—there was no room for him on the strongest pitching staff in baseball.

The bulk of the '94 Bulls spent most of the year at Greenville, and only Marty and Bobby Smith produced well enough to merit a promotion. Smith was sensational at third base, hit a productive .261, and didn't have a Tony Graffanino blocking his way at Richmond. The other position players were so-so at Greenville (Damon Hollins was .247 with 18 homers, Raymond Nunez .263 and 9, Mike Warner only .237), and the pitchers worse. The big disappointments were Jamie Arnold (5-13 with an ERA over 5.00 at Greenville and Durham combined) and Roger Etheridge (2-10, 5.67), followed by Mike D'Andrea and Carl Schutz, both with ERAs approaching 5.00.

The report cards were mixed for those who were held back at Durham. Wonderful Terrific Monds III hit .279 and stole 28 bases for the Bulls; but David Toth and Miguel Correa, each in his sixth season, batted only .245 and .236, respectively. The young pitchers Jeff Bock, Matt Byrd, and Carey Paige, all had winning records and ERAs around 3.00. But the big star of the '95 season in Durham was the new Durham Bulls Athletic Park, where an astonishing 390,486 fans (about 5,600 per game) paid not so much to see Matt West's understocked young Bulls finish next to last in the Carolina League as to savor the charms of what many were calling the best minor-league park in the land. Midway through the season, while the forlorn old DAP sprouted weeds, the Bulls' owners applied for Triple-A status, pointing out that North Carolina's Charlotte franchise, in the AAA International League, was drawing 1,000 fewer fans per game than Durham.

When Marty went home to Trenton after his successful year at Greenville, again to pour concrete during the off-season, he reluctantly hoped to go to another organization either by trade or draft. Not lost on him was the fact that Jon Nunnally, the outfielder who once had beaten him out by one vote as Florida's junior college player of the year, had been picked up in the Rule 5 draft by Kansas City and had jumped all the way from Kinston to the Royals' starting outfield in '95. Chuck LaMar had left the Braves to become general manager of the expansion franchise at Tampa–St. Petersburg, only a two-hour drive from Trenton, and Marty found some hope in that. "Of course, you don't want to go to one of those expansion teams," his father told him.

"Try me," said Marty.

ABOUT THE AUTHOR

Despite a successful career as a journalist and author, PAUL HEMPHILL still rankles over his release forty years ago by the woeful Graceville Oilers of the Class D Alabama–Florida League on a morning after he had struck out all four times he came to bat. "It was politics," he says.